List of Figures, Tables, and Maps

Figures

Tables

Maps

precious cropland is lost every year contributing to a decline in food production (Brown 1995; Vital Signs 2007–2008, 20; Assadourin 2007, 20).
Hence, the need to increase food output requires massive use of chemicals
in agriculture, which further necessitates more water for irrigation. While the
world's total irrigated area has stayed stable due to increasing expenses in
constructing new systems, soil salinization and shortages of water (aquifer
depletion and competition for water) are still quite large (Postel 2000).

The irrigated area is uneven around the world. In Asia in 2000, 42 percent
of arable land was irrigated, while in Sub-Saharan Africa only four percent
of land was irrigated. Irrigated areas in India, Pakistan, the United States, and
China account for half of the global total. China and India each have almost 20
percent of their total area under irrigation (Alder and Pauly 2006). In China,
"Water scarcity is one of the more difficult issues facing the government of
China. In rural areas over 82 million people find it difficult to procure water. In
urban areas, the shortages are even worse. . . . Future water needs in China are
expected to continue growing at a rapid pace. . . . And water scarcity in China
will affect the entire world" (Brown 1995, 66–74). The same could be said
about India, Pakistan, and many other less-developed, predominantly agricultural
economies. In the Middle East the availability of fresh water has always been
a critical issue. Like everywhere else, irrigation consumes the largest share of
water. In Saudi Arabia 90 percent of the nonrenewable fossil water supplies are
used for irrigation (Vidal-Hall 1989, 23–25). Syria, Jordan, Israel, and Iraq, along
with Turkey, face acute water shortages. Mismanagement of these scarce water
resources has further contributed to the already-existing serious problem.

URBANIZATION

Globalization and the changes in lifestyles have greatly spurred the domestic
and international movement of people in search of economic opportunities. This
migration of mostly unskilled populations puts tremendous pressure on the already
overstressed economic and social infrastructures of mainly urban governments. It
is estimated that most of the future urban population increase—88 percent from
2000 to 2030—will be in cities of the developing countries (Lee 2007, 3–21).
In Asia and Africa the urban population will double to 3.4 billion by 2030 (Lee
2007, 3–21; Vital Signs 2007–2008, 52). China now has 16 of the world's most
populated cities. The United Nations projections are that in the coming decades
more people will live in cities than in rural areas (UN Population 2006).

Rising urban populations considerably strain water supplies for dispos-
ing of waste products. The sheer quantity of sewage alone is a major problem. Lack of financial resources, and modern technology and bureaucratic

ineptitude further complicate the problem. Scarcity of water in urban areas is not only an issue in developing countries but also in many European countries and the United States. "People in the United States and Europe on average have a greater ecological footprint than people in the developing world. They use nearly twice as much fresh water, for example, and more than twice the cropland as people in low-income countries and they produce 17 times as many carbon emissions" (World Wildlife Fund 2006).

Due to massive urbanization, "the environmental challenges that cities face vary with the level of economic activity (McGranahan et al. 2001, chapter 4). The poorest cities and their slums typically have the worst local hazards, such as diseases spread by dirty water and lack of toilets" (Smith and Ezzati 2005, 291–333).

INDUSTRIALIZATION

Industries are one of the major consumers and polluters of water resources. They use water to produce energy, run steam turbo generators, and act as coolant. They also pollute water ways (lakes and rivers) by dumping waste materials. With rapid industrialization the demand for water is increasing in developing countries such as India and China. The absent, or more often lax, regulatory laws and bureaucratic mismanagement further exacerbate the water situation. Highway construction and mining also impact water quality. In India these activities "have damaged mountain slopes by covering large surface areas with debris, leading to greater run-off and an alarming rate of sedimentation, the combined impact of which has been to cause surface water drought even in high rainfall regions" (Bandopadhyaya 1988, 90). Most of South Asian rivers are totally polluted mainly due to the unregulated dumping of industrial waste." As a city industrializes, problems at the metropolitan scale, such as air pollution from industry and traffic, tend to worsen first. But a city's burden on the global environment often increases with economic growth as residents buy more cars, bigger houses, and other consumer goods" (Xuemei and Hidefumi 2000, 135:158; McGranahan 2001). The greenhouse effect/global warming will also impact both the quality and quantity of available water.

GLOBAL CLIMATE CHANGE

Despite the absence of substantive, reliable evidence and consensus about the "extent and geographical distribution" (Raleigh and Urdal 2007, 674) of climate changes, there is an increasing sensitivity and realization that these

Table 1.2. Environmental Migration Episodes

Origin, Period	Destination	Environmental Push Factors (Water Scarcity)	Moving	Conflict in Destination	Conflict Intensity
Bangladesh 1970s–1990s	Bangladesh (Chittagong Hills)	Drought, Water Scarcity, Floods	600,000	Ethnic Strife, Insurgency	High
Rwanda (Rural South) early 1990s	Rwanda (North), Zaire	Water Scarcity	1.7 Million	Ethnic Tension, Genocide, Civil War	Very High
Bangladesh (various regions) 1950s	India, West Bengal, Assam, Tripura	Water Scarcity	12–17 Million	Hindu-Muslim Violence	High
El Salvador 1950s–1980s	Honduras, United States	Water Scarcity	300,000	Border Dispute	Very High
Mauritania 1980s–1990s	Senegal, Senegal River Valley	Water Scarcity	69,000	Border Skirmishes, Riots	High
Brazil (Northwest) 1960s–present	Central and Southern Amazon	Water Scarcity	8 Million	Clashes Between ? And Squatters	Medium
Pakistan 1980s–1990s	Urban areas - Karachi and Islamabad	Water Scarcity	NA	Ethnic Discord, Urban Violence	Medium

Source: Adapted from Reuveny 2007, 656–673.

resolutions" (Gleick 1993B, 80) depending on the relative power of the basin states. However, there are several high-potential regions, especially those where there is a river basin shared by at least two countries (Postel 1996, 38), such as the Nile, Euphrates-Tigris in the Middle East, Indus in South Asia, Mekong in East Asia, and Amu Darya and Syr Darya in Central Asia. "In these regions water is evolving into an issue of high politics" (Gleick 1993, 80; Chou, BeZark, and Wilson 1997, 96:105; Fredericksen 2009, 76–78). Water scarcity has also been a major push factor, forcing populations to migrate to other destinations and thus causing conflicts. It is also to be noted that hydrological infrastructures such as dams have been used as "defensive and offensive weapons during wars" (Gleick 2008). Dams not only regulate water but could also be used to deny water to downstream countries (Vajpeyi 1996). As recently as 2010 China's actions renewed long-simmering disputes between China and India on the Bramhaputra's water. The Brahmaputra River's headwaters are in Chinese-controlled Tibet which provides water to the Indian state of Arunachal Pradesh, claimed by China. In 2010 China tried to block an Asian Development Bank loan to India's projected dam in Arunachal Pradesh, raising tension in the region. Since then both countries have increased their military presence in the region. Several skirmishes and intrusions have been reported. In 1950 Israel and Syria clashed, in 1981 Iran bombed a hydroelectric dam in Iraqi Kurdistan, and the proposed Ataturk Dam in Turkey on the Euphrates River has increased tensions between Syria, Iraq, and Turkey. On the completion of the Turkish dam, the flow of the Euphrates to Syria could be reduced by 40 percent and to Iraq by 80 percent (*The Economist*, May 12, 1990: 54–59). So far Turkey has ignored Syrian and Iraqi protestations.

The above discussion points out the factors responsible for shortage of water and the dire need to take action now especially in those countries such as China and India which have large urban populations and economies of scale. However, it should be pointed out that even those developed countries that seemed to have adopted efficient water-management policies do not have a model which fits all. They, like other countries, are also searching for workable solutions. The need, therefore, is to adopt flexible and inclusive water management policies that seek cooperation among policymakers at national, regional, and international levels—policies that will satisfy urban, rural, industrial, and environmental sectors to achieve sustainable development. With careful planning, open and candid discussions, and political and economic commitment to ecological sustainability for the future, it can be done.

The book analyzes the increasing demand for water in the economic and social development of countries in the Middle East, Asia, and Africa, and the dire need to efficiently manage this vital resource. As pointed out earlier, several environmental and human-generated factors such as urbanization, industrialization, climate change, and irrigational needs have created almost a crisis situation in many countries and, therefore, intense competition to utilize available water resources. As a result, transboundary rivers, lakes, and streams, which are shared by more than one country, pose potential both for conflict and cooperation. In Chapter One, Dhirendra Vajpeyi presents a broad framework related to increased demand for water and the potential causes for conflict and cooperation between countries that share transboundary water resources. Paul William's discussion in Chapter Two, "Euphrates and Tigris Water: Turkish-Syrian and Iraqi Relations," is about how Turkey's growing population and its commitment to improve the standard of living of its people, have put increasing pressure on its water resources. Turkey's assertive policies in exploiting water resources have raised tension with its neighbors—Syria and Iraq. These differences are further aggravated by several political factors such as Turkey's governing Justice and Development Party's (JDP) unwillingness to apply the principle of "Integrated Water Resource Management" (IWRM) to water sharing in the region. Political instability in Syria and Iraq could provide the water issue as an excuse for them—a "fig leaf" excuse—to distract their populations from domestic turmoil.

The Middle East/Northern African region is home to several water-scarce countries. It is also a very politically unstable region with a complex record of conflicts including over water. Teagan Ward and Hillery Roach, in Chapter Three, "Hydropolitics and Water Security in the Nile and Jordan River Basins," observe that transboundary basins located in this region provide a context for international water conflicts to arise as riparian nations compete for water security. They point out that the pursuit for water security has already led some riparian countries to undertake unilateral projects that have led to armed conflicts. The Nile and Jordan River basins act as ideal case studies to analyze several key questions: How do riparian states in transboundary basins achieve water security; is a "water war" plausible in the near future; or will water scarcity lead to cooperation between unfriendly nations to conserve this vital resource? Ward and Roach also point out Egypt's virtual veto power over Nile waters in the past and recent challenges by other countries to Egypt's lion's share of water usage. Will the recent changes in Egypt affect the outdated, colonial-era arrangements for water sharing? Ward's analysis of the Jordan River basin reminds us about past conflicts between Israel, Jordan, and Syria, and the potential for cooperation and conflict in the future.

Sheila Rai and Sanghmitra Patnaik, in Chapter Four, "Water Disputes in South Asia," discuss the water scarcity in one of the poorest and water stressed regions in the world. Twenty major rivers criss-cross the South Asian subcontinent (India, Pakistan, Bangladesh, Nepal, and Bhutan). Several of these rivers—such as the Ganges, Brahmaputra, and Indus—are shared by more than one country. Water disputes have arisen between India and Pakistan, India and Bangladesh, and, to some degree, between India and Nepal. Both authors analyze water disputes in the context of political and military terms. India and Pakistan have fought four major wars over Kashmir—a major area from where several rivers flow to Pakistan. So far, water has not been mentioned as a core issue in these conflicts but both countries have made recriminating, shrill noises and threats on water sharing. Rai and Patnaik do not rule out an armed conflict, even if it is limited, between the two nuclear neighbors.

Pia Malhotra-Arora, in Chapter Five, "Sino-Indian Water Wars" discusses the water resources shared by the two biggest emerging economies of Asia— India and China. Both countries are committed to improving their water related infrastructures. Both share major sources of water (Brahmaputra, Indus, and Sutlej Rivers) and a long-simmering, explosive border dispute. In recent times there have been several water-sharing related disputes, short of armed confrontations, between them. She points out that in the absence of a water-sharing mechanism or water treaty between the two countries, extreme distrust of each other and political rivalry in the region could trigger more than verbal-diplomatic dissonance.

The collapse of the Soviet Union in 1991 resulted in the emergence of five independent republics in Central Asia. Under Soviets these countries were a major source of petroleum and agricultural products in general and cotton in particular. In Chapter Six, "Conflict and Cooperation: The Aral Sea Basin," Vajpeyi and Brannon provide not only social, economic, and political background on the region but also old and new problems these countries face in an attempt to improve the quality of life for their citizens. Sloppy planning under the Soviets in managing water resources is one of the crucial issues, which has proved intractable in the post-Soviet era. Scarcity of water resources, poor management, and the absence of agreed-upon arrangements to share water have generated ethnic, economic, and political tensions, environmental degradation, health issues, and overall stagnation in the region. The chapter also analyzes efforts both domestic and international to diffuse these tensions and potential conflicts in this strategic region of the world.

In Chapter Seven, "Conflict and Cooperation mong the Riparian Countries of the Volta River Basin in West Africa," Owusu analyzes current and past cooperation and conflict among the six riparian countries of the Volta River in West Africa by focusing primarily but not exclusively on transboundary water relationships between two main countries—the downstream Ghana and the upstream Burkina Faso. Owusu also points out that traditional cultural respect and perspectives on nature and centuries-old informal mechanisms have played a crucial role in mitigating potential water and other natural resources related conflicts in the region alongside more recent international arrangements such as the Volta Basin Authority (VBA). Combined efforts— traditional and modern—have created a more conducive environment for conflict resolution in the region.

The concluding chapter presents a brief summary of main points analyzed in earlier chapters and then several policy options and recommendations related to efficient use of water, and measures that could be undertaken by national and international agencies including non-governmental organizations.

REFERENCES

Bandyopadhyay, Jayanto. 1988. "The Ecology of Drought and Water Scarcity." *Ecologist* 18 (2/3).

Barnett J. and Ager N. 2007. "Climate Change, Human Security, and Violent Conflict." *Journal of Political Geography* 26 (6): 639–655.

Barringer, Felicity. 2011. "Groundwater Depletion is Detected From Space." *The New York Times*, May 31.

Biswas, Asit. 1994. "Sustainable Water Development: A Global Perspective." *Water International* 17 (2).

Briscoe, John. 1993. "When the Cup is Half-Full: Improving Water and Sanitation Services in the Developing World." *Environment* Spring.

Brown, Lester R. 1995. *Who Will Feed China?* New York: W. W. Norton and Company, Inc.

Chou, Sophie, Ross BeZark, and Anne Wilson. 1997. "Water Scarcity in River Basins as a Security Problem." In *Environmental Change and Security Project*, 95–105. Washington, D.C.: Woodrow Wilson Center, available athttp://wilsoncenter.org/topics/pubsacf26e.pdfaccess20070726.

Detraz, Nicole, and Michele M. Betsill. 2009. "Climate Change and Environmental Security for Whom the Discourse Shifts." *International Studies Perspectives* 10.

Dinar, Shlomi. 2010. "Scarcity and Cooperation along International Rivers." *Global Environmental Politics*. February: 109–135.

Foster, Gregory D. 1989. "Global Demographic Trends to the Year 2010: Implications for National Security." *The Washington Quarterly* Spring; Frederiksen, Harald. 2009. "The World Water Crisis and International Security." *Middle East Policy* Winter 16 (4): 76–88.

Gleditsh, Nils Peter. 1998. "Armed Conflict and Environment: A Critique of the Literature." *Journal of Peace Research* 35 (3): 381–400.

Gleditsch, Nils et al. 2006. "Conflicts Over Shared Waters: Resource Scarcity or Fuzzy Boundaries." *Political Geography* 25: 361–382.

Gleick, Peter H., ed.. 1993. *Water in Crisis: A Guide to the World's Fresh Water Resources.* New York: Oxford University Press. Gleick, Peter H. 1993. "Water and Conflict: Freshwater Resources and International Security." *International Security* 18 (1): 79–112.

Gleick, Peter H. 2008. *Water Conflict Chronology.* Oakland: Pacific Institute www.worldwater.org/conflictintro.htm.

Homer-Dixon, Thomas. 1999. *Environment Security and Violence.* New Jersey: Princeton University Press.

Jeffrey, Leonard. 1989. *Environment and the Poor: Development Strategies for a Common Agenda.* United Kingdom: Transaction Books.

Kaplan, Robert. 1994. "The Coming Anarchy." *Atlantic Monthly* February.

Klare, Michael. 2006. "Resource Wars." *Foreign Affairs* 80 (3): 49–61.

Malen, Irna Vander, and Antionette Hildering. 2005. "Water Cause for Conflict or Cooperation." *Journal on Science and World Affairs.*

Postel, Sandra. 1996. "Dividing the Waters: Food Security, Ecosystem Health, and the New Politics of Scarcity." Washington D.C. Worldwatch Institute Paper 132.

Rachman, Gideon. 2011. *Zero-Sum Future American Power in an Age of Anxiety.* New York: Simon and Schuster.

Raleigh, Clionadh, and Henrik Urdal. 2007. "Climate Change, Environmental Degradation, and Armed Conflict." *Political Geography* 26: 674–694.

Reuveny, Rafel. 2007. "Climate Change-Induced Migration and Violent Conflict." *Political Geography* 26: 656–673.

Shanker, Thom. 2010. "Why We Might Fight," *The New York Times*, December 12.

Starr, Joyce R. 1991. "Water Wars." *Foreign Policy* Spring.

"Climate Change and Crops 2011," *The Economist*, May 14.

Vajpeyi, Dhirendra, and Tingting Zhang. 1998. "Dam or Not to Dam: India's Narmada River." In *Water Resource Management-A Comparative Perspective*, edited by Dhirendra Vajpeyi. London: Praeger.

Vidal-Hall, J. 1989. "Wellsprings of Conflict." *South* May.

Zawahari, Neda. 2008. "International Rivers and National Security: The Euphrates, Ganges-Brahmaputra, Indus, Tigris, and Yarmuk Rivers." *Natural Resources Forum* 32 (1): 280–289.

Chapter Two

Euphrates and Tigris Waters—Turkish-Syrian and Iraqi Relations

Paul Williams

As elsewhere, Turkey's water usage has grown in parallel with its population and standards of living. While the country is not exactly "water rich" on a per-capita basis, national planners base their developmental objectives through the year 2023, the Turkish Republic's centennial anniversary, on the presumption that Turkey has enough water to meet its myriad agricultural, industrial, and household needs.

The country's official development targets involve five transboundary rivers overlapping its territory. Turkey's upstream position in three of these basins minimizes its hydrological dependence on what its neighbors choose to do in their respective areas of these basins. Of course, just as Turkish officials periodically criticize what these neighbors have done in river basins where Turkey lies downstream (i.e., the Maritsa and Orontes basins), downstream states also protest Turkey's upstream actions in the Coruh, Kura-Araks, and Euphrates-Tigris River basins. At a September 2009 Euphrates-Tigris crisis summit among Iraq, Syria, and Turkey, for instance, Turkey's energy minister, while acknowledging downstream states' concerns, "maintained that Turkey could not 'allow our own water and energy management to run into problems'" (Jongerden 2010, 140). Such assertions contradict the current Turkish foreign-policy paradigm based on "zero problems" with neighbors (Davutoglu 2010).

After discussing Turkey's water supply and usage, this chapter looks more closely at Turkey's transboundary river basins and its extant and prospective utilization of these basin water resources. It then examines disputes over these basins and resolution (or non-resolution) thereof before offering concluding remarks.

TURKEY'S WATER SUPPLY AND USAGE

Overview

Turkey is not unique as an "upstream state." Yet, various facets of its water resources—from basic data to official positions on their use—reflect the pervasive political influence of Turkey's transboundary water disputes with its downstream neighbors, notably in the Euphrates-Tigris basin. Major discrepancies exist even on fundamental estimates of how much water exists in Turkey. United Nations Food and Agriculture Organization (UNFAO 2010a) estimates of the country's available water resources exceed those of Turkey's General Directorate of State Hydraulic Works, or *Devlet Su Isleri* (DSI) in Turkish. Both place Turkey's total internal renewable water resources at 227 billion cubic meters or cubic kilometers per year (km^3/year), comprising 186 km^3 of surface water and 41 km^3 of groundwater (DSI 2009b, 9; UNFAO 2010a). The UNFAO (2010a) deducts 13.44 km^3 of external sources to reach total renewable water resources (TRWR) of 213.6 km^3/year. According to DSI (2009b, 8), however, "not all the renewable water resources can be utilized because of economic and technical reasons," leaving only 112 km^3/year (nearly 100 km^3 less than the UN's final estimate): 98 km^3 of surface water and 14 km^3 of groundwater.

Estimates of per-capita water resources vary accordingly. The most recent UN estimates suggest that Turkey lies above the "water stress" threshold of 1,000–1,667 m^3/year identified by Falkenmark, Lundqvist, and Widstrand (1989, 260). Based on an interim population estimate of 73.9 million, UNFAO (2010a) placed Turkey's per-capita water supply at 2,890 m^3/year in 2008, *above* the respective Iraqi and Syrian figures of 2,512 m^3 and 791.4 m^3 (UNFAO 2010b; 2010c). By contrast, according to Turkey's Ministry of Foreign Affairs (2004, 2), both Turkey and Syria, at 1,830 and 1,420 m^3/year, respectively, were already close to or inside this threshold in 1993, while Iraq, at 2,110 m^3, remained above it. However, the DSI (2009b, 10) has estimated, using an interim population estimate of 70.6 million, that Turkey's available supply had fallen to 1,586 m^3/year in 2007.

Turkey's officials, influenced by Malin Falkenmark's benchmark "water competition" intervals, have deployed them to highlight and contrast the country's dire circumstances with its misconceived "water rich" image. DSI's (2009a, 51; 2010, 37) Turkish-language reports cite 1,652 m^3/year, suggesting that this could drop to 1,120 m^3/year by 2023 for a projected population of 100 million, while the same agency's (DSI 2009b, 10) English-language report offers an even grimmer prospect of "less than 1,000 m^3/capita/year" by 2023. Whichever number cited, all fall under 10,000 m^3/year, which

Falkenmark, Lundqvist, and Widstrand (1989, 260) associated with "limited management problems," but Turkish sources characterize as "water rich" and thus inapplicable to their country (DSI 2009b, 10, 46; Ministry of Foreign Affairs 2004, 2).

Turkey's politicized "water rich" image has not been easy to dispel. It arose in part from earlier misestimations of its total water availability and projected consumption of Euphrates-Tigris water, as well as by proposed offers of alternative supplies for its Arab neighbors (Williams 2001, 32–34). First, a 1984 government study overestimated excess runoff in Turkey's 26 drainage basins at two-thirds of the total (Kolars and Mitchell 1991, 291, 294–295). Then the 1989 Southeast Anatolia Project or *Guneydogu Anadolu Projesi* (GAP) Master Plan underestimated future maximum Euphrates water consumption at 10.4 km^3/year (Kolars 1994, 75), inadvertently matching a 1990 joint Syro-Iraqi demand of 700 m^3/second (m^3/s). In addition, Turkish leader Turgut Özal's "Peace Pipeline" proposal, related to a 1987 Protocol pledging Turkey to deliver an average of 500 m^3/s (15.75 km^3/year, half the mean annual flow of Euphrates water at Syria's border), implied that Turkey could compensate for any shortfall there from its domestic rivers. By 1992, Turkey had already embarked on image control, with its foreign minister stating that, "Turkey is not a country which has abundant water resources. We may soon face problems in meeting our own needs" (Beschorner 1992, 44).

Turkish officials have stressed how the national population will be able to consume the country's potential exploitable volume when all relevant projects get built. According to government sources, Turkey's annual water use expanded by nearly half in two decades—from 30.6 km^3 in 1990, 27 percent of the maximum utilizable supply (i.e., 112 km^3), to 46 km^3 in 2008, 41 percent—and is targeted to reach the symbolic milestone of 100 percent by 2023, the Turkish Republic's centennial anniversary (DSI 2009b, 16, 22). The present volume includes 12.4 km^3 of groundwater, nearly 91 percent of the utilizable volume of underground sources (DSI 2009b, 17). Per-capita annual usage rose by nearly 100 m^3—from a volume of 542 m^3 in 1990, when Turkey had 56.5 million people, to a total of 643 m^3 in 2008, when the population had grown by another 15 million (DSI 2009b, 4, 5; Turkstat 2011). By contrast, the UNFAO's (2010a) estimate of "total water withdrawal per capita" for 2007 is just slightly higher than the above 1990 figure.

Infrastructure

Dams meet an official Turkish objective of maximizing the country's benefits from its two dozen river basins. Turkey's hydraulic officials have long been infused with "techno-scientific optimism, belief in mega projects, and willingness to put economic development over other policy objectives" (Yuksel 2010, 1473). For example, "The fact that one-time heads of the State Water Works (DSI in Turkish) which was created in 1953 to ensure efficiency in hydroelectric power plants' (HEPP) planning and construction, have often gone on to hold influential positions in Turkish politics demonstrates the centrality of dam construction to the Developmentalist position" (Yuksel 2010, 1474).

Indeed, the founding of DSI, charged with water-resources management pursuant to 1954's Law No. 6200, imparted a key impetus to dam building in Turkey. While three large dams (the first—Cubuk I—was built in 1936 to serve Ankara) existed in Turkey prior to its creation, DSI oversaw the construction of 654 dams—inclusive of 241 "large-scale projects" and 413 "small-scale projects"—through 2008, and another 20 (nine large-scale projects and 11 small-scale projects) in 2009 (DSI 2010, 38–46). In each of the five decades spanning 1960 to 2010, an average of 51 dams built within the framework of large-scale projects came online, with construction accelerating to 63 per decade after 1980 (DSI 2010, 38–40). Today, Turkey's large dams can hold approximately 140 m³ of water (DSI 2009b, 18). In the past half century, an average of 85 large dams built within the framework of small-scale projects came online each decade, with building increasing to 125 per decade after 1980 (DSI 2010, 41–46).

SECTORIAL PATTERNS AND TRENDS

Consumptive Water Uses

Agriculture

Most of Turkey's water consumption goes to irrigation. Between 1990 and 2008, irrigation's water use rose from 22 km³ to 34 km³, nearly three-quarters of total water consumption, and by 2023 it could increase by more than double to 72 km³ per annum. According to this projection agriculture's *share* of water is expected to fall to 64 percent of the total (DSI 2009b, 16–17). Of the current 34 km³ of water for irrigation, nearly one-fifth, or 6.77 km³, was sourced from groundwater (DSI 2009b, 17). The projected decline in the relative percentage of abstracted water for agriculture corresponds to comparative declines in rural population, from 80 percent of the total in 1927 to nearly 30 percent in 2007, as well as in agriculture's contribution to GNP, from one quarter in the 1980s to 11 percent in 2007 (DSI 2009b, 4, 24). Turkey has approximately 78 million hectares (mha) of land, almost 28 mha (36 percent) of which is arable; nearly 22 mha (80 percent) of this arable land is cultivated, three-quarters via rainfall and one-quarter via irrigation; and nearly 8.5 mha (62 percent) of irrigational land is actually irrigated (DSI 2009b, 11). Nearly 92 percent of irrigated land is served by surface irrigation (DSI 2009b, 25).

Industry and Households

As Turkey's population has grown and the standard of living has risen, so has its non-agricultural water usage. While domestic and industrial water usage made up just over one-quarter of the country's total water consumption in 2008—7 km^3/year (15 percent) went to households and 5 km^3/year (11 percent) went to industry—water consumed in these sectors is projected to increase nearly 150 percent and 350 percent, respectively, by 2023, with 18 km^3/year (16 percent) going to household users and 22 km^3/year (one-fifth) going to industry (DSI 2009b, 17). According to the DSI (2009b, 23) domestic water consumption increased nearly 37 percent over the 1990–2008 period, from nearly 5 km^3/year to 7 km^3/year, although Turkey's Statistics Institute (Turkstat 2011) reports a nearly 41 percent increase over the 1994–2008 period, from 3.2 km^3/year to 4.6 km^3/year, in quantity abstracted to municipal water supply networks. As a percentage of total consumption, however, domestic water use actually dropped from 17 to 15 percent, while industrial water usage, which rose 45 percent between 1990 and 2008, should exceed household usage by 4 km^3/year by 2023 (DSI 2009b, 22, 23).

Turkey's average per-capita household water supply grew slightly over the past two decades. Estimates based on a combination of Turkstat (2011) population statistics and DSI's (2009b) aggregate domestic water consumption figures show that Turkey's per-capita water consumption increased from nearly 249 liters per day (l/d) in 1990 to 267 l/d in 2008, although DSI (2009b, 23) states explicitly that average daily per-capita water supply rose from 195 liters to 250 liters, adding that, "Turkey aims to save water by reducing the daily use to 150 liters per person per day through the application of modern techniques." Per-capita water supply abstracted to municipal water-supply networks remained considerably smaller than overall per-capita domestic water uses. According to Turkstat (2011), mean per-capita water supply to municipalities equalled 211 l/d in 1994 and 215 l/d in 2008.

Average individual water consumption varies extensively across Turkey's municipalities and 81 provinces. The General Directorate of State Hydraulic Works supplies domestic and industrial water to cities with populations over 100,000 (Law no. 1053 of 1968). A 2007 amendment to this law authorized the same agency to provide water to the "3,225 settlements with municipal administrations" (DSI 2009b, 13). According to Turkstat (2011) data, munici-palities in more populous and urbanized provinces enjoy smaller average per-capita abstractions of water than those in less populous and more rural provinces. Each of the nearly 36 million people living in cities located in 14 provinces with municipal populations of over one million used an average of 194 l/d, as opposed to 260 l/d for the typical resident living in cities located in the 16 provinces with municipal populations of between 500,000 and one million, and 236 l/d for the typical urban dweller located in the 51 provinces with municipal populations under half a million. Moreover, dams supplied the first category with 59 percent of its water on average, but only 16 percent of the water abstracted by the last two categories. Rates of urbanization also matter. In 2008, three-quarters of Turks resided in provincial and district centers. According to additional computations based on Turkstat (2011) data, while municipal residents of the ten least urbanized provinces, containing nearly 2.8 million municipal residents who accounted for less than half of their respective provincial populations, abstracted nearly 236 l/d on average, their counterparts in the 12 *most* urbanized provinces, containing nearly 30.5 million city residents accounting for at least three quarters of their respective provincial populations, abstracted a daily average of 186 liters. Istanbul, where the 2008 urban population of 12.4 million made up nearly the entire provincial population and each city resident had access to 146 l/d on average, exemplifies this disparity.

As Table 2.1 shows, Turks lack uniform access to water services. The UNDP (2010, 169) indicates that, while drinking water is nearly universally available, "population with improved access" to sanitation equals 90 percent. DSI (2009b, 23) reports that 83 percent of the population, averaging 94 percent of the urban population but only 62 percent of the rural population, had "access to improved sanitation, including the households at least having connection to public sewer, septic system or simple pit latrine." Thus, "improved sanitation" does not mean upgraded sewage and wastewater treatment. By 2008, 69 percent and 62 percent of the rural population of Turkey remained without access to water-supply networks and sewage systems, respectively, while 86 percent and 84 percent lacked water and wastewater treatment.

Table 2.1. Turkey's Water Access Coverage by Service Category (%)

Year	1994		2008		
Service	Total	Urban	Total	Urban	Rural
Water-supply network	67	88	82	99	31
Sewage	52	69	73	88	28
Water treatment	23	35 (2001)	41	50	14
Wastewater treatment	10	35 (2001)	46	56	16

Source: Total/urban: Turkish Statistical Institute (Turkstat) 2011; rural: author derivations based on Turkstat 2011

Non-consumptive Water Usage

Consumptive usage forms the crux of many salient water disputes between Turkey and its basin neighbors. Even the Turkish dams built for non-consumptive water usage have invited controversy because they entail initial filling of "dead storage" and altered timing of flows from "live storage" to generate hydroelectric power (HEP). Turkey's 2007 per-capita power usage was estimated at 2,068 kWh—a 700-percent increase since 1973 and a 160-percent increase since 1990 (International Energy Agency 2009, III.572). Its electricity consumption has been met increasingly by imported natural gas (Ozturk, Bezir, and Ozek 2009, 606; Yuksel 2010, 1470–1471), which supplied three-fifths of Turkey's net thermal electricity and half its total electricity of 198 Terawatt hours in 2008 (TWh = 1 billion kilowatt hours) (DSI 2010, 49).

Turkey seeks more electricity from HEP. Turkey was reportedly operating 175 hydroelectric power plants (HEPPs), building 94 and planning 542 by the end of 2008 (DSI 2009a, 40, 66), and these numbers had risen to 213, 145, and 200, respectively, by the end of 2009 (DSI 2010, 49, 50), with the latter source including another 1,100 not counted in the earlier report. HEPPs with ten-plus megawatts (MW) of installed capacity accounted for 98 percent of Turkey's total installed HEP capacity in 2008 (European Commission 2011), while 25 HEPPs with at least 100 MW of installed capacity supplied 82 percent (DSI 2009a, 71). By 2010, DSI (2010, 52) was building another 17 HEPPs with installed capacity of at least ten MW, for a total of over 3,000 MW.

Estimates of Turkey's HEP potential vary. DSI's (2009b, 19) recent English-language report puts the country's "gross theoretical viable hydroelectric potential" at 433 TWh, but "economically viable potential" at only 140 TWh. However, its Turkish-language annual activity reports (DSI 2009a, 40; DSI 2010, 23) contend that the latter could be boosted to 180 TWh. As Figure I shows, Turkey's weather-dependent HEP output has fluctuated from year to year (even month to month within years), instead of rising steadily. While Turkey's gross HEP output grew 2.4 percent/year between 1990 and 2008, it shrunk from its post-Cold War peak of 46 percent of total electricity output in 1993 to a low of 17 percent in 2008, as electricity output had increased 14 percent/year (European Commission 2011). Installed HEP capacity doubled over the 1990–2008 period, increasing from 6,764 MW to 13,828 MW, but total generation capacity increased by over 150 percent, from 16,318 MW to 41,817 MW (European Commission 2011), so even HEP's share of Turkey's total installed capacity fell from a post-Cold War high of 48 percent in 1993 to 33 percent in 2008.

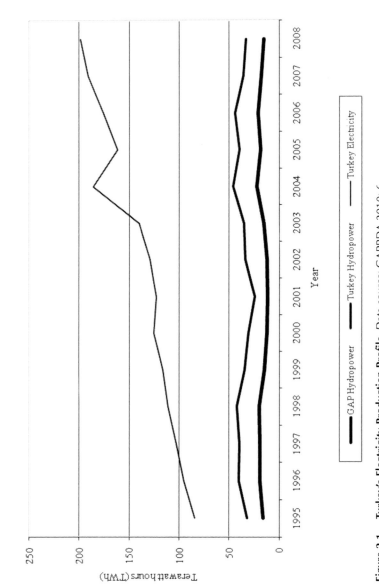

Figure 2.1. Turkey's Electricity Production Profile *Data source:* GAPRDA 2010: 6.

TRANSBOUNDARY WATERCOURSES
IN TURKEY'S ECONOMY

Transboundary watercourses figure prominently in Turkey's development programs. According to DSI (2009b, 47), "Transboundary waters constitute 40 percent of Turkey's water potential." Turkey is upstream from Armenia, Azerbaijan, Georgia, and Iran in the Kura-Araks basin, Georgia in the Coruh basin, and Syria and Iraq in the Euphrates-Tigris basin. Conversely, it lies downstream from Lebanon and Syria in the Orontes basin and downstream from Bulgaria in the Maritsa basin.

THE KURA-ARAKS BASIN

Geographical and Hydrological Characteristics

The provinces of Ardahan, Erzurum, Igdir, and Kars in northeastern Turkey provide the headwaters and main tributaries of these rivers, which join in downstream Azerbaijan before reaching the Caspian Sea. The basin covers two thirds of the South Caucasus region (DSI 2009b, 49), including more than half of Georgia, which occupies 18 percent of the catchment area; 80 percent of Azerbaijan, which has 29 percent of the basin area; and all of Armenia, which also has 18 percent of the catchment area (Kibaroglu et al. 2005, 39–40). Turkey lies upstream from Georgia on the Kura River, which flows nearly 210 km in Turkey, another 390 km in Georgia, and a final 915 km in Azerbaijan. The main stem of the Araks River flows nearly 548 km in Turkey before forming the Turkish-Armenian border. The various headwaters and smaller feeder streams of the 1,700 km Arpacay River tributary also arise in Turkey before forming a more northerly Turkish-Armenian boundary section of the Araks River. The tributary Sarisu River rises in Turkey before crossing into Iran, from where it later joins the main Araks branch to form Iran's boundaries with Azerbaijan and Armenia. Turkey contributes a relatively small fraction of mean annual flow and occupies a minor portion of total basin area. Of the basin's combined average annual discharge of 32 km^3, Turkey provides approximately 1 km^3/year to the Kura and 4.63 km^3/year to the Araks and has only 14 percent of the 190,000 km^2 catchment area (Kibaroglu et al. 2005, 39, 41).

Turkey's Uses of Kura-Araks Water

Due to unpropitious topography, Turkey has somewhat minor developments in the combined basin. As of 2005, Turkish planners had been slating to build two dams on the Kura (Koroglu and Besikkaya) and one on the Araks (Bayburt) and were already operating two additional dams on that latter branch: the Arpacay (a joint project with Armenia built before the Soviet Union's collapse) and Demiroven (Kibaroglu et al. 2005, 39).

The Kura River, starting in Turkey's Ardahan province and crossing into Georgia, is less significant for Turkey. In 2005, less than 3,000 ha—albeit reportedly six percent of the basin's irrigable land—were being irrigated, mostly from more than two dozen small lakes, but dams were being planned to irrigate nearly 51,000 ha and produce HEP (Kibaroglu et al. 2005, 42). The Araks looms larger in Turkey's development plans. With the Bayburt Dam reportedly 95 percent complete by the end of 2009, its 52-cubic hectometer (hm^3 = 1 million cubic meters) reservoir will supply 10.32 hm^3 of water to Kars residents and irrigation water for 5,237 ha in the Selim Plain (DSI 2010, 225). In 2009, construction started on the Kars Dam on the Kars River, an Arak feeder, in order to generate 19 GWh/year of HEP and irrigate 29,414 ha (DSI 2011a). These would add to a number of extant HEP and irrigation projects on the Araks. A fraction of the network used to irrigate 62,000 ha in the Igdir Plain was under renovation at the end of 2009 (DSI 2010, 226; DSI 2011b). This area draws from Turkey's half of the 0.53 km^3 Arpacay Dam reservoir (Kibaroglu et al. 2005, 42). This dam also waters 7,650 ha across three projects, including the Arpacay Plain, presently undergoing expansion to 11,400 ha (DSI 2010, 225). These add to the nearly 67 GWh/year of HEP and 18,000 ha of net irrigation affiliated with Cildir Dam and Lake (DSI 2011a) and the 8,323 ha watered by Erzurum's Demirdoven Dam (DSI 2011c). In general, "because of rather unfavourable hydrological conditions . . . hydropower generation projects are of minor importance" (Kibaroglu et al. 2005, 43), leaving most projects focused on irrigation and drinking water.

THE CORUH RIVER BASIN

Geographical and Hydrological Characteristics

The Coruh River makes its 426 km descent from its headwaters, which arise at an altitude of 3,000 meters northwest of the Erzurum-Kars Plateau, to its Black Sea alluvial delta in Batumi, Georgia, picking up the Tortum and Oltu tributaries during its 400 km journey through Turkey, which the river departs near the town of Muratli. Nearly 91 percent of the basin's 21,100 km^2 drainage area lies in Turkey (primarily Artvin province) and the rest in Georgia (Kibaroglu et al. 2005, 47; DSI 2009b, 49). Thus, Turkey contributes more territory and water (a mean flow of 6.3 km^3 per year) to the Coruh.

Turkey's Uses of Coruh Water

Given the sheer elevation drop involved, Turkey has focused on this river system's HEP potential. The Coruh Master Plan project should provide 5.9–6.4 percent of the country's HEP potential (DSI 2009a, 68; DSI 2010, 52; Ozturk, Bezir, and Ozek 2009, 614). Turkey operates four HEPPs in this basin: Borcka, Muratli, Murgul, and Tortum I, with the latter two having installed capacity of 31 MW and providing an average annual output of 112 GWh (DSI 2011d). The former two come under the auspices of said master plan. Conceived in 1982, this scheme envisages construction and operation of a cascade of ten HEP dams, consisting, in successive order starting at an altitude of 1,420 meters above sea level (masl), of Laleli, Ispir, Gullubag, Aksu, Arkun, Yusufeli (the reservoir crest of which will lie at the medium elevation of 710 masl), Artvin, Deriner, Borkca, and Muratli (Berkun 2010, 656). Planned irrigation is constrained to 30,000 ha "due to the basin's topographical limits" (Kibaroglu et al. 2005, 50).

Components of the master plan are already complete. Borcka and Muratli, the lowest-lying dams and those closest to the Turkish-Georgian boundary, have been generating a combined average annual energy output of 1,483 Gwh from 415 MW installed capacity since 2005 and 2007, respectively (DSI 2009a, 68, 71), with Borcka supplying 2,422 GWh until the end of 2009 (DSI 2010, 230). To be the sixth of Turkey's largest dams, each with at least 100 MW installed capacity (DSI 2009a, 71), the Deriner Dam-and-HEPP, three-fifths finished by the end of 2009, should provide 2,118 GWh/year from an installed capacity of 670 MW (DSI 2010, 230). During 2009, construction started on the Gullubag Dam-and-HEPP, third from the top of the cascade and slated to produce 285 GWh/year from installed capacity of 84 MW (DSI 2010, 52). In all, this plan's dam-and-HEPPs will add installed capacity of 2,536 MW and supply 8,231 GWh/year of HEP (DSI 2010, 52).

THE EUPHRATES-TIGRIS BASIN

Geographical and Hydrological Characteristics

These characteristics alone give a rough initial sense of the high significance these two rivers possess, not only for the Turkish economy, but also for the larger basin economy. While the Euphrates River basin spans 444,000 km^2, of which nearly one-third, one-fifth, and 46 percent lie in Turkey, Syria, and Iraq, respectively, the Tigris River Basin spans 387,000 km^2, of which nearly 15 percent lies in Turkey and three-quarters in Iraq. Syria possesses a mere 1,000 km^2 of the basin area, a short leg of its boundary with Turkey (Kibaroglu et al. 2005, 55–57).

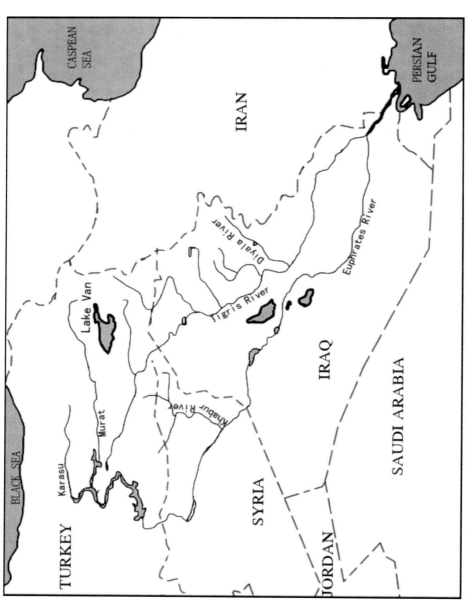

Figure 2.2.   The Euphrates-Tigris Basin

Both branches of the conjoined transboundary watercourse system originate nearly 30 km from each other. At 2,700 km, the "longest river in south-west Asia west of the Indus" (Kolars 1994, 51), the Euphrates flows for nearly half that distance in Turkey before crossing into Syria (DSI 2009a, 48). Its headwaters— the Karasu and Murat rivers—form at 4,417 and 5,047 masl, respectively, north of Erzurum and on Mount Ala north of Lake Van (Kolars and Mitchell 1991, 4). Some 45 km northwest of Elazig municipality, they join prior to reaching Keban Dam (see Table 2.3). Afterwards, the main channel receives numerous feeder streams and Malatya province's Tohma River tributary before reaching the Karakaya Dam in Diyarbakir; takes water from the Kahta River upstream from the Ataturk Dam and the Nizip River downstream from Birecik Dam; and finally passes southwest through a gorge near Hilvan before leaving Turkey at Karkamis, the site of the river's fifth main dam (Kibaroglu et al. 2005, 56).

In Syria, the river's left bank joins the Balikh and Khabour tributaries. After its confluence with the latter at Deir es-Zor, the Euphrates River receives no regular incremental flows of water (Kolars 1994, 51). Three hundred sixty km from the Syrian border, the river reaches its 100,000 km^2 alluvial plain in Iraq and then drops only 53 m in altitude over the next 735 km to the Gulf, losing water to various distributaries before reaching Nasiriya, where one part fissures into a skein of channels that drain into Lake Hammar and another part joins the Tigris River at Qurna, where the confluence flows into the 200 km long Shatt al-Arab estuary of the Persian Gulf (Kibaroglu et al. 2005, 56–57; Kolars 1994, 51).

Within Turkey, the Tigris starts close to the Euphrates headwaters, but quickly turns further east. At 1,840 km, "the second longest river in southwest Asia" (Kolars and Mitchell 1991, 6), this river rises in eastern Turkey near Lake Hazar, at 1,150 masl and traverses Diyarbakir province before demarcating a 32 km section of the Turkish-Syrian boundary that starts at the Turkish city of Cizre (Kibaroglu et al. 2005, 57; Kolars and Mitchell 1991, 6). The river reaches its alluvial plain between Iraq's Tikrit and Samarra, but, in contrast to the Euphrates, receives its larger increment of water from tributaries that flow from the Zagros Mountains, partially from Iran: the Greater and Lesser Zabs (downstream from Mosul, Iraq) as well as the Adhaim and Diyala (Kolars 1994, 52).

Estimates of mean annual runoff of these rivers vary. Natural flows, always highly variable across seasons and years, no longer exist in any calculable sense (Kibaroglu 2008, 184). Turkey's Ministry of Foreign Affairs (2010, 2–3) implies that Turkey provides just over 56 km^3/year—31 km^3/year for the Euphrates and 25 km^3/year for the Tigris—two thirds of the rivers' combined annual flow. UNFAO (2010d) gives Turkey's collective contribution as 49.43 km^3/year—28.1 km^3/year to the Euphrates (although natural flow of 26.29 km^3/year is also cited) and 21.33 km^3/year to the Tigris, 28.4 percent of Turkey's cited 173.8 km^3/year of "actual" surface TRWR. Others (Kibaroglu

2008, 184–185; Kibaroglu et al. 2005, 56–58) cite Turkey's contribution of 90 percent of the Euphrates's mean flow of 32 km³/year (28.92 km³/year) and 40 percent of the Tigris's mean flow of 52 km³/year (20.84 km³/year), a collective share of 49.76 km³/year, comparable to UNFAO (2010d) numbers.

One matter complicating resolution of Euphrates-Tigris disputes centers on the exact origins of the Balikh and Khabour tributaries of the Euphrates. As Kibaroglu et al. (2005, 56) state, "The Khabour sub-basin together with its transboundary tributaries and its springs is the most complicated element of the system; various branches of the Khabour originate either from Turkey or from Syria and are estimated to have a significant potential of 200 MCM/ year [0.2 km³/year]." Leading experts claim that, since the catchment area of these springs lies in Turkey and can thus be impacted by groundwater pumping there, Turkey may account for up to 98 percent of Euphrates flow (Kolars and Mitchell 1991, 106–107; Kolars 1994, 51).

Turkey's Use of Euphrates-Tigris Water

These waters are being harnessed to expand Turkey's agricultural and HEP output and to improve living standards in the southeastern region overlapping this basin. Some changes have taken place and GAP cities' drinking-water and wastewater treatment coverage rates reached 2001 national averages (Table 2.2). This region's laggard quality—per-capita GDP was 47 percent of the national mean in 1985 (Nippon Koei Co. Ltd. and Yuksel Proje A.S. 1990, 1)—and pronounced ethnic divisions have fomented violent unrest. With the 1989 GAP Master Plan, which converted an array of irrigation and HEPP projects (first named the "Southeast Anatolian Project" in 1977) into an integrated "multi-sector social and economic development program for the region" (DSI 2009b:,36), development of this river basin in Turkey has come under the GAP Regional Development Administration (GAPRDA).

Development of Southeast Anatolia and increased exploitation of Euphrates-Tigris water remain inextricably linked. State "planners are quick to note that the twin rivers represent over one quarter of Turkey's freshwater resources and a similar percentage of Turkey's hydroelectric potential" (Harris and Alatout 2010, 148). GAP also accounts for one-fifth of national irrigable agriculture (Berkun 2010, 649; Yuksel 2010, 1473–1474). GAP encompasses ten percent of the country's territory and population and host 13 projects (seven in the Euphrates basin and six in the Tigris basin) consisting of 22 dams and 19 HEPPs. These will have 7,490 MW of installed capacity and generate 27.387 TWh of HEP. 1.8 mha of cropland will also come under irrigation (DSI 2009a, 84–88; GAPRDA 2008, 5) (Table 2.3). GAP is also supposed to raise

Table 2.2. The GAP Region (2008)

Province	pop.	pop growth: 2007–08(%)	urban(%)	wsn*(%)	dwt*(%)	ss*(%)	wwt*(%)
Adiyaman	585067	4	56	99	-	91	0
Batman	485616	27	72	98	-	92	-
Diyarbakir	1492828	22	70	99	57	94	52
Gaziantep	1612223	33	87	98	51	97	85
Kilis	120991	21	68	100	59	96	-
Mardin	750697	7	56	98	1	73	-
Sanliurfa	1574224	33	56	99	50	93	12
Siirt	299819	28	60	98	-	97	-
Sirnak	429287	31	63	94	-	82	-
GAP	7350752	24	68	98	35	92	35
Turkey	71517100	13	75	99	50	88	56

* wsn, dwt, ss, ww = municipal population with access to water-supply network, drinking-water treatment, sewage system and wastewater treatment, respectively
Source: provinces/Turkey: Turkish Statistical Institute (Turkstat) 2011; GAP: author computations based on Turkstat (2011)

Table 2.3. Euphrates-Tigris Basin Dams (Operating or under Construction in 2008)

Major DAM-and-HEPP complexes	Construction (in order of completion)	River/Province	Reservoir Volume (km³)	Installed capacity (MW)	Nominal Annual HEP (TWh)
Keban (non-GAP)	1965–1975	Euphrates/Elazig	31.000	1,330	6.000
Karakaya	1976–1987	Euphrates/Diyarbakir	9.580	1,800	7.354
Ataturk	1983–1992	Euphrates/Sanliurfa	48.700	2,400	8.900
Kralkizi	1985–1997	Tigris/Diyarbakir	1.919	94	0.146
Dicle	1986–1997	Tigris/Diyarbakir	0.595	115	0.444
Batman	1986–1998	Tigris/Batman	1.175	198	0.483
Karkamis	1996–1999	Euphrates/Maras	0.157	189	0.652
Birecik	1993–2000	Euphrates/Sanliurfa	1.220	672	2.518
Ilisu	2007–	Tigris/Mardin	10.400	1,200	3.833
TOTAL			104.746	7,998	30.330
GAP (operational)			63.346	5,468	20.497
GAP Master Plan				7,490	27.387

Sources: all dams except Kralkizi and Ilisu: DSI (2009a), 71; Kralkizi: DSI (2011e); Ilisu: Kibaroglu et al. (2005), 62–63; total/GAP (operational): author computations

regional per-capita income over 200 percent and employ 3.8 million people (DSI 2009b, 38).

The project has faced recurring delays. Yuksel (2010, 1473) writes that, "Although current justifications for this mammoth project [GAP] mention irrigation and regional development as key objectives, the earlier plans were articulated squarely in terms of providing a secure electricity supply." Indeed, GAP's hydropower targets have come online more rapidly than its irrigation components. "GAP's original schedule called for the irrigation of one million hectares of land with Euphrates waters, and 625,000 hectares with Tigris waters by the year 2002" (Kolars 1994, 67), a goal that proved overly ambitious. Even the master plan recommended completion by 2005 of only 894,000 ha (55 percent of planned irrigation) and 5,300 MW of installed capacity, 70 percent of the HEP target (GAPRDA 1990, 10). By the end of 1996, only seven percent of irrigation targets and 56 percent of HEP targets had been reached (GAPRDA 1997, 64–65).

Financial shortfalls plagued this project. By 2000, only 44 percent of the project's US$32-billion cost had been met (GAPRDA 2000, 5). In 1998, Turkey's Council of State mandated completion by 2010 (GAPRDA 2000, 6), but the later-admitted inadequacy of GAP's public-investment-budget allocation—6.2 percent/year over 1999–2005—made this goal farfetched (DSI 2009a, 67; GAPRDA 2010, 5). In 2004, GAP's dam-and-HEPP installations, which supplied nearly 49 percent of Turkey's HEP and 15 percent of its electricity (Figure I; GAPRDA 2010, 6), had met part of the master plan's 2005 "priority" goals. Excluding Keban Dam-and-HEPP, which came online prior to GAPRDA's existence, the Euphrates hosts the Ataturk, Birecik, Karakaya, and Karkamis dams and two stand-alone HEPPs (Sanliurfa and Cagcag), while the Tigris hosts Batman, Dicle, and Kralkizi and is awaiting completion of Ilisu Dam by 2014 (DSI 2009a, 70). Thus, three-quarters of GAP's HEP potential has been realized (DSI 2010, 66).

Conversely, GAP's irrigation progress lags behind. By the end of 2005, only 245,613 ha—roughly 13.5 percent of total GAP land—were being irrigated (GAPRDA 2010, 7). In 2008, the GAP Action Plan prioritized nearly 1.06 mha, roughly 59 percent of the original target, for completion in 2012 (DSI 2009a, 85). By 2010, after two consecutive years of enhanced GAP shares of the public-investment budget (12.1 percent in 2008 and 14.4 percent in 2009), 300,397 ha of GAP land, 16.5 percent of the total target (GAPRDA 2010, 5, 7) or 28 percent of the Action Plan's priority target (DSI 2010, 66), had been brought under irrigation. In fact, the uncompleted fraction of GAP's irrigable land makes up nearly 47 percent of the 3.22 mha of Turkey's total irrigable area that is not yet being irrigated. The Euphrates area has come out ahead here. By 2010, according to DSI (2010, 67), while the 256,898 ha being irrigated in the Euphrates Basin represented 22 percent of that basin's GAP irrigation target and 86 percent of all GAP irrigation, the 43,499 ha being irrigated in the Tigris Basin accounted for seven percent of that basin's irrigation target and 14 percent of all GAP irrigation.

TURKEY IN THE DOWNSTREAM POSITION

The Maritsa Basin

Bulgaria generates the headwaters of three transboundary tributaries of this river system. Upon leaving Bulgarian territory, the 500 km central Maritsa stream forms a short 15 km boundary between Bulgaria and Greece and then a 187 km boundary between Greece and Turkey, then it enters the Aegean Sea. On its way south to the sea, however, its right bank picks up water from the Arda tributary, which travels its first 240 km through Bulgaria and its final 30 km through Greece, while its left bank takes in the Tundja River, which also originates in Bulgaria before demarcating a 15 km stretch of the Turkish-Bulgarian boundary and finally flowing another 30 km through Turkey, which adds its own Ergene tributary to the Maritsa nearly 30 km from the estuary (Kibaroglu et al. 2005, 26–28).

The upstream state in this river basin also happens to hold the bulk of both the basin area and its annual runoff. Bulgaria sits on nearly two thirds of the 50,000 km² drainage area, while 26 percent lies in Turkey and eight percent in Greece, which, however, has four-fifths of the Maritsa's 188,000 km² alluvial delta zone, winter home to 300 species of birds and enjoying protected wetland status under the Ramsar Convention. Similarly, Bulgarian tributaries supply 71 percent of the basin's average annual runoff of 8 km³, while Turkey provides 23 percent and Greece supplies six percent (Kibaroglu et al., 28, 36).

Turkey's portion of the basin area is geographically located in Europe and represents one of the most developed parts of the country. According to Turkstat (2011) data, the Edirne and Kirklareli provinces are 66 and 65 percent urban and their municipal populations had an average per-capita water supply of 154 l/d and 257 l/d, respectively, in 2008. Even though this region is highly industrialized and industrial runoff generates much waterborne pollution, Turkey's Ergene basin also contains productive agriculture. Of the 1.24 mha estimated to be arable, approximately 26 percent is irrigable, but only 44 percent of irrigable land was being irrigated as of 2003 (Kibaroglu et al. 2005, 29). Seven dams have been supplying water to 60,000 ha, about two-fifths of Turkey's total Maritsa irrigation (DSI 2011f, 2011g). If all planned projects come to fruition, 257,000 ha may come under irrigation, drawing on 2.15 km³ of water (Kibaroglu et al. 2005, 29). Presently under construction on the Turkish-Bulgarian section of the Tundja tributary is the Tundja Dam, which should provide irrigation water for nearly 16,000 ha and flood control for 2,500 ha and have 11.68 MW installed capacity, capable of generating 37 GWh/year of HEP (DSI 2011f).

The Orontes Basin

The main stem of this river crosses Lebanon (upstream), Syria (midstream), and Turkey (downstream). Originating in the Bekaa Valley and flowing north between the Lebanon and Anti-Lebanon mountain ranges for 35 km before reaching Syria, it flows for another 325 km in Syria until it crosses the Turkish border, after which it traverses its final 88 km through Turkey's Hatay province, taking the confluence formed by the Karasu and Afrin tributaries (which originate in Turkey but border and traverse Syria, respectively, before re-entering Turkey) before meeting the Mediterranean Sea (Kibaroglu et al. 2005, 66). Nearly half of the 37,000 km² catchment area lies in Turkey, another 44 percent in Syria, and the remaining six percent in Lebanon, the uppermost riparian state, which generates only 11 percent of the estimated 2.8 km³ discharge, while Syria supplies 43 percent and Turkey 46 percent (Kibaroglu et al., 66–67). Hatay faces tight constraints on the extent to which it can develop all of its planned water uses. Less than half urbanized, municipal residents of the province had access to 183 l/d of water on average in 2008 (Turkstat 2011). At present, approximately 22,000 ha are being irrigated in the basin (DSI 2011h). If further plans materialize, it may be possible to bring up to 100,000 ha under irrigation, generate 180 GWh/year of HEP, supply 37 hm³ of drinking water and provide flood control for 20,000 ha (Kibaroglu et al. 2005, 69).

Disputes and Resolution Efforts between Turkey and its Riparian Neighbors

A central point to be underscored here concerns the nature of the relationship between Turkey's water-related disputes and its other conflicts with neighboring states in the transboundary river basins in question. While Turkey's water-related disputes have the distant potential to escalate into overt armed conflict (Klare 2001, 173–182), evidence is just as scant to support the possibility that Turkey can achieve "water peace" (Conca and Dabelko 1997), wherein functionalist or even "epistemic community"-driven (Kibaroglu 2008) basin-centric cooperation may impel a more broadly cooperative relationship between Turkey and its neighbors. In short, while exchanges of information and viewpoints occur among basin-state technical officials (Beschorner

1992/1993, 42), the quality of riverine cooperation is more likely to track the status of overall relations than vice versa (Brunée and Toope 1997, 47).

The Maritsa Basin

The main axis of historical disputes in this basin involves Bulgaria and Turkey. With the industrialization of Bulgaria during the Cold War its needs for water increased. In the Bulgarian part of the basin, there exist 21 dams capable of holding about 3 km³ of water (over half of the total basin runoff that Bulgarian territory contributes), 2.5 million people, and fertile agricultural land in the area of Plovdiv. The region has reportedly experienced water stress and quality deterioration (Kibaroglu et al. 2005, 29). Bulgaria has historically served as a font of negative externalities: In addition to a considerable volume of agricultural, livestock, and heavy-metal effluents generated there, its dams have aggravated scarcity and flooding as well as sedimentation in Greece and Turkey. As recently as 2005, inundation damaged large swaths of property in Greece and in the Edirne vicinity of Turkey (Kibaroglu et al. 2005, 30–31). Turkey's officials frequently underscore the importance of controlling floods, which inflict US$100 million/year of damage to its territory (DSI 2009b, 28).

Even before the end of the Cold War these two parties have agreed on certain issues. In 1968, both countries signed an agreement committing themselves to "good neighborly" limits on mutual harm, data exchange on flooding, and dispute settlement by joint commission. In 1975, they signed another technical accord on the use of boundary waters for HEP and irrigation (Kibaroglu et al. 2005, 33). The end of the Cold War provided a fresh impetus to cooperation, not least because of the sudden decline in post-Soviet economies. During the 1990s, Bulgarian water use and industrial waterborne pollution decreased considerably (Kibaroglu et al. 2005, 30). This created an opening for further Turkish-Bulgarian cooperation in 1993, when Turkey agreed to purchase nearly 16 hm³ of irrigation water from Bulgaria during a drought period. In 1998, both countries decided on a later-aborted project to build three joint dam-and-HEPPs on the Arda tributary and Turkey assented to buy the HEP (Kibaroglu et al. 2005, 33). As part of a larger 18-dam "Border Dams Project" (Yavuz 2011), construction started in 2009 on the aforementioned joint Tundja Dam project (DSI 2011f), originally conceived as part of the two countries' 1968 accord, but not revived until 2002 (Kibaroglu et al. 2005, 34). The two countries are also using EU funds to implement a flood forecasting system on their border (DSI 2009b, 29).

Turkish-Greek agreements on the Maritsa predate those between Turkey and Bulgaria. In 1934, Turkey and Greece signed an agreement specifying permitted flood- and erosion-control infrastructure and providing for data exchange, prior notification, and dispute settlement, and then in 1955, signed an unpublished agreement on construction of flood-control measures (Kibaroglu et al. 2005, 31–32). However, it was not until after substantial improvement in bilateral relations in 1999 that Greco-Turkish basin cooperation acquired fresh momentum. Under the environmental component of the European Commission's (EU) Community Initiative Program INTERREG III A/ Greece—Turkey, "priority will be given to the integrated management of the cross-border waters in accordance with the Water Framework Directive and to the management of ecosystems of exceptional ecological significance" (Kibaroglu et al. 2005, 32). The 2000 European Water Framework Directive contains explicit measures oriented towards shared management among member states, coordination between member states and non-member states, and environmental conservation and protection (UNDP 2006, 221). As Bulgaria and Greece, which signed the UNECE Water Convention and have their own joint agreements dating back to 1964 and 1971, had already been cooperating after the Cold War within the framework of the latter INTERREG program (Kibaroglu et al. 2005, 34), even before the latter joined the EU in 2007, this program and the Directive could serve to bring about tripartite arrangements to address unresolved issues of water allocation and quality as well as minimum freshwater inflows into the delta region.

The Kura-Araks Basin

In this basin, Turkey has not been generating the heaviest downstream impacts. For example, while Turkey plans to develop its section of the Kura River, the most significant pollution on that tributary originates from "Georgian industrial sites and urban conglomerations" (Kibaroglu et al. 2005, 43), which affect Azerbaijan. Furthest downstream, Azerbaijan has received industrial pollutants and agricultural pesticides emanating from Armenia and Georgia (Kibaroglu et al. 2005, 41). Turkey could have a larger impact upon the Araks River, but little of this will emanate from industrial activity. While several Turkish provinces in the area show "comparatively good environmental conditions," watershed degradation, erosion, and agricultural runoff remain key problems (Kibaroglu et al. 2005).

Turkey has numerous agreements with Georgia, Armenia, and Iran dating back to Soviet times. In fact, today's basin-centric relations between Turkey and Georgia (on both the Kura and Coruh) as well as between Turkey and Armenia (on the Arpacay tributary of the Araks) rest largely on the 1927 Kars Protocol between Turkey and the Soviet Union. This agreement encompasses border delimitation, riverbank protection, equal water shares (unlike the

Maritsa and Orontes basins, where allocations do not exist), compensation provisions, and a joint water-boundary commission (Kibaroglu et al. 2005, 39, 45). In 1964, Turkey agreed with then-Soviet republic Armenia to build the aforementioned Arpacay Dam, constructed between 1975 and 1983 (DSI 2011i). Moreover, the scope of this accord covered equal allocation of the dam's water and creation of a joint operating commission (Kibaroglu et al. 2005, 39, 45). The last agreement on this issue between Turkey and the Soviet Union in 1990 mandated that efforts to prevent or facilitate riverbed adjustments be jointly consensual (Kibaroglu et al. 2005, 45). In 1955, Turkey also agreed to supply Iran at least 1.8 m^3/s of water from the Sarisu tributary and divide Karasu tributary water in half (Kibaroglu et al. 2005).

After the Cold War, these Soviet-era agreements remained in force. Nonetheless, cooperation among the downstream riparians, particularly the Former Soviet Union (FSU) countries of Armenia, Azerbaijan, and Georgia, has not advanced much, as the "intra-Soviet Union mechanism of cooperation, information sharing . . . ceased to function after the break-up of the Soviet Union," and integration of uppermost riparian Turkey began much later (Kibaroglu et al. 2005, 44). In the early 1990s, Armenia and Azerbaijan fought over the disputed Nagorno-Karabakh enclave, resulting in the flight of about one million ethnic Azeris to Azerbaijan. Supporting Azerbaijan's blockade of this enclave, Turkey severed official relations and closed its border with Armenia and has not yet normalized them despite efforts in this direction since late 2008. Although Turkey has faced international condemnation for its alleged genocide against Armenians in 1915, domestic politics and Azerbaijan's threats to withhold natural gas supplies that Turkey needs to fuel its economy and bolster its role as an East-West energy corridor continue to hinder Turkish-Armenian rapprochement (Tekin and Williams 2011,160–161). Turkey's ability to gain Armenia's assent to adjusting the Araks riverbed to facilitate Turkey's ability to use the Arpacay Dam for irrigation has been correspondingly undermined (Kibaroglu et al. 2005, 43–44).

Turkey enjoys better post-Cold War relations with Georgia. This stems partly from Georgia's disinterest in Turkey's plans on the Kura and Araks branches: Georgia, the main source of negative externalities on the Kura, "lacks the basic monitoring capabilities required to . . . assess the water quality of the Kura River and to quantify the pollutants stemming from the Turkish stretch of the river" (Kibaroglu et al. 2005, 46). It also relates to Turkish-Georgian cooperation over pipelines that transport some of Azerbaijan's hydrocarbon supplies via the parallel Baku-Tbilisi-Ceyhan (BTC) oil and South Caucasus gas pipelines, which traverse Georgia on their way to Turkey. Between late 1998 and late 1999, Azerbaijan, Georgia and Turkey signed both the Ankara Declaration expressing support for the BTC and an intergovernmental agreement on this project at the Organization of Cooperation and Security in Europe (OSCE) summit in Istanbul (Baran 2005, 106–107). In 2000, Turkey and Georgia agreed on further technical cooperation and on certain riverbed changes (Kibaroglu et al. 2005, 39), and, in late 2010, decided to build a joint dam on the Kura (Yavuz 2011).

Economic ties work analogously in the Turkish-Iranian relationship. Despite UN and U.S. sanctions on Iran, Turkey imports about 5 km³/year of natural gas from Iran through a pipeline that can deliver twice as much, to the same Erzurum hub that receives Azerbaijan gas (Tekin and Williams 2011, 148, 150, 158–159). Just as Iranian gas deliveries have not always been reliable in winter (Tekin and Williams 2009, 347), Sarisu water to Iran often falls short of Turkey's pledged 1.8 m³/second during dry seasons (Kibaroglu et al. 2005, 46). Still, both countries have agreed to build an Araks dam to generate 192 GW/year of HEP (Yavuz 2011).

The Coruh Basin

As in the Kura Basin, the aforementioned 1927 Kars Protocol also applies to the Coruh Basin, although its practical value has diminished in light of new environmental issues. As opposed to the Kura-Araks, however, development and pollution in the Coruh Basin, which receives urban wastewater and mining discharges, do not have major agricultural characteristics, either in Turkey (because of the topographical conditions that make it more highly conducive to HEP exploitation) or in Georgia, where fishing in this basin holds more importance than water consumption (Kibaroglu et al. 2005, 50, 51). By contrast, one of today's key problems, acknowledged by both parties yet largely unmeasured, consists of the anticipated dramatic alteration of the river's sedimentation patterns caused by Turkey's dams and the consequent effects on Georgia's alluvial delta and Batumi-area coastline, which are shielded from the Black Sea's eroding force by the river's sediment deposits (Berkun 2010, 655).

As mentioned above, two Master Plan dams, the Muratli and Borcka dams, are already operating. They generate up to 1.3–1.4 TWh of HEP per annum and store up to 10 km³ of water (DSI 2009a, 71), exceeding the average annual flow. "Georgia is not dependent on the Coruh for either energy or water; this clearly reduces the potential for conflicts" (Kibaroglu et al. 2005, 50). Less auspiciously, however, Turkey's Deriner and Yusufeli projects, which are not yet online but will generate about 3.8 TWh/year of HEP (DSI 2010, 52), could have worse environmental impacts. While the Deriner Dam-and-HEPP, just upstream of the Borcka, threatens sedimentation blockage, the Yusufeli complex may have adverse effects on plants, mammals (including wild goats and bats), fish (especially migratory salmon), and over 1,400 ha of the 23,000 ha Coruh Valley Wildlife Protection Area (Berkun 2010, 655–656).

The broader Turkish-Georgian ties enumerated above aid cooperation on Coruh basin issues. FSU state Georgia acceded to the various Turkish-Soviet accords regulating their boundary waters, which encompass the Coruh's three-km border segment (Kibaroglu et al. 2005, 51). Both countries belong to the 1992 Bucharest Convention, which mandates controls on land-borne pollution and the dumping of waste into the Black Sea as well as joint response to accidents, and to the Black Sea Environmental Program (Berkun 2010, 652–653)—two Istanbul-based organizations that could facilitate cooperation on the Coruh due to its interface with the Black Sea (Kibaroglu et al. 2005, 52). Further bilateral technical cooperation and consultations occurred in the 1990s, with Turkey seeking to widen the scope of cooperation to enhance mutual gains in contrast to Georgia's narrower focus on compensation for coastal erosion. Turkey, concerned with data inadequacy, assumed responsibility for financing two disused flow-monitoring stations in Georgia, and assented to set up a joint group to monitor the effects of Deriner Dam, which broke ground in 1998 (Kibaroglu et al. 2005, 53). With more Coruh dams coming online without a comprehensive accord in place, Georgia has continued to seek compensation, and, though Turkey produced an environmental impact report on Yusufeli, scientific assessment has not been jointly consensual (Kibaroglu et al. 2005, 53).

The Euphrates-Tigris Basin

Even though previous bilateral accords existed between Turkey and Syria during French colonial administration, and between Turkey and Iraq on flood-control measures, prospective expansion in water uses led to more intractable disputes starting in the 1960s. Between 1965 and 1975, Turkey built the Keban Dam. During this time, while Syria had launched the Euphrates Valley Project, with an irrigation target of 640,000 ha, Iraq was already operating the Euphrates Dam to divert water into Al-Habbaniya Lake (Kibaroglu 2008, 186) and withdrawing 45 percent of mean annual Euphrates flow (Naff and Matson 1984, 90). Even now, Turkey depends on external sources for only one percent of its TRWR and withdraws less than one-fifth of the latter, while Iraq, which withdraws 87 percent of its TRWR, has a 53 percent "dependency ratio," and Syria, which withdraws nearly all of its TRWR, has a 72 percent "dependency ratio" (UNFAO 2010a; 2010b; 2010c).

Thus, downstream states have been cool to Turkish projects. In the first of two bilateral meetings in 1964, Turkish officials pledged to Iraq to maintain a minimum flow of 350 m³/s downstream from Keban and advanced its current position that the two rivers, which join in Iraq, belong to a common water-course, implying that Iraq could compensate for Euphrates shortages from the Tigris. The second meeting between Turkey and Syria aired similar issues (Bilen 1997, 111–112). By 1965, the World Bank approved transboundary basin project loans. Ankara secured World Bank and USAID funding for Keban only by sticking to its previous 350 m³/s pledge (Kut 1993, 4). It also obtained European Investment Bank (EIB) and other European monies for this US$85-million project (Kolars 1994, 62). Turkey also offered to convene a Joint Technical Committee (JTC) to identify each state's water and irriga-tion needs, but Iraq pressed for guaranteed flows and shares (Kibaroglu 2008, 186). The construction of Turkey's Keban and Syria's Tabqa dams by the mid-1970s worsened the effects of drought and led each downstream state to fault its immediate upstream neighbor; Baath Party leadership rivalry pushed Iraq to the brink of war with Syria (Naff and Matson 1984, 93–95).

By 1980, Syria and Iraq had drawn closer on Euphrates-Tigris water issues. Between 1976 and 1987, Turkey built the Karakaya Dam, which also regulates Keban outflows (Bilen 1997, 113). In 1979–1980, Turkey pledged in writing to guarantee at least 500 m³/s of Euphrates flow (Kut 1993, 5) to obtain World Bank funds; additional EIB, Swiss, Italian money, and outside loans met half of the project's US$1.16-billion cost (Bilen 1997, 115). In 1980, Turkey and Iraq formed the JTC. While Syria did not participate in the JTC first meeting in 1982, by 1983 Syria, which had once concurred with Turkey that the two rivers formed a single watercourse, was favoring the Iraqi stance that the rivers should be addressed singly (Bilen 1997, 112). In 1984, at the JTC's fifth meeting, Turkey advanced its "Three-Staged Plan for Optimal, Equitable and Reasonable Utilization of the Transboundary Watercourses of the Euphrates-Tigris Basin." This scheme was to inventory all basin water and land resources, identify actual needs, and jointly compile data, but Iraq and Syria insisted on divisions (Bilen 1997, 117–118; Kibaroglu et al. 2005, 61). The JTC met 16 times, but failed by 1993 for lack of a "clear and jointly agreed mandate" (Kibaroglu 2008, 187). By 1990, in proximity to the Ataturk Dam, Syria and Iraq had agreed to a respective 42–58 split of Euphrates flow at the Turkish-Syrian boundary and were demanding a minimum of 700 m³/s there (Williams 2001, 30).

Tensions escalated when Turkey built its mammoth Ataturk Dam. This dam can supply 328 m³/s to the Sanliurfa Tunnels for irrigation of 476,000 ha (GAPRDA 1997, 15). With this project, Turkey lost its World Bank funding for GAP. It however obtained US$571 million in foreign loans which made up a small fraction of the dam's US$11-billion cost (Kolars 1994, 62). Though the Karkamis and Birecik dams are only equipped for HEP and re-regulation of Ataturk Dam outflows (Ministry of Foreign Affairs 2004, 6–7), the Ataturk Dam controversy made foreign monies even scarcer. This necessitated Turkey's heavier reliance on "Build, Operate and Transfer" (BOT) schemes (where private firms build and operate projects until they secure a reasonable return, at which point they revert to host-government control), as with Birecik Dam (Williams 2001, 30), or on domestic funds.

By the new millennium, six major dams were already operating on Turkey's section of the Euphrates. This feat occurred against considerable resistance, not just from downstream states, but from an array of various domestic and international NGOs—Ataturk, Karakaya and Keban dams were estimated to have displaced about 145,000 people (McCully 2001, 334). Opposition of a similar nature confronted Tigris projects. In 2001, the Ilisu Dam remained blocked by NGO concerns that the dam would flood 52 villages and 15 small towns including Turkey's cultural-heritage city of Hasankeyf and displace up to 20,000 inhabitants, as well as by Iraqi worries over this dam's effects on its marshland delta (Berkun 2010, 651; Kibaroglu et al. 2005, 64–65). By 2006, however, Turkey obtained a US$1.64 billion loan package backed by European export-credit agencies, allowing construction to start in 2007 (Berkun 2010, 650). Coming on the heels of Iraqi claims that Iraq's spring water reserves had plummeted from 40 km^3 to 11 km^3 due to Turkish dams (Jongerden 2010, 138), the 2009 withdrawal of official Austrian, German, and Swiss loan guarantees left Andritz AG as the sole foreign consortium member. Turkey's Prime Minister Recep Tayyip Erdogan of Turkey castigated environmentalists as "terrorists" (Steinvorth 2010).

Syrian and Iraq opposition was not confined to verbal demarches. Their territories also served as bases for the Kurdistan Workers Party (PKK) to carry out its insurgency in Turkey. Lebanon's then Syria-controlled Bekaa Valley provided an initial launching pad for PKK incursions into Turkey's southeast after 1984, one year after the Ataturk Dam broke ground. In 1998 Turkey's troop buildup forced then Syrian leader Hafez al-Assad to expel PKK head Abdullah "Apo" Ocalan, who was captured in Kenya and brought back to Turkey in 1999. During this period, Turkey both appeased and threatened Syria. Turkey's 1987 protocol underlined its commitment to allowing at least half of the Euphrates flow (500 m^3/s) to cross into Syria, but Turkish leaders occasionally threatened to cut Syria off (Williams 2001, 29–31). As the Ataturk Dam's reservoir took nearly eight months in 1990 to fill and its HEP turbines required another 1.5 years (July 1992–December 1993) to come fully online (GAPRDA 1997, 13), this dam infused threats of water blockage with greater potency.

Turkish officials have unfailingly depicted their hydrological projects and operations in law-abiding terms. They contend that: the Ataturk Dam's filling

violated neither legal obligations to give prior notification nor their country's
1987 protocol commitment to Syria; Turkey's mountainous southeast is more
optimal for basin projects than further downstream, where flatter topogra-
phies, higher evaporation rates, and soil gypsum are poorly suited to HEP and
irrigation; and their dams have evened out flow variations, thus providing a
public good rather than worsen water shortages (Bilen 1997, 68–73). According to the Ministry of Foreign Affairs (2004, 6), extra releases of water from
the Keban and Karakaya dams counteracted both the effect of the 1988–1989
drought which lowered Euphrates flow to 50 m³/s and maintained flow
between November 13, 1989 and February 13, 1990—covering the January
1990 filling of the Ataturk Dam—at an average of 509 m³/s.

While Turkey's position emerged out of this earlier period of Turkish-
Syrian hostilities—largely centered on the water-PKK nexus—PKK terrorism
now sours Turkish-Iraqi relations. The 2003 US-led invasion of Iraq, which
consolidated the partial autonomy of northern Iraq's "Kurdistan Regional
Government" (KRG), revived PKK incursions into Turkey. It is difficult to
ascertain the extent to which the completion of GAP, especially its irrigation
targets, which may have stimulated PKK action independent of Syria's support, was slowed by terrorism-related instability in Turkey's southeast or simply by the glacial pace of land redistribution and on-farm training identified by
Kolars (1994, 67–68). As part of the aforementioned "Border Dams Project,"
Turkey has been building a moat-like string of 14—originally 33—new dams
in its Sirnak and Hakkari provinces to deter PKK incursions from Iraq and to
generate HEP (Haber 7 Com 2010; Jongerden 2010, 142; Yavuz 2011).

Turkey's relations with its riparian neighbors in this basin have vastly
improved since the 1980s and 1990s, but it is unclear how this has impacted
river-centric cooperation. While Turkish governments present legalistic
stances even on the use of transboundary waters where Turkey is upstream,
they also reject the notion of formal international water law. Turkey is one
of three states, including Burundi and China, to vote against the 1997 UN
Convention on the Non-Navigable Uses of International Watercourses.
Turkey does not oppose the convention in its entirety, accepting the basic
stipulations contained in articles 5–9 (Ministry of Foreign Affairs 2004,
8–9). Yet, Turkey objected to what its officials perceived as the convention's
excessive enumeration of prior-notification obligations while neglecting to
spell out "sovereignty of states over the parts of transboundary watercourses
located in their territory" (DSI 2009b, 50). While Turkish governments do not
advocate the obsolete principle of "absolute territorial sovereignty," former
Prime Minister Suleyman Demirel exemplified the official Turkish view that
"'water is an upstream resource and downstream users cannot tell us how to
use our resources'" (Bagis 1997, 577).

Practical modes of present cooperation stand in stark contrast to basin states' rigid official positions. In 2001, Turkey's GAPRDA and Syria's General Organization for Land Development (GOLD) signed a joint communiqué, which accelerated contacts and dialogue and went beyond the limited scope of the old JTC's mandate to include provisions for training, joint irrigation research with twin research stations, management of irrigation systems, "participatory rural development projects and soil improvement," and additional joint decision-making (Kibaroglu et al. 2005, 65). In 2005, Iraq, Syria, Turkey, and the United States formed the "Euphrates-Tigris Initiative for Cooperation" (ETIC), which looks "beyond water rights, per se, to themes of environmental protection: development and gender equity, water management and governance, and grassroots participation in a holistic, multistakeholder framework" (Kibaroglu 2008, 192). While ETIC's mission and its participatory framework are more inclusive than the defunct JTC's ever were, the mutual confidence it could foster among the riparians may not suffice to overcome historically high levels of mistrust that have stymied formal riverine cooperation (Kibaroglu 2008, 195).

The Orontes Basin

Although Turkey occupies an upstream position in the previous basin and a downstream position in this one, the two basins have been linked together by the common presence of Syria and Turkey. Turkey had an agreement with Syria on this basin dating back to 1939, when Syria was still under French rule, largely due to the river's demarcation of a 31 km segment of the Turkish-Syrian boundary. However, precisely as a result of that accord, Syria has long refused to recognize Turkey's sovereignty over Hatay, which contains many Arabic speakers. It was Turkey's initial objection to Syrian construction of the Ghab Valley drainage and irrigation project in this basin, dating back to 1950, that eventually led to the aforementioned World Bank policy memorandum requiring basin-wide consensus as a necessary condition for its financing of transboundary watercourse projects (Kut 1993, 4).

Until the past decade, Turkey's relations with Syria had thus festered over the unresolved political status of Hatay province and its main water source. In October 1989, Syrian jets even downed a Turkish land-survey plane flying over this province (Beschorner 1992/1993, 36). An estimated 10 percent of the 1.2 km³ of the Orontes River's mean annual flow that crosses Syria reaches Turkey, with earlier Syrian dam projects anticipated to stem the flow to 25 hm³/year (Ministry of Foreign Affairs 2004, 7). The 1998 Adana Accord, concluded after Syria's expulsion of PKK head Ocalan, set cooperation on a firmer footing. In 2004, both countries signed a trade agreement and one creating a bilateral technical commission to look into a joint dam to generate HEP and provide irrigation for 30,000 ha, two-thirds in Turkey and one-third in Syria (Kibaroglu et al. 2005, 71). Construction on this "friendship dam" started in February 2011 (Haber 7 Com 2011).

CONCLUSION

Given the size of the water resources in question and their economic importance for all three riparian states, it is understandable that the voluble controversy over Turkey's development of its upstream segment of the Euphrates-Tigris River basin often drowns out quieter cooperative efforts, which even entail the building and operating of joint hydraulic installations on border sections of various transboundary rivers. Yet, recent history shows that Turkish collaboration with its basin neighbors tends to follow, rather than lead, overall improvements in their political relations. Thus, the "zero problems" foreign policy pursued by Turkey's Justice and Development Party government should offer brighter vistas for water relations.

Nonetheless, the autonomous motor of Turkey's water-resources development, though not isolated from changes in the tenor of its larger regional relations, is not driven fully by the latter, as the Turkish energy minister's earlier remarks on the GAP scheme attest. One avenue towards enhanced cooperation among Iraq, Syria, and Turkey lies in the possibility that the domestic environmental, financial, political, and social costs of various hydrological projects, which can be sequentially evaluated and used to alter subsequent ones, will cause some of these projects to be modified, postponed, or even abandoned. An ideal candidate in this regard would seem to be GAP irrigation, which has fallen way behind schedule. Tacitly shelving some irrigation projects, coupled with engagement in "integrated water resources management" that incorporates underemphasized estuarine environmental issues, could greatly assist in achieving sustainable solutions. Conversely, Turkey's building of dam-and-HEP installations, even if these do not permanently diminish downstream flows, may continue to block full attainment of riverine peace, both at home and abroad.

REFERENCES

Bagis, A. I. 1997. "Turkey's Hydropolitics of the Euphrates-Tigris Basin." *Water Resources Development* 13: 567–581.

Baran, Z. 2005. "The Baku-Tbilisi-Ceyhan Pipeline: Implications for Turkey." In *The Baku-Tbilisi-Ceyhan Pipeline: Oil Window to the West*, edited by S. F. Starr and

S. E. Cornell, 103–118. Washington: The Central Asia-Caucasus Institute & Silk Road Studies Program.

Berkun, M. 2010. "Environmental Evaluation of Turkey's Transboundary Rivers' Hydropower Systems." *Canadian Journal of Civil Engineering* 37: 648–658.

Beschorner, N. 1992. "Water and Instability in the Middle East." Adelphi (Paper 273). London: International Institute for Strategic Studies.

Bilen, Ö. 1997. *Turkey and Water Issues in the Middle East.* Ankara: Southeastern Anatolia Project (GAP) Regional Development Administration.

Brunée, J., and S. J. Toope. 1997. "Environmental Security and Freshwater Resources: Ecosystem Regime Building." *The American Journal of International Law* 91: 26–59.

Conca, K., and G. D. Dabelko. 1997. *Environmental Peacemaking.* Washington: Woodrow Wilson Center.

Davutoglu, A. 2010. "Turkey's Zero-Problems Foreign Policy." *Foreign Policy* 20 May, available at http://www.foreignpolicy.com/articles/2010/05/20/turke ys_zero_problems_foreign_policy.

[DSI] General Directorate of State Hydraulic Works. 2009a. *2008 Activity Report* [Turkish]. Ankara: General Directorate of State Hydraulic Works, available at http://www.dsi.gov.tr/faaliyet_raporlari/2008_faaliyet_raporu.pdf.

_____. 2009b. *Turkey Water Report 2009.* Ankara: General Directorate of State Hydraulic Works, available at http://www.dsi.gov.tr/english/pdf_files/ TurkeyWaterReport.pdf.

_____. 2010. *2009 Activity Report* [Turkish]. Ankara: General Directorate of State Hydraulic Works, available at http://www.dsi.gov.tr/faaliyet_raporlari/2009_ faaliyet_raporu.pdf.

_____. 2011a. *Province Information: Kars* [Turkish]. Ankara: General Directorate of State Hydraulic Works, available at http://www.dsi.gov.tr/bolge/dsi24/kars.htm.

_____. 2011b. *Province Information: Igdir* [Turkish]. Ankara: General Directorate of State Hydraulic Works, available at http://www.dsi.gov.tr/bolge/dsi24/igdir.htm.

_____. 2011c. *Province Information: Erzurum* [Turkish]. Ankara: General Directorate of State Hydraulic Works. Available at http://www.dsi.gov.tr/bolge/dsi8/ erzurum.htm.

_____. 2011d. *Province Information: Artvin* [Turkish]. Ankara: General Directorate of State Hydraulic Works. Available at http://www.dsi.gov.tr/bolge/dsi26/ artvin.htm.

_____. 2011e. *Dams: Kralkizi* [Turkish]. Ankara: General Directorate of State Hydraulic Works, available at http://www.dsi.gov.tr/baraj/detay.cfm?BarajID=173.

_____. 2011f. *Province Information: Edirne* [Turkish]. Ankara: General Directorate of State Hydraulic Works, available at http://www.dsi.gov.tr/bolge/dsi11/edirne.htm.

_____. 2011g. *Province Information: Kirklareli* [Turkish]. Ankara: General Directorate of State Hydraulic Works. Available at http://www.dsi.gov.tr/bolge/dsi11/ kirklareli.htm.

_____. 2011h. *Province Information: Hatay* [Turkish]. Ankara: General Directorate of State Hydraulic Works. Available at http://www.dsi.gov.tr/bolge/dsi6/ hatay.htm.

_____. 2011i. *Dams: Arpacay* [Turkish]. Ankara: General Directorate of State Hydraulic Works. Available at http://www.dsi.gov.tr/baraj/detay.cfm?BarajID=82.

European Commission. 2011. *Eurostat*, available at http://epp.eurostat.ec.europa.eu/portal/page/portal/energy/data/database.

Falkenmark, M., J. Lundqvist, and C. Widstrand. 1989. "Macro-Scale Water Scarcity Requires Micro-Scale Approaches: Aspects of Vulnerability in Semi-Arid Development." *Natural Resources Forum* 13 (4): 258–267.

[GAPRDA] Southeast Anatolia Project Regional Development Administration. 1997. *Southeastern Anatolia Project*. Ankara: Afsaroglu Printing House.

_____. 2000. *Status Report: Southeastern Anatolia Project (June 2000)*. Ankara: Afsaroglu Printing House.

_____. 2008. *Southeastern Anatolia Project Action Plan (2008–2012)*, available at http://www.gapep.gov.tr/yayinlar.php?lang=en.

_____. 2010. *Southeast Anatolia Project (GAP) Latest Situation (December 2010)* [Turkish]. Sanliurfa: Southeast Anatolia Project Regional Development Administration, available at http://includes.gap.gov.tr/files/ek-dosyalar/gap/gap-son-durum/Son%20Durum-2010.pdf.

Haber 7 Com. 2010. *Border Dams Project Back to the Drawing Board!* [Turkish]. *Haber 7 Com*, 9 March, available at http://www.haber7.com/haber/20100309/Sinir-Barajlari-Projesi-sil-bastan.php.

_____. 2011. *Friendship Dam Turned into a Meeting at Amik* [Turkish]. *Haber 7 Com*, 6 February, available at http://www.haber7.com/haber/20110206/Suriye-Turkiye-dostluk-baraji-temeli-atildi.php.

Harris, L. M., and S. Alatout. 2010. "Negotiating Hydro-Scales, Forging States: Comparison of the Upper Tigris/Euphrates and Jordan River Basins." *Political Geography* 29: 148–156.

International Energy Agency. 2009. *Electricity Information 2009*. Paris: OECD/IEA.

Jongerden, J. 2010. "Dams and Politics in Turkey: Utilizing Water, Developing Conflict." *Middle East Policy* 17 (10): 137–143.

Kibaroglu, A. 2008. "The Role of Epistemic Communities in Offering New Cooperation Frameworks in the Euphrates-Tigris Rivers System." *Journal of International Affairs* 61 (2): 183–198.

Kibaroglu, A., A. Klaphake, A. Kramer, W. Scheumann, and A. Carius. 2005. *Cooperation on Turkey's Transboundary Waters: Final Report—October 2005*. Berlin: Adelphi Research.

Klare, M. T. 2001. *Resource Wars: The New Landscape of Global Conflict*. New York: Henry Holt and Company.

Kolars, J. 1994. "Problems of International River Management: The Case of the Euphrates." In *International Waters of the Middle East from Euphrates-Tigris to Nile*, edited by Asit Biswas, 44–94. Oxford: Oxford University Press.

Kolars J. F., and W. A. Mitchell. 1991. *The Euphrates River and the Southeast Anatolia Development Project*. Carbondale and Edwardsville: Southern Illinois University Press.

Kut, G. 1993. "Burning Waters: The Hydropolitics of the Euphrates and Tigris." *New Perspectives on Turkey* 9: 1–17.

McCully, P. 2001. *Silenced Rivers: The Ecology and Politics of Large Dams*. London and New York: Zed Books.

Ministry of Foreign Affairs. 2004. *Water: A Source of Conflict or Cooperation in the Middle East?* Ankara: Ministry of Foreign Affairs, available at http://www.mfa .gov.tr/data/DISPOLITIKA/WaterASourceofConflictofCoopintheMiddleEast.pdf.

Naff, T., and R. C. Matson. 1984. *Water in the Middle East: Conflict or Cooperation?* Boulder, Colorado: Westview Press.

Nippon Koei Co. Ltd., and Yuksel Proje A. S. 1990. *The Southeast Anatolia Project Master Plan Study: Final Master Plan Report, Volume 1: Executive Summary*. 2nd Edition. Ankara: Prime Ministry of Turkey, State Planning Organization.

Ozturk, M., N. C. Bezir, and N. Ozek. 2009. "Hydropower-Water and Renewable Energy in Turkey: Sources and Policy." *Renewable and Sustainable Energy Reviews* 13: 605–615.

Steinvorth, D. 2010. "Protecting Turkey's Treasures—Environmentalists See One Last Chance to Stop Ilisu Dam," 31 May, available at http://www.spiegel.de/ international/world/0,1518,697801,00.html.

Tekin, A., and P. A. Williams. 2009. "EU-Russian Relations and Turkey's Role as an Energy Corridor." *Europe-Asia Studies* 61 (2): 337–356.

_____. 2011. *Geo-Politics of the Euro-Asia Energy Nexus: The European Union, Russia and Turkey*. Houndsmills, England and New York: Palgrave MacMillan.

[Turkstat] Turkish Statistical Institute. 2011. *Turkstat*, available at http://www.turkstat .gov.tr/Start.do.

[UNDP] United Nations Development Programme. 2006. *Human Development Report 2006- Beyond Scarcity: Power, Poverty and the Global Water Crisis*. New York: United Nations Development Programme, available at http://hdr.undp.org/en/ media/HDR06-complete.pdf.

_____. 2010. *Human Development Report 2010—The Real Wealth of Nations: Pathways to Human Development*. New York: United Nations Development Programme, available at http://hdr.undp.org/en/media/HDR_2010_EN_Complete_reprint.pdf.

[UNFAO] United Nations Food and Agriculture Organization. 2010a. *Country Fact Sheet: Turkey*, available at http://www.fao.org/nr/water/aquastat/data/factsheets/ aquastat_fact_sheet_tur_en.pdf.

_____. 2010b. *Country Fact Sheet: Iraq*, available at http://www.fao.org/nr/water/ aquastat/data/factsheets/aquastat_fact_sheet_irq_en.pdf.

_____. 2010c. *Country Fact Sheet: Syrian Arab Republic*, available at http://www .fao.org/nr/water/aquastat/data/factsheets/aquastat_fact_sheet_syr_en.pdf.

_____. 2010d. *Turkey: Water Balance Sheet*, available at http://www.fao.org/nr/ water/aquastat/data/wbsheets/aquastat_water_balance_sheet_tur_en.pdf.

Williams, P. 2001. "Turkey's H$_2$O Diplomacy in the Middle East." *Security Dialogue* 32 (1): 27–40.

Yavuz, E. 2011. "Water Wars" Threat Gone with 18 Transborder River Dams." *Today's Zaman*, 11 January, available at http://www.todayszaman.com/news-232099-water-wars-threat-gone-with-18-transborder-river-dams.html.

Yuksel, I. 2010. "Energy Production and Sustainable Energy Policies in Turkey." *Renewable Energy* 35: 1469–1475.

Chapter Three

Hydropolitics and Water Security in the Nile and Jordan River Basins

Teagan E. Ward and Hillery L. Roach

"Nations fight over oil, but valuable as it is, there are substitutes for oil. There is no substitute for water. We die quickly without water, and no nation's leaders would hesitate to battle for adequate water supplies"

(Simon 1998).

It is estimated that by 2015 around 3 billion people will live in countries experiencing severe water scarcity (McDonald and Jehl 2003, 58). In the past 25 years, many countries have seen their water supplies reduced by half as their populations have doubled and the demands on water supplies have exceeded the amount of water available (Bulloch and Darwish 1993, 19). "The problem is simply people—our increasing numbers and our flagrant abuse of one of our most precious, and limited resources" (Graves, 1993). The Middle East is the most water-poor region in the world, with 9 out of 14 nations already experiencing water scarcity (McDonald and Jehl 2003, 58). As populations continue to rise, many scholars have argued that competition for this scarce resource could exacerbate the political instability in the region resulting in a "water war" (Allan 2002, 256; Starr 1991, 1).

"Rivers have a perverse habit of wandering across borders . . . and nation states have the perverse habit of treating whatever portion of them that flows within their borders as a national resource at their disposal" (Waterbury 1979, 2). This resulting interdependence on shared water resources has the potential to lead to conflict as riparian nations compete to secure their rights to use and access the rivers' flows. There are currently 263 international river basins in the world that are shared by 145 nations (Wolf et al. 2006, 2). The Danube River basin is shared by 17 riparians alone, which should be an indication of its potential as a site for water conflict (Wolf et al. 2006, 2). However, interdependence on water resources is only one part of the equation.

Peter Gleick suggests that the following characteristics, when present in an international river basin, make water a likely source for conflict: (1) the degree of water scarcity, (2) the capacity to which the water supply is shared between states, (3) the power exerted by the basin states, and (4) the accessibility to alternative freshwater sources (1993). Additionally, the adaptive capacity of riparian states, or the lack thereof, to meet growing water demands through water conservation and importing virtual water may also be a characteristic that could trigger water conflict. For example, basins such as the Nile and the Jordan, which are shared by 10 and 5 riparians, respectively, are already experiencing water scarcity and increased competition for water resources as a result of population growth and increased water demands for economic development (Wolf et al. 2006, 2). In these cases, the hegemons in these basins have already made it clear that they are willing to engage in any means necessary to achieve water security, including armed conflict with their riparian neighbors.

As water resources become increasingly scarce in this region of the world, the risk of conflict erupting between competing riparians is expected to intensify. Historically, nations like Egypt and Israel have built diversion and storage schemes within their own territories to secure the flows of the Nile and Jordan rivers to meet their growing freshwater demands, often resulting in armed hostilities with their riparian neighbors. Today these nations are facing many additional demands on their water resources. How these demands will ultimately play out on the hydropolitical board game is unknown. However, whether we see water wars or basin-wide cooperation in the future may well be dependent upon whether these riparians decide to play as a team or go it alone in their pursuit for water security.

The Nile and Jordan River basins act as ideal case studies to ask the following questions: (1) how do riparian states in transboundary basins achieve water security, and (2) in the face of increasing water scarcity, will efforts to achieve water security lead to increased conflict throughout the region or will they lead riparian states to cooperate in an effort to conserve their shared water resources? To answer these questions, the hydrogeography, history, and hydropolitics of the basins and riparian states in question need to be examined. This background will then be used to demonstrate the potential for water conflict to arise as a result of unilateral attempts to achieve water security in transboundary settings.

THE NILE RIVER BASIN

On January 25, 2011, people from around the world watched, with great trepidation, as thousands of Egyptians took to the streets of Cairo and Alexandria to voice their demands for Egyptian reform and for the resignation of their leader, President Hosni Mubarak, who had been in power for 30 years. For the first time in decades, all eyes were focused on the Nile River basin where nations have been competing for water security and water development rights for decades.

While it was once considered to be the center of civilization, the Nile River basin has become one of the most volatile regions in the world in recent decades. One of the longest rivers on earth, the Nile runs through 10, soon to be 11, riparian states, making basin-wide cooperation over the Nile's waters an extremely difficult task. In addition to being shared by such a large number of countries, the Nile is also distinguished by its highly variable flows, as well its historically asymmetrical distribution of power between upstream and downstream riparians that has the potential to lead to water conflict as riparian nations compete to exploit the waters of the Nile.

GEOGRAPHY AND HYDROLOGY OF THE NILE RIVER BASIN

The Nile River is one of the longest rivers in the world (Sutcliffe 2009, 335–364) with an estimated length of 6,718 kilometers (Dumont 2009, 21). It flows north from its most southern tributary, the Kagera River, which drains the mountains of Burundi and Rwanda, through Lake Victoria and the Sudd, and then across the Sahara, the largest desert in the world, before reaching the Mediterranean

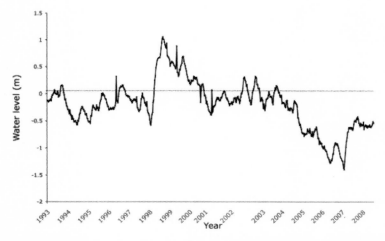

Figure 3.1.   Water levels of Lake Victoria from 1993–2008. Water level of Lake Victoria relative to the 10-year average from September 1992. More data points were available in 2002; thus, the interval is wider than for other years. Radar altimeter data were obtained from the NASA/CNES Topex/ Poseidon and Jason-1 satellite missions. *Source:* Minakawa, et al. 2008.

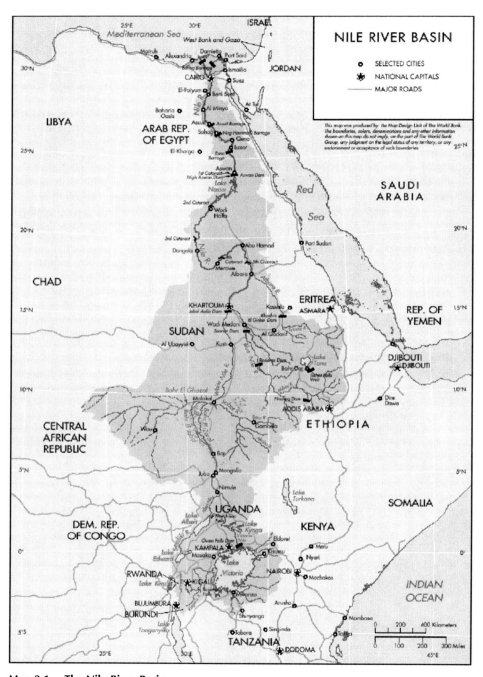

Map 3.1. The Nile River Basin

Sea (Dumont 2009, 1–21). The Nile basin has a total catchment area of 3.1 million square kilometers and is divided into three main sub-basins: the White Nile, the Blue Nile, and the main Nile where the White and Blue Nile sub-basins merge (Dumont 2009, 1–21; Elhance 1999, 55).

The White Nile originates in Lake Victoria, located in east central Africa, and then flows through a succession of rapids and falls before entering the equatorial lakes of Uganda, the Democratic Republic of the Congo, Tanzania, and Kenya. It then flows across the Sudanese border, where it is known as the Bahr el Jebel (Dumont 2009, 1–21; Elhance 1999, 56). In Sudan, the relatively flat reach of the Bahr el Jebel becomes a steeper channel dominated by swamp vegetation before entering the Sudd, the world's largest freshwater swamp (Sutcliffe 2009, 335–364). It is in this vast swampland that the White Nile loses much of its flow as a result of high temperatures, shallow swamps, and dense vegetation leading to millions of cubic meters being lost to evaporation (Bulloch and Darwish 1993, 86). South of Malakal, the White Nile is joined by two other tributaries, the Sobat River from the east and the Bahr el Ghazal in southwestern Sudan (Elhance 1999, 56). Beyond Malakal, the White Nile continues to Khartoum, the Sudanese capital, where it joins the Blue Nile from the east (Dumont 2009, 1–21).

The Blue Nile originates in Lake Tana in the central Ethiopian Highlands (Dumont 2009, 1–21) and then cascades over the Tissisat falls before meandering through an impressive gorge that is up to two kilometers deep (Dumont 2009). It continues its steep drop in elevation as it flows through deep canyons and ravines, which have created significant hydropower potential for Ethiopia (Elhance 1999, 56). Before reaching Khartoum, the Blue Nile is joined by two seasonal tributaries, the Rahad and the Dinda (Elhance 1999, 56). North of Khartoum, at Atbara, the main Nile is joined by the Atbara River which also originates in the Ethiopian Highlands (Dumont 2009, 1–21; Elhance 1999, 56). The main Nile meanders its way north of Khartoum through the arid lava fields of the Bayuda Desert and is interrupted by six rapids, or cataracts, along its course to Aswan in Egypt (Dumont 2009, 1–21; Sutcliffe 2009, 334–361). Beyond Cairo, after flowing for 1,200 kilometers through the Sahara Desert, the Nile forms a flat, triangular delta that is composed of two branches, the Rosetta and the Damietta, which empty into the Mediterranean Sea and the Suez Canal, respectively (Dumont 2009, 1–21; Elhance 1999, 56). "From Khartoum to the Mediterranean Sea, the Nile does not receive any substantial rainfall or other perennial source of water" (Elhance 1999, 57) making the downstream riparians, Egypt and Sudan, extremely dependent upon the Nile's flows to meet their water needs.

While the Nile River's catchment area covers almost 10 percent of the African continent, its average annual discharge at Aswan is only 84 billion cubic meters (Swain 2008, 202). While this amount is substantial, it is dwarfed in comparison to the average annual discharge of other major river systems in Africa: the Congo (1,250 billion cubic meters), the Volta River (390 billion cubic meters), the Zambezi River (230 billion cubic meters), and the Niger River (180 billion cubic meters) (Swain 2008, 202). Part of the reason for the relatively lower average annual discharge of the Nile is due to the highly variable flows of the Nile (Waterbury 1979, 23). The White Nile provides a small but constant flow of water to the main Nile, whereas the Blue Nile contributions vary significantly depending on the seasonal floods (Swain 2008, 202). Throughout the entire year roughly 86 percent of the Nile flow originates in the Ethiopian Highlands and only 14 percent is contributed by the White Nile (Swain 2008, 202). However, during the flood, the contribution to the Nile flow from the Ethiopian Highlands rises to 95 percent (Waterbury 1979, 23). The reason for the disproportionate contribution from the two major branches of the Nile is due to the differences in evaporation rates and degree of seasonal flooding occurring within their catchments. For example, downstream from the Sudd, the discharge of the White Nile during the flood is generally no more than three times the flow during the dry season, whereas the Blue Nile may discharge 60 times as much water during the flood compared to its flow for the rest of the year (Waterbury 1979, 23).

The Nile River basin is currently shared by 10 riparian states including: Rwanda, Burundi, the Democratic Republic of the Congo (Zaire), Tanzania, Kenya, Uganda, Eritrea, Ethiopia, Sudan, and Egypt. The total population of the countries that share the basin is almost 300 million with half of this population completely dependent upon the Nile (Swain 2008, 202). All these countries in the Nile basin are experiencing relatively high population growth. With the population of Ethiopia, Sudan, and Egypt alone expected to be close to 340 million by 2050 (Swain 2008, 202), the demands on the Nile's water resources are expected to grow substantially in the coming years while utilizable Nile flows are projected to decrease as a result of increased abstraction for irrigation, industrialization, and residential uses; water degradation as a result of increased discharge of industrial, agricultural, and wastewater pollutants; and an expected decrease in overall available supply as a result of water shortages associated with climate change (El-Sheekh 2009, 395–405; Chou, Bezark, and Wilson 1997, 100). While the Nile is currently shared by 10 riparian countries, any new water sharing agreements will have the greatest impact on Egypt and Sudan, due to their historical domination of and reliance upon the Nile's flows for survival, and on Ethiopia, where the majority of the Nile's flows originate.

Table 3.1.   Population in the Nile Basin: 1959–2030

Countries/ Year	1959	2000	2010	2020	2030
Burundi	2,213,480	6,473,000	8,519,000	10,318,000	11,936,000
D.R. Congo	13,864,421	50,829,000	67,827,000	87,640,000	108,594,000
Egypt	25,327,000	70,174,000	84,474,000	98,638,000	110,907,000
Eritrea	1,442,300	3,657,000	5,224,000	6,719,000	8,086,000
Ethiopia	27,465,000	65,515,000	84,976,000	107,964,000	131,561,000
Kenya	7,880,000	31,441,000	40,863,000	52,034,000	63,199,000
Rwanda	2,665,000	7,958,000	10,277,000	13,233,000	16,104,000
Sudan	11,030,000	34,904,000	43,192,000	53,309,000	60,995,000
Tanzania	10,078,000	34,131,000	45,040,000	59,603,000	75,498,000
Uganda	6,536,600	24,433,000	33,796,000	46,319,000	60,819,000
Total Nile Basin Population	108,481,801	329,515,000	424,188,000	535,777,000	647,699,000

Source: Data collected from the United Nations Department of Economic and Social Affairs: Population Division (2008)

Table 3.2.   Urbanization in the Nile Basin Countries: 2000–2030

Country	Urban Population In 2000	% Of population in 2000	Projected Urban population in 2030	% Of population in 2030
Burundi	536,000	8.28	2,362,000	19.78
DRC	15,168,000	29.84	53,382,000	48.23
Egypt	30,032,000	42.79	56,447,000	50.89
Eritrea	650,000	17.77	2,780,000	34.38
Ethiopia	9,762,000	14.9	31,383,000	23.85
Kenya	6,204,000	19.73	20,884,000	33.04
Rwanda	1,096,000	13.77	4,550,000	28.25
Sudan	11,661,000	33.40	33,267,000	54.54
Tanzania	7,614,000	22.30	29,190,000	64.15
Uganda	2,952,000	12.08	12,503,000	20.55
Total	85,675,000	26	246,748,000	38.09

Source: Data collected from the United Nations Department of Economic and Social Affairs: Population Division (2009).

Egypt

"Egypt is the Nile and the Nile is Egypt, the saying goes, and it is true that without the Nile, Egypt would be very different. The river has shaped the people, their beliefs and customs, and is a prime concern of every Egyptian government, making Cairo as concerned with affairs in the heart of Africa as it is with events in the Arab world" (Bulloch and Darwish 1993, 26).

Egypt covers an area of about one million square kilometers, but roughly 96 percent of Egypt's population of 80 million people lives within 12 miles of the Nile River valley and delta which only occupy about 5.5 percent of the total area of the country (UPI 2011, 1; Elhance 1999, 61). The landscape of Egypt is incredibly arid and 94.5 percent of its landmass is dominated by desert (Hamza 2009, 75–94). The Nile River supplies almost 96 percent of Egypt's water needs and the other four percent are supplied by underground reserves, small amounts of rainfall, agricultural drainage water, and treated municipal water (Swain 2008, 204; Elhance 1999, 57). Thus, no other country in the basin is as utterly dependent on the Nile's waters for its survival as is Egypt. This obvious vulnerability is at the heart of much of Egypt's psychological response to all perceived threats from its upstream riparians (Waterbury 1979, 63). Historically this feeling of vulnerability has led Egypt to seek water security through both unilateral and bilateral water storage and diversion schemes such as the Aswan High Dam, the Jonglei Canal, and the Al-Salaam Canal (Swain 2008, 204). Egypt continues to rapidly industrialize; however, agriculture still accounts for 17 percent of its Gross Domestic Product (GDP) (Hamza 2009, 75–94). With Egypt's population rising by 1.3 million each year, the demands on its increasingly scarce water supply are also expected to increase in order to provide water for basic human needs, industrialization, and for increasing crop production (Swain 2008, 204). Despite signing water sharing agreements with Sudan in 1929 and 1959, Egypt and Sudan have yet to sign the new Nile Comprehensive Framework Agreement which would create a new water allocation framework for sharing the Nile's waters among all 10 riparians. The military-run government that has taken over from Mubarak has not yet indicated what it plans to do regarding the Nile issue; nonetheless, Nile water security, whether through unilateral or cooperative means, is expected to remain on Egypt's political agenda regardless of who is in charge.

Sudan

Sudan is currently the largest country in the African continent (Swain 2008, 205), and occupies an area equal to almost a third of the continental United States (Waterbury 1979, 9). While historical average population densities in Egypt were 1,000 people per square kilometer, Sudan's population was much more dispersed across its vast territory with average densities of only six to seven people per square kilometer (Waterbury 1979, 9). The northern and southern provinces of Sudan are divided due to religious and ethnic differences, and are also set apart due to their variations in climate with the northern part of the country receiving virtually no rainfall and being highly dependent upon irrigation for agriculture while the southern-most part of the country receives an average annual rainfall of over 1,600 millimeters (Swain 2008, 205). Due to the low rainfall in northern Sudan, where the central government is located, the Sudanese are highly dependent upon the flows of the Nile to meet their growing needs (Swain 2008, 205). Being one of the most downstream nations of the Nile River, Sudan has made an effort to achieve water security by signing water sharing agreements with Egypt and by building both unilateral and bilateral water storage and diversion schemes for flood control and to increase the amount of arable land for irrigation (Swain 2008, 205). Later in 2011, southern Sudan will secede from the rest of Sudan to become the 11th riparian in the Nile basin. What this will mean for water security in the north and how the water rights of this new Republic of Southern Sudan will be included in any water-sharing arrangement between the 10 current Nile riparians is yet to be determined; however, after decades of civil war, the southern portion of Sudan is now pushing to develop its untapped economic potential and with it, the demands on the Nile's water resources are expected to rise.

Ethiopia

Unlike the downstream nations of Egypt and Sudan, which depend upon the Nile's waters for survival, Ethiopia is the origin of eleven rivers including the Blue Nile and the Atbara Rivers (Bulloch and Darwish 1993, 99). While much of Ethiopia is semi-arid, the Ethiopian Highlands experience severe downpours during the rainy season. These rains not only enable Ethiopia to supply much of the main Nile's flows via contributions from the Blue Nile and Atbara Rivers, but also erode the soils from the Ethiopian Highlands and send rich silts downstream to Sudan and Ethiopia (Bulloch and Darwish 1993, 99). So far, Ethiopia is only cultivating 11 percent of the economical irrigation potential for the country; but, there is growing demand for water resources to further develop the country's agricultural production (Swain 2008, 206). Most of Ethiopia's food production is concentrated in the Ethiopian Highlands where 88 percent of the population lives (Swain 2008, 206). As Ethiopia overcomes its long history of rebellion, civil war, disintegration and famines, it faces increased pressure to develop its economy and achieve self-sufficiency in food production by developing its share of water projects on the Nile for irrigation and hydropower facilities (Bulloch and Darwish 1993, 98). However, any dams that Ethiopia builds along the Nile are likely to be seen as a threat to the water security of its downstream neighbors, as 85 percent of the Nile's flow originates in Ethiopia (Swain 2008, 207). Unless a basin-wide cooperative agreement can be negotiated, Ethiopia's development plans may become a cause for conflict in the Nile River basin.

HISTORY AND HYDROPOLITICS OF THE NILE RIVER BASIN

"Hydropolitics in the Nile basin can be understood only if it is recognized outright that without the Nile's water Egypt would cease to exist as a viable state." After all, "no other country in the world is so dependent on the water of a single river that it shares with not two or three but [nine] other states, all located upstream from Egypt" (Elhance 1999, 53–54). While Egypt may be the strongest state in the Nile basin, both economically and militarily, it is also the most vulnerable to matters affecting its national water security due to its position as the most downstream nation in the basin (Elhance 1999:,54).

During the colonial period, Great Britain essentially had control over the entire Nile River from its source in east Africa all the way to the Mediterranean Sea (Elhance 1999, 68). The British had control over Egypt and Sudan, as well as three upper riparian states: Kenya, Tanzania, and Uganda. To achieve full control over the Nile the British signed treaties with other colonizers and initiated an Anglo-Egyptian condominium over Sudan in 1899 that declared that no projects could be built in the basin and no water could be withdrawn upstream from Egypt without Egyptian and British consent (Elhance 1999, 68). Egypt was a strategic and economic ally, important for the British due to the value of its ports in the Mediterranean, the Red Sea, and the Suez Canal for British colonial trade routes (Elhance 1999, 68). This "colonial-era mentality" was inherited by the rulers of independent Egypt and still drives hydropolitics in the Nile River basin today (Elhance 1999, 69).

The 1929 Agreement between Egypt and Britain is a noteworthy example of this "colonial-era mentality" in which Britain, representing Kenya, Tanzania, Sudan, and Uganda, declared that "no works of other means likely to reduce the amount of water reaching Egypt were to be constructed or taken in Sudan or in territories under British administration without prior Egyptian consent" (Elhance 1999, 69). This agreement also allowed Egypt to undertake its own water projects throughout much of the Nile basin territories—essentially giving Egypt a monopoly over the development and use of the Nile's water resources (Elhance 1999, 70). Under this 1929 Agreement,

Egypt received 48 billion cubic meters of water annually, whereas Sudan only received 4 billion cubic meters, and the other riparians were effectively ignored (Bulloch and Darwish 1993, 87).

The growing populations throughout the region pressed upon Egypt, and Britain, the need for perennial irrigation and the need for year-round storage of the Nile's flows to meet growing needs for agriculture and later for industrial use (Dumont 2009, 1–21). This need for year-round storage led to the building of the initial dam at Aswan and inspired the framework for a management plan that was later known as the Century Storage Scheme (Dumont 2009, 1–21). The main components of the Century Storage Scheme, first proposed in the 1920s, included: controlling water runoff from Lake Victoria using a dam at Owen Falls in Uganda that would provide storage for the irrigation needs for Egypt and Sudan while providing hydroelectricity to several upper riparians (Elhance 1999, 71). Several other storage dams were also proposed under this scheme in the Blue Nile basin, but the Jonglei Canal project in southern Sudan was by far the most ambitious of the projects proposed. The canal was intended to act as a bypass around the Sudd swamps to prevent a large fraction of the White Nile's flows from being lost to evaporation (Elhance 1999, 71). In the end, only the Owen Falls Dam and part of the Jonglei Canal were ever built according to the Century Storage Scheme (Elhance 1999, 71). The Jonglei Canal project was resurrected in the 1970s but then had to be abandoned in 1983 due to civil war in the south and destruction of excavation equipment by the Sudan People's Liberation Army (SPLA) (Allan 2010, 2).

One of the reasons that the Century Storage Scheme proposal of 1946 was set aside was due to Egypt's new focus on the Aswan High Dam proposal which would allow Egypt to continue its "colonial-era mentality" and rather than having to negotiate projects under the auspices of political developments occurring upstream, it could focus on controlling the Nile by means of one giant water project located completely within its own territory (Elhance 1999, 75; Waterbury 1979, 99). The new Egyptian leadership in 1952, led by Gamal Abd al-Nasser, felt a strong "need to assert Egypt's national sovereignty and territorial integrity and concretely demonstrate to its own people and to the rest of the world its resolve to transform Egypt into a modern, industrialized nation" (Elhance 1999, 75). It was felt by the Nasserist regime that the Aswan High Dam would enable Egypt to achieve its goals of national water security, economic and agricultural development and would also establish a higher prior use of the Nile's waters by Egypt to provide leverage in future water allocation negotiations (Elhance 1999, 76). While the dam was originally to be financed by the United States and Britain, events that occurred as a result of the 1948 arms embargo and new conflicts erupting between Israel and Egypt over the Gaza raid of 1955, ultimately forced Egypt to sign an agreement with the Soviet Union to finance the Aswan High Dam project in 1958, making the dam a focal point of the Cold War (Elhance 1999, 77; Waterbury 1979, 107).

Although the dam was presented by the new Egyptian regime as a joint undertaking with Sudan since its inception in 1952, the Egyptian leaders made no effort to include Sudan in the process and did not formally inform the Sudanese of their intentions to construct the Aswan High Dam on the Sudanese-Egyptian border near Aswan until 1954 (Waterbury 1979, 68). Bilateral talks between the two states began in 1954 during Sudan's three-year transition period when British administrators were still very much involved in Sudanese politics. The years 1954–1958 were characterized by political conflicts and rising tensions between Egypt and Sudan as a result of the Sudanese voicing their objections to the Aswan High Dam and making continued demands for the renegotiation of the 1929 Agreement. However, a military coup in Sudan in 1958 resulted in the establishment of a new leadership in Sudan that was more open to negotiating with the Egyptian government (Okoth 2007, 86; Wolf 2003, 119). The resulting negotiations between the two states focused on establishing criteria for water allocations for Egypt and Sudan that would later become the 1959 Agreement for the Full Utilization of the Nile Waters (Waterbury 1979, 68). An additional requirement under the Agreement included the establishment of a Permanent Joint Technical Commission (PJTC) that would station water inspectors within each country to collect hydrological data, and supervise studies and the implementation of water projects on the Upper Nile (Waterbury 1979, 73). As part of the Agreement, Egypt agreed to pay Sudan US$43 million as compensation for the flooding of land and the displacement of people that would result from the construction of the project (Elhance 1999, 77). The Agreement completely allocated the Nile's flow at Aswan (assumed to be 84 billion cubic meters) between the two countries, without taking into account any claims or future water needs of the other riparians (Elhance 1999, 77). As a result of the Agreement and the construction of the Aswan High Dam, Egypt would receive a total of 55.5 billion cubic meters from the Nile while Sudan would receive 18.5 billion cubic meters (up from the original four billion cubic meters agreed upon in the 1929 Agreement). The remaining 10 billion cubic meters of water was expected to be lost due to evaporation and seepage from the reservoir (Elhance 1999, 77; Waterbury 1979, 72). Like the 1929 Agreement, this bilateral agreement failed to consider any water claims by the other riparian states.

Construction of the Aswan High Dam began in 1961 and was completed in 1968, creating the longest man-made lake in the world: extending in Egypt for almost 300 kilometers as Lake Nasser and for 180 kilometers as

Lake Nubia in Sudan (El-Shabrawy 2009). While it was expected to produce 10 billion kilowatt hours of electricity each year, the highest recorded figure was only 8 kilowatt hours during the 1980s (Elhance 1999, 78). In addition to providing much of Egypt's electricity, the dam also increased the arable land in Egypt by 30 percent and enabled the use of perennial irrigation throughout much of the Nile Valley (El-Shabrawy 2009). It also provided Egypt with water security; protecting it from floods and offering year-round storage during times of drought. However, in spite of the many benefits associated with the dam, it is also responsible for causing many socioeconomic and environmental problems in the Nile River basin. For example, the dam now holds back the silts, making the Nile soil fertile for thousands of years. This impact has now been offset by the application of 10^6 tons of chemical fertilizers each year (El-Shabrawy 2009), which has resulted in additional challenges for the Nile as these chemical fertilizers re-enter the river in agricultural runoff leading to explosive algal growth and water quality degradation (Elhance 1999, 78). Additionally, this new source of cheap irrigation water encouraged Egyptian farmers to over-irrigate their fields without creating proper drainage ditches (Elhance 1999, 78). These practices have resulted in a rising water table, and as a consequence, many large tracts of once arable farmland have now been abandoned due to water logging and salinity (Elhance 1999, 79). Also, the silts that once replenished the delta and protected Egypt's coastline from subsiding are now entrapped behind the Aswan High Dam resulting in the subsidence of low-lying sections of Egypt's coastline, which is already at risk for flooding as a result of projected sea level rise (Elhance 1999, 58, 79). However, despite the many critiques of the project since its inception, the Aswan High Dam remains "a giant symbol of Egypt's long quest for sovereignty, national security, economic prosperity, and technical accomplishments" (Elhance 1999, 74).

Gamal Abd al-Nasser, who died in September of 1970, did not live to see the completion of the Aswan High Dam (Waterbury 1979, 113). In January 1971, Nasser's successor, Anwar al-Sadat, presided over the dam's inaugural ceremony with the USSR President, Nikolai Podgorny, at his side. Much of Sadat's speech was spent criticizing the United States and praising the new Soviet-Egyptian ties and the anticipated fruits of their joint venture. However, within months of the inauguration of the dam, Sadat decided to cut all ties with the Soviet Union and unilaterally abrogated the Soviet-Egyptian Friendship Treaty that had been signed in 1971 (Waterbury 1979, 113). In October 1975, when officials gathered to watch the filling of Lake Nasser, there was not a Soviet to be seen (Waterbury 1979, 115).

In February 1979, the Egyptian President Anwar al-Sadat signed the Camp David Accords with Israel and declared that there would be no more war between Egypt and Israel, after almost three decades of hostility (Bulloch and Darwish 1993, 79). While his actions were supported by millions across the globe, much of the Arab world saw his actions as a great betrayal (Bulloch and Darwish 1993, 79). Back in Cairo, opinion was deeply divided. Many of the senior officials, ministers, and military officials were very concerned by Sadat's actions and several of them resigned. The Egyptian people, however, appeared to be in support of Sadat's actions as they were tired of wars (Bulloch and Darwish 1993, 79).

Within a year of Sadat's diplomatic detente with Israel, several plots to overthrow the Egyptian president were unveiled. While the reasoning behind these plots was partially due to Sadat's effort to make peace with Israel, these plots were also justified in order to prevent Sadat from agreeing to divert water from the Nile to irrigate the Negev Desert in Israel, an idea discussed during the peace talks at Camp David (Bulloch and Darwish 1993, 80). The idea to divert roughly one percent of the Nile's flow through a pipeline to Israel had been discussed for years by hydrologists (Bulloch and Darwish 1993, 80). The project was to be financed by both nations and was to provide work for both Israelis and Egyptians. It was also hoped that the project could lead to cooperation with other states through the extension of the pipeline through Lebanon and Jordan to create a regional water network (Bulloch and Darwish 1993, 80). Sadat supported the arrangement, but did not realize the degree of opposition brewing both at home and abroad, and after several warnings including from Washington, D.C., he dropped the idea of cooperating with Israel over water (Bulloch and Darwish 1993, 83). Thus, this proposed project with Israel illustrates that "water came close to causing the downfall of Sadat long before the bullets of fundamentalist extremists killed him in 1981" (Bulloch and Darwish 1993, 80).

After signing his initial agreement with Israel, Sadat was concerned that the greatest threats to Egypt and to the Nile were events occurring in Africa, particularly in Ethiopia. Ethiopia was incensed when it heard of Sadat's plan to divert the Nile's waters to the Negev Desert as it would involve the allocation of Nile water to an area outside of the Nile basin, a decision that could only be made with the consent of all of the Nile basin states (Bulloch and Darwish 1993, 84). However, Egypt was much concerned with developments in Ethiopia. The Egyptian intelligence had reported that Israeli engineers were helping Ethiopia to plan new dams to be constructed on the Nile (Bulloch and Darwish 1993, 84). This perceived threat from Ethiopia and Israel planning new developments on the Nile was enough to make Egypt re-assert its military dominance over its upstream neighbors, with Sadat voicing a warning that "the only matter that could take Egypt to war again is water" (Bulloch and Darwish 1993, 84). Ethiopia might very well end up being the instigator for water conflict in the Nile River basin due to the fact that it "has its hand on the taps that supply Sudan and Egypt" (Bulloch and Darwish 1993, 99). While the potential to harness the Nile in Ethiopia has always been apparent, decades of civil war and famine meant that this was an empty threat. After Nasser's death, relations between Egypt and Ethiopia became increasingly tense. Sadat was often cited using overt threats of war against any country that tried to affect the flow of the Nile (Mohamoda 2003). Covert operations were undertaken against riparian countries to destabilize them and to limit the capacity of other states to develop the Nile. Egypt gave aid to various armed groups against riparian countries, including Eritrea against Ethiopia in 1962, the support for Somalia in armed conflicts with Ethiopia in 1960, 1964, and 1977–79, eventually leading to conflict with Kenya after the country joined Ethiopia in 1977 to fight against the Somali aggressors (Kagwanja 2007, 325). However, the end of civil war and the push for economic development and food security put Ethiopia in a much better position to harness its hydroelectric power potential (Bulloch and Darwish 1993, 99). Ethiopia plans to construct several major dams and irrigation schemes along the Blue Nile within the next few years. These projects are dependent upon Chinese investment and expertise as well as financial support from the World Bank (Cascao 2009, 254). Surely, these proposed projects are seen as a direct threat to the water security of Sudan and Egypt.

While Sudan and Egypt have been engaged in cooperative water agreements over the Nile since the 1950s, Sudan also has plans to harness the Nile through additional hydropower dams and irrigation schemes (Cascao 2009, 257). Protracted civil war between North and South Sudan, political instability throughout the state, the ongoing conflict in the Darfur region, and lack of international funding or support for hydropower and irrigation projects have hindered Sudan's plans and Sudan has had a very limited ability to develop its largely untapped water development potential on its own (Cascao 2009, 257; Wichelns et al. 2003, 543). However, the Peace Agreement with Southern Sudan in 2005, in addition to Sudan's extensive exploitation of its oil resources, have made conditions for investing in water development projects much more favorable in recent years (Cascao 2009, 257). Sudan is now determined to utilize its full water development potential in the coming years through investment in multiple hydraulic facilities—generating high levels of concern in Egypt (Cascao 2009, 257).

Egypt has also been pursuing several of its own water projects to meet the demands of its growing population. Since the late 1990s, Egypt has undertaken three projects to extend the Nile's reach out to the Sinai and south-western desert by 2017: the West Delta Irrigation Project, the North Sinai Agriculture Development Project (Al-Salaam Canal), and the South

Valley/Toshka Development Project, which would reclaim thousands of hectares of land for agricultural development (Cascao 2009, 249). These projects have received much criticism and are considered as the "'pharaonic' monument building of President Mubarak" just as the Aswan High Dam was considered to be Nasser's "pyramid" (Cascao 2009, 249). Within the Nile River basin, these projects are viewed as continued attempts by Egypt to prevent other riparians from making use of their share of the Nile's waters.

Despite these unilateral development projects by Ethiopia, Sudan, and Egypt, all of the Nile basin riparians have been engaged in cooperative efforts since the 1990s through the Nile Basin Initiative (NBI) which aims "to achieve sustainable socioeconomic development through the equitable utilization of, and benefit from, the common Nile Basin water resources" (Swain 2008, 209). Contrary to the promises of many of the Nile's riparians to strive for basin-wide cooperation, these countries are obviously still engaging in unilateral, large-scale projects within their own territories. Moreover, while the NBI has helped to alleviate some international tensions over the Nile, the demands on the Nile's water resources are still increasing at an unsustainable rate (Swain 2008, 210).

WATER SECURITY AND THE NILE RIVER BASIN: MOVE TOWARDS REGIONALISM OVER BILATERALISM

As discussed above the Nile River is unique among international rivers in that it is shared by 10 relatively young riparian nations, experiencing water stress due to growing demands, and the Nile the sole source of freshwater available throughout the arid portion of its basin. Additionally, its unique colonial heritage has resulted in very asymmetrical power dynamics throughout the basin; notably Egypt's domination of the Nile's flows since 1929 as a result of its long-held prior use rights and economic and military superiority over the upstream riparians, and, until fairly recently, the underutilization of the Nile's flows by upstream riparians that lacked the economic investment, political will, and technological know-how to harness the Nile's flows. All of these factors have meant that much of the hydropolitical history of the Nile basin has been defined by Egypt's unilateral pursuit for water security: to tap the Nile's resources before its upstream neighbors do, no matter what the cost.

Egypt's historical obsession with water security is especially obvious through its water-sharing agreements with Sudan and its continued pursuit of unilateral water storage and diversion schemes, often constructed without giving consideration for the future water claims of its upstream neighbors. The Aswan High Dam is just one example. Resulting in substantial socio-economic and irreversible environmental impacts, the dam allowed Egypt to establish a more secure source of water within Egyptian territory, to achieve greater food security through the resulting widespread, perennial irrigation, and to hold a stronger bargaining position with its upstream riparians for future water allocation discussions as a result of a higher level of prior use of the Nile's waters by Egypt (Elhance 1999, 76). As discussed above, since the 1950s, Egypt has continued to pursue greater water security through numerous water diversion projects including the Jonglei Canal in Sudan, the Al-Salaam Canal (North Sinai Agriculture Development Program), and several additional agricultural development projects to increase cultivation in the Egyptian deserts. Sudan and Ethiopia are also attempting to pursue greater water security through the development of hydropower facilities and water diversion projects within their own territories. Both of these countries have substantial water development potential that has been left largely untapped until now.

However, despite many unilateral attempts by the Nile riparian states to achieve water security, the Nile's flows are not inviolable. It took eight years of drought during the 1980s to force the Nile basin countries to acknowledge the water crisis they were now confronting. "The drought which first hit the Ethiopian hills in 1979–1980 lasted until late 1987, and at its worst in 1983–1984 the Nile flow measured at Aswan was only 42 billion cubic meters, half its normal flow" (Bulloch and Darwish 1993, 87). This drought was so severe that Lake Nasser dropped to 148 meters in the summer of 1987, the lowest in its 30-year history, and Egypt had to modify many of its water laws and regulations and introduce new, more efficient irrigation practices to adapt to this new era of inadequate water resources (Bulloch and Darwish 1993, 88). "Those years of drought changed the national mood in Egypt, shaking people out of their comfortable assumptions about the Nile and forcing them to think about the dangers to that vital asset. For the first time, people worried about the water crisis. The records of water flows and lake depths made them realize, perhaps for the first time, that the Nile was not inviolable" (Bulloch and Darwish 1993, 88). This water crisis forced the Nile basin countries to make national, and regional, water security a top priority and acted as a catalyst for the creation of the NBI to improve regional water security through increased basin-wide cooperation.

Most of the Nile basin countries believe that the treaties originally agreed upon by Egypt and their colonial masters are illegal. Uganda called for the rejection of the colonial-era treaties and in 2004 the Ugandan president questioned Egypt's monopolization of the Nile (Kagwanja 2007, 328).

Water stress is starting to take its toll in the EAC countries due to large-scale droughts, a drop in the level of Lake Victoria, and the over abstraction of water to generate power. The decreased level of Lake Victoria has caused a severe power shortage in many countries by undermining the production of the Owen Falls Dam hydroelectricity facility.

Poverty is prevalent in the Lake Victoria basin and the waters provide a livelihood for many people in the area. The falling water levels are sure to impact many of their jobs. The amount of land that is mismanaged or degraded around the lake is increasing, reducing the output of agriculture in the basin (El Zain 2000, 7). This, coupled with an increasing population and possible future food scarcity, makes cooperation around Lake Victoria a necessity. The EAC's top priority is water and while they largely focus on the waters of Lake Victoria, as demand increases, they have agreed to act as a block in future Nile negotiations (EAC 2010).

EGYPT'S NEW STRATEGY?

Egypt, under President Mubarak, moved away from the rhetoric of war over the Nile waters and began dealing more amicably over the issue. Its foreign policy has shifted from confrontation to cooperation and from fostering instability under Sadat to promoting peace in the Nile basin (Kagwanja 2007). Egypt and Ethiopia have had a long history of strained relations, particularly under the Sadat presidency when Egypt was funding Ethiopia's opposition. "Egypt recognizes each state has rights to equitable utilization of its waters in accordance with international law . . . existing water agreements do not hinder the utilization of the Nile by and of the Riparian states" (Kagwanja 2007, 328).

Egypt's new strategy is to continue to support the claim that the colonial water agreements are still binding while allowing countries to move forward with Nile projects, so long as they are not big enough to significantly affect the volume of water that reaches Egypt. Its strategic interest of maximizing its share of the Nile waters has remained the same but its actions appear to be giving other riparian countries some leeway in developing the Nile projects. Egypt has even partnered with some riparian countries to support food production. But why promote cooperation now?

Egypt's overall water supply is not increasing, but its population and food demand certainly are. However, decreased rainfall in the Ethiopian highlands, variable rainfall in Uganda, with Sudan rapidly approaching its allocation of Nile waters under the 1959 agreement, and increased claims of the "maldistribution" of the Nile waters, have all led to the need for measures to sustain the Nile waters through cooperation with other countries to ensure Egypt's supply despite a lack of pressure from Ethiopia and Uganda. The recent move of Egypt away from its defensive posture towards cooperation has allowed for the creation of the NBI, but is this initiative enough to stop potential conflict?

THE NILE BASIN INITIATIVE

In 1999, the NBI was created involving all 10 riparian states. The mission of the NBI was to explore the mechanisms required to establish a permanent cooperative framework, and in 2002 the NBI secretariat was created. The goal of the NBI is to develop the Nile in a sustainable, equitable, and cooperative manner, and to ensure the future supply of water. In doing this it hopes to share the socioeconomic benefits of such cooperation and promote peace and stability in the region (NBI 2010). While the initiative indicates a move toward cooperation among riparian states, several roadblocks have impeded its progress in achieving any meaningful progress. The first problem stems from a mutual distrust between riparian countries. The long history of conflict between countries makes it difficult for them to trust one another and cooperate. The EAC countries and Egypt and Sudan have been involved in talks outside of the cooperative framework of the NBI, excluding other riparian countries and furthering the general lack of trust. Second, the issue of the status of the colonial treaties is not resolved. Egypt and Sudan actively defend the colonial treaties while other riparian countries believe that the 1929 Nile Water Agreement should not be allowed to continue and a new negotiated settlement should be created. Although, the Nile basin countries do seem to agree that the 1929 treaty should be defended or challenged through peaceful means. Finally, there is a conflict of interests in hydroelectric power generation. Many countries would like to create their own hydropower plants while others want to export some of the existing power already generated by current facilities. These three issues have led to a stalemate on negotiations of new agreements on the allocation of the Nile water between riparian countries.

No Nile state claims that there is a crisis concerning the Nile and the use of its waters to date. Because there is no crisis yet, hence there isn't any particular urgency to resolve the problems within the NBI framework. As time passes, it becomes more and more likely that any future relations between riparian countries will be in the form of bilateral, contractual agreements as opposed to multi-lateral frameworks for development and sustainability involving all 10 riparian countries (Abdullah Ali 2009).

In order for the NBI to develop into meaningful cooperation on the development of the Nile basin, riparian states must change their approach from state-centric to basin-based strategy (Abdullah Ali 2009). None of the Nile basin countries have ratified the 1997 UN Convention on the Law of the Non-navigational Uses of International Watercourses calling for the equitable and reasonable utilization of water (United Nations 1997, Article 5) and requiring states to "take all appropriate measures to prevent the causing of significant harm" (United Nations 1997, Article 7) to other states sharing an international watercourse. While some upstream riparian countries have called for similar measures, none of them have signed the convention and many abstained from voting. This indicates that they are still in the state-centric mindset concerning the management of the Nile waters (Swain 2008, 11). The NBI, though a move towards cooperation, has been ineffective in designing a legal framework in which to solve the problems concerning the allocation of the Nile waters and for developing the Nile for mutual benefit. Most progress has been made on small issues of little or no real importance while the larger issues have been ignored. The emphasis of the NBI on consensus has largely contributed to its standstill in coming to an agreement over the Nile waters. Meanwhile tensions between and within countries continue to mount.

Egypt and Sudan remain firmly against a proposed new agreement in favor of the colonial era agreements (Ethiopian Reporter 2010) that ensure their access to the Nile water. On May 14, 2010, four Nile countries, Rwanda, Ethiopia, Uganda, and Tanzania, signed the Cooperative Framework Agreement (CFA) on the Nile waters (Sudan Tribune 2010). In response to the new CFA, Egypt threatened legal action if the process of implementing the agreement moves forward. The signing of the CFA is largely seen as a setback to real cooperation through the NBI and has the potential to ultimately end the initiative if the four countries try to push it forward towards implementation.

While the signing of the CFA was one setback to cooperation among Nile countries, it has not been the only one. Ethiopia has recently accused Egypt, on the basis of solid evidence, of funding rebel groups to destabilize Ethiopia (Ethiopian Reporter 2010). Prime Minister Meles Zanawi of Ethiopia boasted that Egypt could not win a war against Ethiopia over the Nile. Egypt responded, maintaining that relations between the two countries are amicable and that Egypt is not involved with any group within Ethiopia (Bulletin 2010). Despite numerous efforts at cooperation, the rhetoric of conflict continues between Egypt and Ethiopia but the balance of power has been shifting. Egypt is still the dominant power in the Nile basin, although other countries have been gaining ground in recent years and could soon present a real challenge to Egypt. In the short term Egypt is more concerned with instability within one of its greatest allies in the Nile basin, Sudan.

On January 9, 2011, South Sudan went to the polls to vote in a referendum to determine the country's future as one state or a separate North and South Sudan. Ninety-nine percent of southerners voted for succession of the South from the North (B. N. Staff 2011). The Comprehensive Peace Agreement for Sudan outlines power sharing, wealth sharing, conflict resolution, and security arrangements but it makes no mention of an agreement on the Nile waters in the event that the South secedes (Comprehensive Peace Agreement 2002). The Comprehensive Peace Agreement does stipulate that it is not intended to address the ownership of natural resources but that the parties agree to establish a process to resolve this issue (2002, Chapter 3, Section 2.1). This referendum also affects Egypt which favors a united Sudan to negotiate sharing of the Nile waters with Sudan's support. The vote for the South to secede indicates that there may be a higher chance of conflict over the Nile's resources in the coming years, particularly as South Sudan seeks to develop its water resources.

On January 25, 2011, Egyptians took to the streets in an 18-day protest that removed President Hosni Mubarak from power, replaced by the Supreme Council of the Armed Forces. During these 18 days, the police forces largely disappeared from the streets of Egypt and the military was forced to take over policing activities. These events could have an impact on conflict or cooperation in the Nile basin. First, Egypt's government could be viewed as weak by riparian countries that may seek to act while Egypt's military is busy with internal affairs. Burundi took advantage of the uprising to sign the controversial Nile pact joining the four other riparian countries (Staff 2011). Second, the new Egyptian government could stress the importance of cooperation in their weakened state as exhibited in several calls for Nile basin cooperation by the new Egyptian government (Staff 2011). However, there has also been a push to form a ministry in the Egyptian government dedicated to "preserving Egypt's historical rights to the Nile waters" (Salem 2011). While indicating a desire for cooperation with other Nile basin countries, Egypt is determined to preserve its current quota of Nile water. The real question is will the new government leadership opt for cooperation or conflict?

In the past, several efforts to seek viable, acceptable agreements to share the Nile waters among the basin countries show mixed results. In June of 1990, an African Water Summit, led by Dr. Bhoutros Bhoutros-Ghali, was held in Cairo. It was attended by delegates from 43 African nations and voiced the need for regional cooperation over the Nile's water resources (Bulloch and Darwish 1993, 90). One idea that was discussed in detail at the Cairo conference was the need to share information, such as hydrological data, between riparians to improve emergency preparedness, project planning, and to aid in regional modeling efforts. Additionally, the conference emphasized the potential for Nile riparians to meet their national and regional economic development goals through the sharing of resources and expertise with their riparian neighbors. For example, "Egypt, with its wealth of hydroelectric generating capacity, could export cheap electricity to the less populated upstream African countries in exchange for water" (Bulloch and Darwish 1993, 91). While basin-wide cooperative efforts began as early as the 1960s under the auspices of the United Nations Development Program (UNDP) and the World Meteorological Organization (WMO) whereby Egypt, Kenya, Sudan, Tanzania, and Uganda launched a Hydromet Survey Project to regulate the flows of the Nile and the water level of Lake Victoria, the cooperative framework that we see today was not created until the 1990s. In the late 1990s, there was a move away from bilateralism and confrontation towards cooperation amongst all of the riparian countries and regional actors. The move towards regionalism over bilateralism resulted from the reduction in conflict within the riparian countries. Internal conflicts that diverted attention away from the Nile waters in countries like Ethiopia, allowed Egypt to have veto power over all Nile projects (dams, irrigation, hydroelectric plans, etc.) with few objections. But the tide may be shifting with the creation of several multilateral initiatives by riparian states.

After two years of deliberations between the Nile riparians and the World Bank, the NBI was finally launched in February 1999, and included all the Nile basin countries with the exception of Eritrea (Swain 2008, 209). The NBI, composed of a council of water ministers from Nile basin countries, was created as a transitional arrangement to guide Nile management activities until a more permanent arrangement for sustainable development of the Nile River basin could be agreed upon (Swain 2008, 209). The NBI's shared vision was "to achieve sustainable socioeconomic development through the equitable utilization of, and benefit from, the common Nile Basin water resources" (Swain 2008, 209). This vision led to the formation of two regional action programs: the Eastern Nile and the Nile Equatorial Lakes, responsible for cooperative water development and management plans to be implemented in the basin (Swain 2008, 209). Despite the transient nature of the NBI, efforts to establish a permanent Nile River Basin Commission were not attempted until 2007 (Swain 2008, 209). While the NBI led to a relative increase in the number of bilateral development projects within the basin, many Nile basin countries are promising basin-wide cooperation while simultaneously advocating and promoting the unilateral construction of large-scale hydrological projects within their own territories (Swain 2008, 210).

The combination of a stillborn NBI, the rhetoric of war in the face of increased pressure on the Nile, and the recent changes in both Egypt and Sudan indicate that the Nile basin countries may be moving away from the framework of cooperation back towards their state-centric approach of bilateral agreements. While an agreement may be struck between upstream Nile countries, it is unlikely that Egypt and Sudan will agree to give up their disproportionately large share of the Nile waters. If upstream countries move forward on any development initiative that significantly reduces the flow of the Nile, it is likely that Egypt and/or Sudan will attempt to resolve the conflict first through diplomatic efforts, reserving military action as a last resort. With the increasingly bold gestures and actions, particularly of Ethiopia, it becomes more likely that diplomatic efforts may fail, resulting in armed conflict over the Nile waters. The current events in both Egypt and Sudan could put added pressure on the Nile's water, making conflict more likely than ever before.

Thus, as Egypt, Ethiopia, and Sudan continue their pursuit for water security via unilateral means, they are impeding basin-wide cooperative efforts that have the potential to lead to more sustainable utilization of the Nile's waters to achieve greater economic gains throughout the region. Additionally, their focus on unilaterally tapping the water-development potential of their territories has the potential to lead to armed hostilities as tempers rise in the race to secure the Nile's diminishing flows to meet the needs of their growing populations and economies.

The events of 2011 may also prove to be highly instrumental in changing the management framework for allocating the Nile's flows in the future. Early in 2011, the "25 January Revolution" in Egypt resulted in the resignation of President Hosni Mubarak, who had been in power since the assassination of Anwar al-Sadat 30 years ago. Despite his seeming support for basin-wide cooperation, he was virulently opposed to the idea of Egypt giving up its prior use rights over the Nile's flows agreed upon in the 1959 Agreement between Egypt and Sudan that failed to include the water claims of any of the other Nile basin riparians. Thus, while Mubarak was in power, the hidden message that continued to be heard by the upstream riparian states was "that Egypt [was] quite able and willing to resort to force if necessary—and any interference with the Nile without prior consultation would certainly be a *casus belli*" (Bulloch and Darwish 1993, 97). With Mubarak no longer in power and the new military-run government not yet releasing any plans regarding the Nile issue, the upstream riparian nations have taken this opportunity to end Egypt's stronghold on the Nile's flows. In 2010, members of the NBI proposed the Nile Comprehensive Framework Agreement (CFA) to replace the NBI and guide the equitable utilization of the Nile's waters between all 10 riparian nations.However, in order for this agreement to come into effect, it needed six signatories. On February 28, 2011, Burundi became the sixth state to sign the agreement along with Ethiopia, Kenya, Rwanda, Tanzania, and Uganda (UPI 2011, 1). The Democratic Republic of Congo is also expected to sign the agreement later this year which would leave Sudan and Egypt at the whim of their now-united upstream neighbors. How Egypt and Sudan will react to this new agreement and the expected reduction in their share of the Nile's flows is not yet clear. However, as all of the Nile riparians attempt to meet the needs of their swelling populations, their water demands for irrigation and hydroelectric projects are also expected to increase—all of this in the face of growing water scarcity due to climate change. While this cooperative agreement has the potential to lead to more sustainable development of the Nile's water resources throughout the region, these additional pressures have the potential to act as catalysts for conflict unless Egypt and Sudan can be persuaded to participate in this CFA.

It is to be noted, Southern Sudan is scheduled to become the eleventh riparian in the Nile River basin later this year–making negotiations over this increasingly scarce resource even more complicated. Southern Sudan is a vital territory for the Nile's flows as it is the home of the Sudd, a vast wetland in which the White Nile flows for a time before its confluence with the Blue Nile in Khartoum. After decades of civil war with the northern provinces of Sudan, this new republic is expected to have increasing demands for water resources as it works to develop its economy and its water development potential within the Nile River basin. How the upstream and downstream nations within the basin will react to the addition of a new player remains unclear; however, stability throughout this area may well act as an impetus for the formation of a multilateral water development project to benefit the entire region.

As the Nile's riparians seek to develop their economies and provide job opportunities and a higher standard of living for their citizens, we must acknowledge the fact that larger quantities of water are going to be required in order to meet these growing industrial, agricultural, and residential demands. These increased demands come at a time when water resources are becoming increasingly scarce and less secure as a result of increased competition between riparian nations, who are also trying to develop their economies through increased agriculture and hydropower production, and reduced Nile flows as a result of climate change. In order to meet these growing demands without placing additional stress on the Nile's diminishing flows, efforts for basin-wide cooperation must also insist on the use of water conservation measures; more efficient irrigation technologies and practices; and on select-ing less water-intensive crops. These efforts will become particularly impor-tant as the political unrest throughout the region results in inflated oil and food prices which may force these relatively poor nations to seek energy and food security within their own borders, leading to greater utilization of the already-diminished Nile flows.

In conclusion, the hydropolitical map of the Nile basin is being redrawn as a result of the departure of the Egyptian President Hosni Mubarak and the resulting attempts of the upper riparians to pressure Sudan and Egypt to accede to their demands for larger shares of the Nile's waters through the Nile CFA. As the 10, soon to be 11, riparians continue their quest for water security and economic development in the face of water scarcity and popula-tion growth, the pressures on the Nile River's water resources will intensify. These growing pressures have the potential to act as a catalyst for conflict unless a basin-wide cooperative management framework can be agreed upon by *all* of the riparians that results in increased water security throughout the region.

THE IMPLICATIONS OF CLIMATE CHANGE
FOR THE NILE BASIN

Africa is home to 84 percent of the world's dry productive land affected by desertification. Sudan and Ethiopia have the largest share of productive dry land on the continent with 473 million hectares (El Zain 2000, 9). Desertifi-cation, due to changes in rainfall, has greatly impacted the amount of tillable land in most of the Nile countries, thus reducing agricultural production and the ability of the country to sustain a subsistence economy. Water levels in Lake Victoria and Lake Tana are extremely vulnerable to the variations in rainfall as their primary source of renewable water (Conway 2005, 102). The marked fluctuations in rainfall over the last several decades have had a significant impact on all of the riparian countries from acute water shortages in Egypt to severe drought in Sudan and Ethiopia. Chart 1 shows the decreas-ing annual levels of Lake Victoria, which have an impact on everything from hydropower generation to agricultural production and more generally, the water supply.

Both Ethiopia and Sudan have experienced periods of persistent drought. In Sudan, the droughts of the 1980s impacted nearly 90 percent of the coun-try's agriculture causing severe shortages of food and the loss of livestock (El Zain 2000, 7). Many subsistence farmers fled to the cities and by 1988, Khartoum was home to the world's largest population of internally displaced

Table 3.3.   Figures of the Internally Displaced Persons in Khartoum

Year	Total Population of Khartoum	# Of IDPs in Khartoum	IDPs as % of the population in Khartoum
1988	2,110,000	1,800,000	85
1993	3,512,145	750,000	21
1998	4,372,000	920,000	21

Source: (Bedri 1998)

persons (IDP) putting more stress on scarce water resources. As the drought subsided, you can see a marked decrease in the population of Khartoum.

Sudan and Ethiopia are both extremely vulnerable to famines due to a high level of poverty combined with periods of drought due to variations in rainfall, causing a lower than average agricultural production for a population that is unable to cope with these fluctuations. Further decreasing agricultural production in Ethiopia is the extremely high rate of erosion. Every year an estimated 1.285 billion tons of topsoil are being washed down the Nile basin from the highlands that are home to 80 percent of the nation's people and 70 percent of the nation's cattle, having implications for the sustainability of the population in the Ethiopian highlands (El Zain 2000, 7).

While other areas of the Nile basin have also been impacted by climate change, Ethiopia and Sudan have been impacted the most. Most of the evidence on rainfall shows periods of reduced annual rainfall followed by periods of increased rainfall making it difficult to determine any long-term trends in precipitation (Conway 2005, 103). It is clear, however, that when rainfall is lower than average it has a negative impact on all Nile riparian countries due to reduced water levels in the two main sources of the Nile—Lake Tana and Lake Victoria—and decreased flow to downstream countries. Times of reduced rainfall have put further constraints on the Nile waters and on the people that depend on the waters for their livelihood and food, making it more important than ever for an agreement on the development of the Nile to be developed and implemented.

The impacts of climate change and an increased demand on the Nile by growing populations, development, and agriculture, have led to several altercations between countries over the allocation of the Nile waters. From 1929 until recently, agreements over shared resource were largely bilateral, with Egypt and Sudan acting together to preserve their shares of the Nile waters. In the late 1990s, there was a move away from bilateralism and confrontation towards cooperation amongst all of the riparian countries and regional actors. The move towards regionalism over bilateralism resulted from the reduction in conflict within the riparian countries. Internal conflicts that diverted attention away from the Nile waters in countries like Ethiopia, allowed Egypt to have veto power over all Nile projects (dams, irrigation, hydroelectric plans, etc.) with few objections. But the tide may be shifting with the creation of several multi-lateral initiatives by riparian states.

While water conflict is a possibility in the Nile River basin, it is dependent on many factors that are currently undecided within the region such as the succession of South Sudan and the changes in Egypt. It is possible that the NBI framework will be revived; however, it appears that Egypt and Sudan are still concerned with maintaining their water allotment. As the water stress increases, other nations may become more active in either attempting to reach a settlement or engage in conflict. If conflict does occur in the Nile basin there is no way of knowing the potential scale of it but one thing is for sure: water conflict is a real possibility.

THE JORDAN RIVER BASIN

"The Jordan River carries a flow equal to only 2 percent of the Nile's, is no more than 340 kilometers long, and is an unimpressive, muddy brown stream compared to the serenely rolling river that spreads its wide expanse through the heart of Cairo" (Bulloch and Darwish 199, 28).

The Jordan River, a relatively small river basin in comparison to the Nile, is shared by five riparian states and flows from Mount Hermon down to the Dead Sea. While the Jordan River may not be the most impressive when it comes to size or length, it has a great potential for conflict as populations continue to rise and the river begins to run dry. The Jordan River basin is a major area of concern as three of the five entities that share the transboundary waters of the Jordan are expected to experience "absolute water scarcity" by 2025 (i.e., they will be unable to provide enough water to sustain their currently growing populations) (Seckler, Barker, and Amarasinghe 1999).

Due to the arid nature of the region, these co-riparians are all experiencing serious water deficits (Phillips et al. 2007, 16). In 2010, much of the Jordan River basin experienced one of its hottest and driest years on record (Garcia-Navarro 2010,1). As Israel's top rabbis begged for divine intervention, the price of fruit and vegetables skyrocketed as a result of farmers being charged more for exceeding their water quotas (Garcia-Navarro 2010, 1). After nearly seven years of drought, the general fear was that these water scarcity realities may be here to stay.

As the available water resources of the region continue to diminish, Israeli and Palestinian representatives continue to engage in final status negotiations for the Israeli and Palestinian occupied territories, which are expected to result in another influx of refugees and immigrants to the area. The question is, will the Jordan's riparians respond to the influx in population in the same way they did in the 1950s when they unilaterally developed their water resources resulting in all-out water conflict, or will they engage in the multilateral basin-wide management of their scarce resources to achieve greater water security throughout the region.

GEOGRAPHY AND HYDROLOGY OF
THE JORDAN RIVER BASIN

The Jordan River basin has a catchment area of roughly 17,300 square kilometers (Elhance 1999, 87). The river originates from a group of springs located on the western and southern slopes of Mount Hermon, which to flow south for 228 kilometers until the river meets the Dead Sea (Elhance 1999, 87; Murakami 1995, 69; Murakami and Musiake 1994, 118). Within its basin, "there is no unclaimed water, no untapped stream or virgin spring or undiscovered groundwater" (Ward 2002, 189). While the Jordan's historic natural flow is estimated to be between 1,470 and 1,670 million cubic meters (mcm) per year (Rumman 2010, 253), today its annual flows are estimated to have dropped to only 70,000 mcm as a result of massive diversion schemes for irrigation (Bromberg 2008, 3).

The headwaters of the Jordan River originate in southern Lebanon as the Hasbani River, in northern Israel as the Dan River, and in Syria as the Banias River (Rumman 2010, 253). The annual average flows of the Hasbani, the Dan, and the Banias Rivers are 160, 260, and 160 million cubic meters per year respectively (Rumman 2010:,253). The upper Jordan River is then formed a few kilometers south of Israel's northern border at the point where these three rivers merge. On average, these springs provide close to 50 percent of the flow of the upper Jordan River with the rest of the river's flows supplemented with winter rainfall runoff (Elhance 1999, 89).

The upper Jordan River flows south through the Huleh Valley until it reaches Lake Tiberias, also known as Lake Kinneret or the Sea of Galilee, which acts as the main natural storage reservoir of the basin and occupies an area of 166 square kilometers (Elhance 1999, 91; Elmusa 1997, 55). From here, it flows south for 10 kilometers until it merges with the Yarmouk River, its main tributary. This river forms a border 40 kilometers long between Syria and Jordan before it becomes a border between Jordan and Israel (Elhance 1999, 89; Elmusa 1997, 57–58). The Yarmouk discharges between 400 and 500 million cubic meters per year into the Jordan River; however, its flows have also been drastically reduced over the years due to multiple water diversions in Syria and Jordan (Pearce 2006, 170; Kliot 2000, 192). The lower

Jordan River forms a border 40 kilometers long between Jordan and Israel before it becomes the border between Jordan and the West Bank (Elhance 1999, 89).

The Jordan River continues to flow south through the Jordan Valley and into the Dead Sea, the saltiest and lowest body of water on earth (Amro 2006; Pearce 2006, 170). Due to the multiple diversions on the upper Jordan River and its tributaries, very little water now enters the Dead Sea from the Jordan Valley. The current discharge of the Jordan River into the Dead Sea is estimated to be no more than 50 million cubic meters per year, less than five percent of its natural flow (Rumman 2010, 253). As a result, the Dead Sea is becoming saltier and lake levels are falling at a rate of up to two meters per year (Elhance 1999, 90).

This reduction in surface waters has led the Jordan River riparians to over-pump groundwater from the aquifers located in the West Bank and in Israel's coastal plain to meet their growing water demands (Solomon 2010, 401). The Middle East and Northern Africa have the least actual renewable water resources per capita in the world; however, the countries in this region withdraw the highest percentage of their total renewable water resources compared to other regions in the world (MENA Development Report 2007). As Solomon points out, "by 2000, the people living in the heart of the [Jordan River] basin were withdrawing 3.2 billion cubic meters of water, well in excess of the 2.5 billion cubic meters that is recharged each year by natural rainfall" (2010, 401).

As mentioned above, the Jordan River basin is shared by five riparians: Lebanon, Syria, Israel, Jordan, and the West Bank (Phillips et al. 2007, 16). The basin is located in a predominantly arid climate with over half of Jordan, Israel, and Syria receiving less than 250 mm of precipitation per year (Amery and Wolf 2000, 7). The current population in the Jordan River basin is roughly 12 million people (Solomon 2010, 401); however, as the population swells in coming years, demands on the basin's increasingly scarce water resources are expected to mount. Additionally, the water quality of the Jordan River continues to decline as a result of increasing pollution from human—mostly agricultural and waste disposal—activities (Elhance 1999, 91). The future of the Jordan River basin's water resources does not look promising. Moreover the basin has a long and volatile history that has already witnessed armed conflicts between its riparians over securing the Jordan's flows. There is no wonder that "today, the Jordan remains the likeliest of all the river systems of the Middle East to cause a new conflict, not only because it is shared by [five] . . . mutually antagonistic states but also because it is over-exploited, of low quality and capable of improvement only by complicated and extensive joint action" (Bulloch and Darwish 1993, 36).

Jordan

Jordan is 80 percent desert and ranks among the nations with the scarcest available renewable water resources per capita in the world (Murakami 1995, 167; Simon 1998). The amount of available water resources in Jordan amounts to far less than most countries in the Middle East and is expected to drop to less than 125 cubic meters per person per year in the next 25 years (Mohsen 2007, 28; Shuval 2000, 609). This is considered to be the Minimum Water Requirement (MWR) for human survival (Shuval 2000, 609). Jordan's population has been growing at a rate of 3.7 percent per year, mainly due to migration from the West Bank and the Gaza Strip, and is expected to reach 7.9 million by 2010 (Simon 1998; Murakami 1995, 167; Lowi 1993a, 158). If living standards are to remain the same, water demand will double during this time period. However, as living standards rise, the demands on the water supply will be even greater (Lowi 1993a, 158). The main surface waters in Jordan are the Jordan, the Zarqa, and the Yarmouk rivers. Due to diversions and over-pumping by Syria and Israel, these waters have become increasingly unreliable (Mohsen 2007; Ward 2002, 189). The Zarqa, which is the only river that flows entirely within Jordan, has been seriously impacted by pollution from nearby industry in Amman (Mohsen 2007). As a result of these reduced surface flows, Jordan relies on groundwater resources to sustain its population (Mohsen 2007).

The struggle for Jordan merely begins here though, as they must also deal with Saudi Arabia overdrawing water from the Disi aquifer on the border between the two countries (Elhance 1999, 91, 107; Bulloch and Darwish 1993, 24). This underground aquifer can produce up to 100–120 million cubic meters per year at safe yield which could then be pumped to Aqaba and eventually to Amman and Zarqa. However, Saudi Arabia began pumping water from the aquifer in 1983 at a rate of 25 million cubic meters per year and is reported to have increased their withdrawals to 250 million cubic meters per year (Elhance 1999, 107). At this rate, this resource may be completely exhausted within 25 years time (Elhance 1999, 107). As populations continue to rise in Jordan, this may result in a more antagonistic situation as Jordanians seek out alternate drinking supply sources for Amman (Bulloch and Darwish 1993, 25). Despite the potential for conflict to arise over the Disi aquifer, Jordan is merely buying time by draining their underground sources. As these water resources are further depleted, Jordan will need to transition toward more sustainable water management strategies if it plans to sustain its growing population (Murakami 1995, 169).

Lebanon

While Lebanon's capital was once known as the "Paris of the Middle East," its national economy and infrastructure were left in ruins after the 1975 civil war (Elhance 1999, 98). Despite Lebanon's struggles at home, it holds a "highly valuable comparative advantage over the other riparian states sharing the Jordan Basin as it is the only water-rich, and perhaps, water-surplus state located close to the basin" (Elhance 1999, 99). However, being home to the headwaters of the Hasbani and the Litani Rivers has also made Lebanon a territory of interest to its less water-endowed neighbors, leading to armed conflict with Israel on multiple occasions. Although it is more than likely that water was merely a secondary cause for the conflict rather than a *casus belli* in itself.

Syria

While Syria, unlike its neighboring riparians, is still expected to have significantly more water at its disposal than the Minimum Water Requirement in the next 25 years (Shuval 2000, 609), its water resources are unevenly distributed across its territory (Elhance 1999, 98). The majority of Syria's population is concentrated in the western region where the water resources are more plentiful, while the more arid eastern region is sparsely populated (Elhance 1999, 98). Unlike Jordan and Israel, however, Syria has access to additional water sources outside the Jordan River basin, namely the Orontes River and the Euphrates-Tigris system (Elhance 1999, 98). However, both of these rivers originate outside Syrian territory, in Lebanon and Turkey, making Syria vulnerable to the water schemes of its upstream riparians (Elhance 1999, 98). Syria depends mainly on the Euphrates for its water, so its main concerns are over relations with Turkey (Sosland 2007; Bulloch and Darwish 1993). As Turkey continues to alter the flow of the Euphrates and as Syria continues to face an ongoing food deficit for its ever-expanding population, many of the major cities in Syria will have to start rationing water to deal with water scarcity (Sosland 2007; Bulloch and Darwish 1993; Gleick 1993). If water shortages continue, all additional sources of water supply, such as the Yarmouk and Jordan, will become increasingly more important to Syria as it strives to achieve water security to meet the needs of its growing population (Bulloch and Darwish 1993). In fact, Syria has already made several

attempts to increase its water security through bilateral diversion schemes
on the Yarmouk River. Despite Syria's continued animosity toward Israel,
Syria may be "the most important agent for unleashing comprehensive water
accords not only in the Jordan Basin but in the Euphrates-Tigris and Orontes
basins as well" (Elhance 1999, 110).

Israel

While the state of Israel came into being in 1948, its quest for water security
in the region began much earlier as Zionist leaders identified the need to
secure water resources to meet the water, and agricultural, needs of a much
larger Jewish state (Elhance 1999, 107). For the first two decades after its
founding, Israel, as the most downstream riparian in the Jordan River basin,
asserted its prior use rights through substantial settlement activity and water
withdrawals within the occupied lands (Elhance 1999, 108). However,
Israel's main concern has always been over water security as it is surrounded
by unfriendly Arab countries that could easily sabotage water supplies if they
did not remain safely within Israel's borders (Pearce 2006, 171; Gleick 1993).
While many argue that water had nothing to do with the Six Day War, Pearce
observes that: "Before the war, less than a tenth of the Jordan River's basin
was within Israel's borders; by the end, the basin was almost entirely controlled by Israel" (2006, 168). Knowing that almost a third of Israel's water
supply is tied to the territory it occupied after the Six Day War, it is difficult
to pretend that the creation of more secure access points to water supplies did
not play a more significant role in the Israeli-Arab conflict of 1967 (Simon
1998). Even so, Israel, like Jordan, is expected to reach the Minimum Water
Requirement in the next 25 years (Shuval 2000, 609). Unlike Jordan, however, Israel also has access to multiple underground aquifers—two in Israel
and two in the West Bank that have been severely over-exploited (Seckler,
Barket and Amarasinghe 1999; Lowi 1993b). Aquifers on the coast are
experiencing saltwater intrusion from over-pumping and those in the West
Bank, while becoming more polluted over time, have also been the center
of several disputes over whether this water should rightfully be in the hands
of the Palestinians (Postel 1993; Starr 1991). Israel is home to a growing
population with increasing demands for fresh water, and Israel has managed
to develop some hugely successful water-saving strategies that are now being
used throughout the world (Simon 1998).

The West Bank

The territory of the West Bank comprises mostly hilly regions in the north,
west, and center; valley lands in the east; and desert in the south (Elhance

1999, 99). Until its occupation by Israel in 1967, the Palestinian people relied upon rain-fed agriculture to meet their growing needs (Elhance 1999, 99). While there were only a few wells drilled in the West Bank prior to the 1967 occupation, by June 1967 there were 314 wells in the western slopes and the Jordan Valley (Elhance 1999, 99). However, the Israelis placed stringent restrictions upon Palestinian water use and irrigation development after the occupation, which have seriously limited development activity throughout the Palestinian territories—namely, the West Bank and the Gaza Strip (Elhance 1999, 99). While the Palestinians' access to the surface waters of the Jordan River has been relatively non-existent since the 1967 occupation, the underlying aquifers in the West Bank have acted as an additional source for conflict between Israelis and Palestinians for decades. While the aquifers located in the West Bank are recharged predominantly by the rains falling over the Palestinian-occupied territories, 80 percent of these flows end up flowing naturally westward where they are extracted largely from within Israel's pre-1967 borders (Rabbo 2010, 154; Bulloch and Darwish 1993 44). Thus, the Israelis have control over the majority of the surface and ground waters of the Jordan River basin, including the flows in the occupied West Bank, which leaves the Palestinians at a serious disadvantage when it comes to their water security and ability to meet growing water demands for economic development (Abdeen 2010, 67). For example, the average Israeli consumes roughly 350 million cubic meters (mcm) of water a year while the average Palestinian uses only 100 mcm per year, the minimum water requirement for domestic, urban, and industrial use (Abdeen 2010, 67; Rabbo 2010:,154). In addition to poor access to water resources throughout the Palestinian territories due to Israeli restrictions, shortages in drinking water can also be attributed to the fact that 70 percent of the available water resources are used by the agricultural sector and an average of 44 percent of the water supply is lost in the system as a result of faulty infrastructure due to leakage and unregistered connections (Rabbo 2010, 155).

Despite continued political instability throughout the Palestinian occupied territories, if an independent Palestinian state does emerge as a result of the peace negotiations, it will most certainly demand a fair share of the Jordan's flows as well as the right to an increased share of the water stored in the aquifers in the West Bank (Elhance 1999, 107). Enduring peace throughout the region would have significant implications for the sharing of the Jordan River basin's water resources as water demands would likely increase throughout the region as a result of an influx of refugees to the area—and growing water scarcity due to climate change. Despite the growing demands, peace throughout the region may in fact lead to increased water security throughout the basin as Jordan River riparians would be more likely to engage in more sustainable, basin-wide management of the Jordan's flows when they are no longer having to play the zero-sum game and outcompete their water-hungry neighbors.

HISTORY AND HYDROPOLITICS OF
THE JORDAN RIVER BASIN

Hydropolitics in the Jordan River basin can only be understood when it is recognized that Israel's survival is dependent upon its ability to control the flows of the Jordan, just as Egypt's survival is dependent upon the flows of the Nile. While Israel only has to share the flows of the Jordan with four riparians, it is surrounded by antagonistic states that would not hesitate to sabotage Israel's water supplies if they did not remain safely within its borders. The most powerful riparian, both economically and militarily, Israel is the only downstream nation that has been able to physically change its riparian position in a basin by occupying upstream territories by force (Sosland 2007; Elhance 1999, 109; Bulloch and Darwish 1993, 41). Even before the war of 1967, Israel has not hesitated to "warn its neighbors that any attempt by them to significantly alter the flow of the Jordan River would invite a military response" (Elhance 1999, 108).

The independent Jewish state of Israel was created in 1948. It was realized early on that the success of this new nation would depend on its ability to exploit the Jordan Valley's then untapped water supply, electric power, and agricultural potential (Amro 2006; Lowi 1993b). Following the Arab-Israel war of 1948–1949, Israel and Jordan experienced massive influxes of immigrants and refugees and found their resources strained considerably. As a result, they both became independently engaged in the creation of national water schemes (Lowi 1993a, 80). Throughout this period, the Jordan River basin riparians were frequently engaged in armed hostilities over objections to both the unilateral attempts of Israel and Jordan to tap the Jordan River's resources as well as Israel's pursuit of development projects in contested territory (Lowi 1993a, 80). In 1951, Israel began to drain the Huleh Lake and marshes to increase the flow of the upper Jordan. The drainage project ended up spilling over into the demilitarized zone agreed upon in the 1949 armistice agreement and as a result, Israeli and Syrian troops engaged in firefights (Bulloch and Darwish 1993, 33). "The Huleh drainage drew the attention of the Arabs to the importance of water in their conflict with Israel and led to the realization that upstream countries had their hand on the water tap, and might be able to exploit this form of pressure" by diverting the headwaters of the Jordan away from downstream Israel (Bulloch and Darwish 1993, 33).

Israel, incessantly aware of its vulnerable riparian position in relation to its hostile upstream neighbors, was "determined to change the hydrological map so that it could control its own resources and ensure supplies for all the Jews who wanted to settle in Israel" (Bulloch and Darwish 1993, 33). To achieve this desired level of water security, Israel began the creation of a National Water Carrier, a large pipeline capable of carrying over 493 million cubic meters of water per year from Lake Tiberias down to Rosh Haayin near Tel Aviv. Years later, with the aid of extensions, the carrier was able to bring water from the north and central regions to the country's urban centers and to agricultural settlements as far south as the Negev Desert (Pearce 2006, 170; Amro 2006; Dolatyar and Gray 2000, 105). This carrier allowed Israel to increase the amount of cultivated land from 1,600 square kilometers in 1948 to over 4,000 in 1980 (Amro 2006). However, by constructing this carrier, the Israelis were seen as hijacking the waters of the Jordan River as they unilaterally constructed this diversion without seeking agreement from their Arab neighbors (Zeitoun 2008, 68; Pearce 2006, 167).

In 1953, in an effort to retaliate against Israel's unilateral attempts to divert the Jordan's flows, Syrian artillery shelled the construction and engineering sites for Israel's National Water Carrier which were located behind the town of Tiberias (Amro 2006). Israel was then forced to move the main pumping station to a more secure location. At the same time, Jordan was becoming increasingly concerned about decreases in the flow of the Jordan River downstream as a result of the Israeli water project upstream (Lowi 1993a, 80).

In order to thwart any increasing conflict in the area, in 1953, President Eisenhower stepped in and appointed Eric Johnston to mediate between Israel, Syria, and Jordan and to negotiate an agreement for the sharing of water resources within the basin (Phillips et al. 2007, 18; Elhance 1999, 112). The idea was to "lessen the possibility of conflict in the region by promoting cooperation and economic stability" (Bulloch and Darwish 1993, 52). One of the key objectives of the agreement was to guarantee the availability of water for the irrigation of crops by the riparian states, with less emphasis placed on meeting domestic (and industrial) needs (Phillips et al. 2007, 19).

As Johnston was working to negotiate his own proposal for sharing the water resources between the co-riparians of the Jordan River basin, he considered several other plans, namely the Main Plan (1953), the Arab Plan (1954), and the Cotton Plan (1954) (Phillips et al. 2007, 20). The Main Plan was to build several dams in the upper and middle reaches of the tributaries of the Jordan which would also be linked to irrigation schemes throughout the basin. The Main Plan also envisaged the use of Lake Tiberias as a storage reservoir. However, unlike the other proposed plans, the primary goal of this plan was to optimize the use of water for irrigation in the basin as a whole, regardless of political boundaries (Phillips et al. 2007, 20). In contrast, the Arab Plan would have strategically placed irrigation and hydroelectric schemes on the Yarmouk and Jordan Rivers above Lake Tiberias to avoid the use of Lake Tiberias as a storage reservoir due to its control by Israel and its potential for high evaporation rates (Phillips et al. 2007, 20). Despite many differences between these two plans, they both emphasized the need to use all of the Jordan's available resources exclusively within the Jordan River basin (Phillips et al. 2007, 22). In contrast to the other two plans, the Cotton Plan included the flows of Lebanon's Litani River in its proposal, which increased the total available resources to be allocated within the basin, and also considered the transfer of the Jordan River's water resources outside of the basin (Phillips et al. 2007, 22).

Johnston's initial instructions for negotiating an agreement were as follows: (1) the Litani River was not to be included because it flows entirely within Lebanon and is not a part of the Jordan River basin, (2) out-of-basin transfers could be permitted in some cases, and (3) a form of joint management of water resources should be sought (Phillips et al. 2007, 23). The key elements of Johnston's final plan as outlined by Phillips et al. were: (1) no consideration of the uses of the Litani River, (2) the optimization of the use of the Jordan River basin waters within the basin itself, but no specific objection to out-of basin transfers by Israel for their National Water Carrier, (3) the development of hydroelectric facilities as feasible, (4) the allocation of 35 mcm per year to Lebanon from the Hasbani River, (5) the allocation of 132 mcm per year to Syria from the combined flows of the Yarmouk, Banias, and Jordan Rivers, (6) the allocation of 760 mcm per year to Jordan from the Jordan and Yarmouk Rivers, (7) the allocation of the remaining flows to Israel, and (8) the creation of a neutral authority to oversee the water allocations to the co-riparians (2007, 26).

The Johnston Plan of 1955 recommended 52 percent of the water to be allocated to Jordan, 36 percent to Israel, nine percent to Syria, and three percent to Lebanon (Bulloch and Darwish 1993, 52). Nevertheless, both Israel and the Arab states rejected the plan, asking for larger shares (Amro 2006). Even though the plan was rejected, Israel and Jordan managed to follow an unwritten agreement that each country would not exceed its share according to the plan (Amro 2006; Simon 1998).

Despite's Johnston's efforts, conflict erupted in the area once more in 1964, when Israel completed its National Water Carrier which was capable of diverting 60 percent of the water that once reached the lower Jordan River (Friends of the Earth-Middle East 2006; Dolatyar and Gray 2000, 104). "This project is one of the very few examples in the world where water is being diverted from an international river basin by one riparian state to areas outside the basin, without the consent of other riparian states and peoples sharing the basin" (Elhance 1999, 115). In response to this unilateral plan, the Arab nations agreed to engage in an "all-Arab" plan to divert some of the headwaters of the upper Jordan that would deprive Israel of 35 percent of their carrier's anticipated source of water (Wolf 2003; Simon 1998). This would have resulted in a reduction in almost half of the water that was supposed to be transported by the National Water Carrier (Simon 1998). Israel saw this as a major threat to its national security and launched a series of tank and air strikes to destroy the diversions being built in Syria in 1967 (Solomon 2010, 402; Dolatyar and Gray 2000, 105; Simon 1998; Wolf 1993).

Twelve months later, the Six Day War erupted. It was fought mostly over land and security issues, but it was fueled by problems over water (Pearce 2006; Dolatyar and Gray 2000, 105; Simon 1998). This war, between Israel, Syria, Egypt, and Jordan, began due to the Egyptian president Nasser's re-blockade of the Suez Canal, Israel's only shipping route to the Red Sea and Indian Ocean (Solomon 2010, 402). As Arab forces assembled along every Israeli border, Israeli forces launched a surprise attack both on the ground and from the air destroying the much larger Egyptian-led air force (Solomon 2010, 402). Israel also managed to drive Jordanian troops out of the West Bank, and sent the Syrian troops retreating to Damascus, abandoning Golan Heights in the process (Solomon 2010, 402). Whatever the cause of the Six Day War, the result was that Israel had achieved a much greater degree of water security because it now occupied the West Bank, which gave it control of the western aquifer, and the Golan Heights, which gave it control over the headwaters of the Jordan River (Pearce 2006, 168). Thus, by the end of the war, the Jordan River basin was almost entirely controlled by Israel (Pearce 2006, 168).

Israel was not the only riparian engaging in water diversion schemes in an effort to improve its water security: Jordan too was eager to develop its agricultural potential and so began the design of a canal to divert the flows of the Yarmouk in 1957. The construction of the East Ghor Canal began in 1962. It was only one part of a much larger scheme known as the Greater Yarmouk Project (Murakami 1995, 296). This much larger project would have also involved the construction of two dams on the Yarmouk (Mukheiba and Maqarin) for water storage and hydropower, the construction of a 47 kilometer West Ghor Canal that would connect with the East Ghor Canal, and construction of several other dams and pumping stations that would increase Jordan's ability to tap its limited water development potential (Murakami 1995, 296). However, when the Six Day War began in 1967, only

20 percent of the Great Yarmouk Project was completed (Murakami 1995, 297) and two of the most important projects out of the scheme, the Mukheiba and Maqarin dams, had to be abandoned as a result of the war (Murakami 1995, 297). Much of the system was put out of commission in 1969 as a result of military raids by Israel (Murakami 1995, 297). In the wake of the 1967 war, the Palestinian Liberation Organization (PLO) engaged in an intensive campaign against Israeli settlements in the Jordan Valley. After an unsuccessful military campaign against the PLO, Israel decided to destroy Jordan's irrigation system in an effort to pressure Jordan to curtail the Palestinian Liberation Organization's violent campaign in the Jordan Valley (Murakami 1995, 297). The conflict over the East Ghor Canal was arbitrated by the United States and resulted in the East Ghor Canal being repaired in exchange for Jordan's pledge to terminate any PLO activity within Jordan's territory (Murakami 1995, 297). By 1978, the construction of the East Ghor Canal, Jordan's national water carrier, was completed and water from the Yarmouk River could then be diverted to meet the growing agricultural demands throughout the Jordan Valley (Murakami 1995, 78). This canal, which now extends for 96 kilometers, was renamed the King Abdullah Canal in 1987 (Pearce 2006, 170; Shuval 2000, 612; Bulloch and Darwish 1993, 35; Lowi 1993a, 155). The construction of Jordan's national water carrier resulted in a substantial increase in Jordan's total irrigation capacity in the Jordan Valley (Lowi 1993a, 155).

Meanwhile, Israel's increasing water demands made the prospect of gaining access to Lebanon's Litani and Hasbani rivers tempting. Israel invaded Lebanon both in 1978 and 1982, though the reasons given for the invasions by Israel were to eliminate terrorist groups or to create more defensible borders (Bulloch and Darwish 1993, 37). While Israel had to withdraw on both occasions as a result of international pressure, Israel held on to a 10 kilometer-wide Security Zone along its border with Lebanon that just happened to give Israel access to both rivers (Bulloch and Darwish 1993, 41). While the primary reason behind these invasions may be debatable, the outcome certainly changed Israel's reign over the region's water supplies.

The Maqarin Dam (also known as the Al-Wuheda or Unity Dam), was originally designed in 1957 as part of the Greater Yarmouk Project. This project was revived through a bilateral riparian agreement between Jordan and Syria in 1988; however, after initial work had been completed, Israel put a stop to the dam arguing that its rights as a co-riparian of the Yarmouk were not acknowledged (Murakami 1995, 78). Later, after the U.S. Department of State got involved in negotiations, the plan for constructing the dam on the Yarmouk was re-discussed once more by *all* of the Yarmouk riparians and the dam was scheduled for completion in 2008 (Fischhendler 2008, 96; Wolf 1996, 66). However, due to Syria's unilateral efforts to tap the waters of the

Yarmouk at a rate much higher than agreed upon in the Johnston Plan, there is a question as to whether the Unity Dam remains a smart investment given the anticipated decrease in average annual flows from this over-tapped resource (Kliot 2000, 196). It has been said that this proposed dam, if completed, "will probably take the last of the Jordan's regular flow—the last of a river holy to Jews, Christians, and Muslims alike, which has watered civilizations for 10,000 years" (Pearce 2006, 170).

In 1994, the unwritten water agreement between Jordan and Israel that had evolved from the Johnston Plan of the 1950s was replaced by a water agreement within the Israeli-Jordan peace treaty that ended a state of war that had lasted almost half a century (Amro 2006; Ward 2002, 190; Postel and Wolf 2001). "The treaty included an Israeli concession to supply an additional 50 million cubic meters of water per year to help meet water-famished Jordan's minimum needs, as well as commitments to cooperate on joint water resource development and to confront the challenge of regional scarcity" (Solomon 2010, 404). Interestingly enough, despite the open hostilities between these two countries for decades, experts from both nations had secretly been meeting for years to exchange information and coordinate water operations in what have become known as the "Picnic Table Talks," which aided in the timely achievement of the peace treaty (Solomon 2010, 405; Wolf 2000, 87).

In September of 1993, an unprecedented event occurred on the lawn of the White House; the PLO leader, Yasser Arafat, shook hands with his long-time adversary, the Israeli prime minister, Yitzhak Rabin, in what marked the start of the Oslo peace process (Solomon 2010, 404). The 1993 signing of the Declaration of Principles between the PLO and Israel (Oslo I) and the 1995 signing of the Oslo II Interim Agreement were the initial steps in an ongoing peace negotiation process between these entities (Zeitoun 2008, 64). The mediated negotiations of the 1990s focused on five issues including: the right of return of Palestinian refugees, the status of Jerusalem, territorial borders, the future of Jewish settlements in the West Bank, and water (Zeitoun 2008, 64). Oslo II was intended to be an interim agreement to be followed by a Permanent Status Settlement (Jayousi 2010, 43; Kerret 2010, 49). Article 40 of Oslo II outlined the basis for cooperation in the water and sewage sectors and was based upon the following objectives: Israel would recognize Palestinian water rights in the West Bank, both sides would engage in the development and coordinated management of additional water resources and systems, additional water allocations would be made available to the Palestinians for a variety of uses, and both entities would engage in the development of a permanent Joint Water Commission (Jayousi 2010, 43; Kerret 2010, 50).

Despite the collapse of the peace negotiations in 2000, several aspects of this agreement still hold. While Israel has recognized Palestinian water rights in the West Bank, specific allocations are to be negotiated as part of the Permanent Status Settlement, which has yet to occur (Kerret 2010, 52). Moreover, the Palestinians have been hesitant to develop additional water resources until they have negotiated their rights to share Jordan River flows. In the meantime, Israel has moved toward the unilateral development of additional water resources through the construction of several desalination facilities along its coastline. While offering Israel greater water security, these unilateral efforts have also diminished the impetus for engaging in more cooperative water-development schemes throughout the basin. Despite the breakdown of the Accords, water officials from both camps have continued to coordinate over the management of their water resources through the ongoing efforts of the Joint Water Commission (Zeitoun 2008, 64).

In addition to the ongoing Israeli-Palestinian conflict, Israel and Lebanon almost engaged in their own water conflict in 2002 over unilateral attempts by southern Lebanon to divert a modest amount of water from the Wazzani Springs to serve several villages. Given that these springs feed the Hasbani River, which is responsible for providing one-quarter of the supply for the Jordan River, this unilateral diversion was considered as "a deliberate provocation that was a potential cause for war" by Israel's prime minister Ariel Sharon (Solomon 2010, 405). International diplomatic intervention by the United States, the United Nations, and the European Union in 2002 averted an escalated conflict between the two riparians (Solomon 2010, 405). However, it was later determined that the small nature of the pumping station and diversion planned by Lebanon would not have adversely impacted Israel's water supply (Amery 2002, 319). In fact, one of the reasons for this conflict was Lebanon's unilateral attempt to utilize the waters of this transboundary spring. Israel considers it a "very dangerous precedent" (Amery 2002, 319).

Since Israel's conflict with Lebanon in 2002, additional conflicts have erupted throughout the region as a result of changes in political leadership in Gaza and Lebanon. A Hamas-led government in 2006 "led to a freeze on the limited cooperation that did exist between Israeli and Palestinian water technicians" and resulted in a deduction of international donor projects aimed at developing the Palestinian water sector (Zeitoun 2008, xiv, 119). Israel's perceived vulnerability due to the Hamas-led government's refusal to acknowledge the right of Israel to exist, led to "the Israeli assault on the main electrical power plant in Gaza in June 2006 [that] denied tens of thousands of people access to water" (Zeitoun 2008, xiv). During the conflict between Israel and Hezbollah in the summer of 2006, Israel damaged water towers of over 50 villages in southern Lebanon in an effort to assert its military superiority over these extremist groups (Zeitoun 2008, xiv). While these conflicts were mainly over terrorism, sovereignty, and national security, water was clearly identified as the Achilles heel of Israel's neighbors.

Despite these conflicts since the collapse of the Oslo Accords, efforts to forge peace between the Jordan River riparians, and Israel and Palestine in particular, have been revived through the Annapolis, Maryland peace talks of November 2007 and the Direct Peace Talks of 2010. U.S. President Barack Obama and U.S. Secretary of State Hillary Rodham Clinton, still maintain that a Permanent Status Settlement is within reach. Palestinian, Israeli, and Jordanian water officials continue to discuss the merits of establishing a Jordan River Basin Commission for the multilateral management and development of the region's water resources despite continued political instability throughout the area.

WATER SECURITY AND THE JORDAN RIVER BASIN

The Jordan River is a unique international river due to its deep-held resonance for Christians, Jews, and Muslims alike. Despite the relatively small size of the basin, it has been a site of great historical and cultural importance for thousands of years. However, "in recent years, all that saved much of the lower Jordan from becoming a desiccated channel has been the agricultural runoff, raw human sewage, diverted saline spring water, and contaminated wastes from fish farms that have been pumped into it" (Bromberg 2008, 1). This great tragedy has been exacerbated by decades of war and regional conflict that have ravaged the basin for the past 60 years.

The Jordan River, while only shared between five riparians, flows through one of the most water-scarce and politically volatile regions in the world. With very few alternative water sources to be had, much of the history of this basin over the past 10,000 years has been defined by riparian attempts to secure water rights to the Jordan's flows. While the conflict of the past 60 years is predicated on territorial disputes between mutually antagonistic states, it has also been exacerbated by severe water scarcity throughout the region as well as the lack of a formalized, equitable water sharing agreement between the riparians. Additionally, the Jordan River basin is also characterized by strong power asymmetries between its riparians with Israel acting as the predominant hydro-hegemon in the basin. Israel's military, technical, and economic superiority over its riparian neighbors in addition to its vulnerable riparian position have made Israel the Egypt of the Jordan River basin, ready to strike at its neighbors with due force at any perceived threat to its water supply.

What is going on today . . . and how could lead to conflict or cooperation—current state of water resources—drought, fires, desalinization/water
conservation—are these leading to less cooperative efforts?

CLIMATE CHANGE AND DROUGHT

Politics—- Hamas in Palestinian Territories and uprising in Jordan (after
Egyptian revolution) what does this mean for the region? What would the
end of protracted conflict in the region mean for the future of the Jordan
River basin? As a result of enduring peace throughout the region, an influx
of refugees (see Jordan and number of Palestinian refugees there) and a
push for economic development are expected. Simultaneously, this increase
in population is expected to result in increased demands for water resources
that are becoming increasingly scarce as a result of climate change. Is
desalinization just offering these countries a false sense of security or will
desalinization and water re-use be the answers to solving the water woes of
this water-scarce region?

Unilateral efforts in the past and the conflicts that resulted. What has
ultimately occurred is that Israel has been able to change from being a downstream riparian to an upstream one . . . based on increasing its occupied territory as a result of the 1967 Six Day War. Israel remains the hydro-hegemon
of the region and continues to be paranoid over water security matters. . . .
see recent perceived threat by Lebanon.

Ongoing conflict—still no final status negotiations completed. . . . Water
continues to be a principle topic for discussion. Syria's cooperation is contin-
gent upon Israel giving up the Golan Heights, which will not happen any time
soon. There is some possibility that Israel—Palestine- and Jordan might be
able to come to some kind of cooperative basin agreement to improve water
security throughout the region. Additional projects that offer some promise
for regional water security include the Red-Dead Canal and the Peace Pipeline and other multilateral desalination investments.

WATER SECURITY: A CATALYST FOR WATER WARS OR
BASIN-WIDE COOPERATION?

"Water will determine the future of the Middle East" (Bulloch and Darwish,
1993, 32).

*"The red flag for water-related tension between countries is not water
stress per se, but rather the unilateral exercise of domination of an international river, usually by a regional power"* (Wolf 2003, 118).

Kofi Annan stated in 2000 that "fierce competition for fresh water may well become a source of conflict and wars in the near future" (Postel and Wolf 2001). If the wars of the next century are going to be fought over water, the Middle East may well end up being a prime site for conflict to erupt. Aaron Wolf suggests that the likelihood for conflict increases significantly whenever two factors come into play. The first factor is that some large or rapid change has to have occurred in the basin's physical setting such as the construction of a dam, a river diversion, or an irrigation scheme, or in its physical setting, such as the formation of new international rivers as a result of changes in national boundaries (Wolf 2003). The second factor is that existing institutions are unable to absorb or effectively manage the change. This can happen when there is no treaty actively delineating the water rights and responsibilities of each nation (Wolf 2003).

In the case of the Jordan River basin, multiple river diversions by all parties have resulted in reduced surface flows in the region. This, in combination with the relatively new national boundaries and the absence of a treaty, make the Jordan River basin a very likely site for water conflicts to take place. The Nile River basin, on the other hand, is shared by ten riparian states, many of which only became independent nations within the latter half of the twenty-first century. The post-colonial era was marked by many of these relatively new nations asserting their sovereignty through unilateral projects including the constructions of dams, river diversions, and irrigation schemes, often with complete disregard for the water rights of neighboring riparians. While historically there have been several bilateral agreements allocating the Nile's flows, the NBI has yet to achieve a consensus over the water rights and responsibilities of each of the riparians. This combination of increasing water demands, the sheer number of players in the Nile's water negotiations, and the power relations present in the basin make the Nile River basin another likely site for water conflicts to occur.

While the ultimate achievement of water security does not have the potential to lead to conflict, the individual steps taken by riparian states to achieve water, and national, security can be a *casus belli*. What are some examples where unilateral actions to achieve water security have led to conflict? Aswan High Dam, Sinai Pipeline, National Water Carrier, etc.

While the discussion above leads us to believe that water wars, as a cause of war unto themselves, are unlikely and that Israel and Egypt's continued warnings of war should anything happen to their water resources are merely paper tigers. . . . I would argue that as water resources become increasingly scarce in the Middle East, as populations continue to grow either through high birth rates or immigration, the impacts from global climate change become more acute, and the political climate continues to shift in an effort to achieve economic development throughout the region, the stresses on the region's water resources are going to be intensified and may well become a catalyst for armed conflict to erupt once more.

It all depends on how water security is achieved. Hydro-hegemons—Israel and Egypt . . . is that what led to conflict over water resources? The general trend is for nations to undertake water projects unilaterally . . . . . . and ultimately, in a transboundary situation, this leads to conflict . . . and while water security may be achieved, it may be achieved at the cost of national security as relations with other riparian states become more volatile. Over time, as water resources become increasingly scarce, there is the potential for basin-wide cooperation as riparian states become more aware of their interdependence on their shared resources for regional security, economic development, and long-term water security.

However, despite these dire predictions, water security can be achieved through cooperative efforts leading even the most violent of neighbors to join forces in conserving their water resources.

Also have to consider what might happen if peace comes to the region and this new wave of democracy that appears to be spreading across the Arab world. . . . Will it lead to more immigrants, more pressure on providing food, jobs and economic prosperity . . . greater need for water resources in the region. . . . the *only* way to deal with this while maintaining water security for the future is going to be through the development of effective basin-wide cooperative management institutions.

CONCLUSION

The threat of future water wars is imminent. We are currently facing an unprecedented demand for freshwater resources that we simply do not have (Gleick 1993). Global climate change is expected to result in rising temperatures that will have the effect of both increasing water losses to evaporation as well as increasing water demands from a more thirsty population (Gleick 1993). From 12 climate models, it is predicted that we will see a 10–30 percent decrease in runoff in the Middle East by 2050 (Milly, Dunne, and Vecchia 2005). If these predictions turn out to be correct, we will have a major water crisis on our hands and the threat of a water war may again become a reality.

Nonetheless, it is in the face of these challenges—rising water demands, decreasing available supplies, and increasing environmental degradation and water quality concerns—that the desire for water security may well become the catalyst for cooperation between riparian states trying to co-exist in transboundary basins. The creation of basin-wide cooperative water management solutions that combine the building of desalination plants and hydropower facilities in water-rich areas; the widespread implementation of water re-use, water-use efficiency, and conservation measures; and the facilitation of regional coopera- tive solutions and institutions, have the potential for averting imminent water wars and creating win-win solutions for riparian states attempting to achieve regional security in the face of water scarcity and political unrest.

Desalinization

Due to the fact that 98 percent of the world's water is seawater, the most obvi- ous long-term solution to alleviate the water scarcity in the Jordan River basin is desalinization (Mohsen 2007; Simon 1998). Two-thirds of the world's desalinization plants are already located in the Middle East and this number is expected to rise (Bulloch and Darwish 1993). Desalinization is appealing because the majority of nations with serious water deficits border the sea making the conversion of saltwater a very accessible solution (Simon 1998). Currently, desalination plants are extremely costly to run and depend on a constant supply of energy, usually in the form of coal or oil, to produce only a limited amount of freshwater (Simon 1998; Bulloch and Darwish 1993). As more research is done, desalinization plants are now being combined with renewable energy sources in an effort to reduce the use of fossil fuels (Pearce 2006; Simon 1998). The use of solar-powered desalinization plants in the Middle East, where there is an abundance of untapped solar energy from the sun's rays, may be the most appealing solution for the water scarcity prob- lems in the region (Mohsen 2007; Simon 1998). While desalinized water is becoming relatively inexpensive so that it can be used for drinking water and municipal use, the majority of the water used by humans is for agriculture and industry (Simon 1998). Currently, desalinized water remains too expensive for these uses so we must look elsewhere if we want to find a more feasible short-term solution to water shortages.

Water Conservation

In order to conserve what water resources we have left, it has been argued that consumers need to be charged the "actual" cost of water based on the amount used (Simon 1998). When people are being charged for water on a "more use/ more pay" basis, they are much less likely to waste it (Simon 1998). Higher prices would provide people with the incentive to conserve (Simon 1998).

The most widely used irrigation method is surface irrigation with an effi- ciency rate of only 40–50 percent (Bulloch and Darwish 1993). However, in Israel, farmers have been able to double their production rates over the past 20 years by using the same amount of water (Simon 1998). They are able to do this because they have developed drip irrigation, which has a 90 percent efficiency rate (Simon 1998; Bulloch and Darwish 1993). Drip irrigation and micro-sprinklers, another new development out of Israel, have dramatically increased the efficiency of irrigation in the region by reducing the amount of water lost through evaporation (Simon 1998). The sharing of these new technologies has great potential as a means for cooperation between water-scarce nations in the Middle East.

Regional Agreements and the Creation of Effective Institutions for Transboundary Resource Management

From 1986 to 1991, Turkey's President Turgut Ozal lobbied a project called the "Peace Pipeline" that would involve two pipelines transporting water from the Seyhan and Ceyhan rivers in southern Turkey down to Syria, Jordan, Saudi Arabia, and other Gulf States (Mohsen 2007, 35; Lowia 1993, 159; Starr 1991). While this project could have led to peace and cooperation in the region, it was rejected because of water security issues and financial reasons (Starr 1991). Southern Arab states did not want to rely on states upstream for their water as it would give them too much power over their water supply (Mohsen 2007; Starr 1991). It was also estimated that the price of water delivered through such a pipeline would exceed the costs of local desalinated water (Starr 1991).

An alternative regional-scale project involves the voluntary trading of water permits between nations (Fisher 2006). This allows parties to have short-term access to other parties' water supplies at a set price. This project provides a win-win situation for buyers and sellers as the buyers are able to get water that they value higher than the money used to buy it and sellers receive money that they value higher than the water they traded in return (Fisher 2006). This notion is very appealing because it allows for more flexibility with regard to water allocations as it can benefit all parties involved even in times of drought (Fisher 2006). However, before such a project can get underway, a certain degree of trust must be developed between participating parties.

- Cooperation and conservation are vital if we are going to win the fight against water scarcity without "water wars." If the nations in the Jordan River basin can cooperate with regard to conserving this vital resource, it is likely that cooperation on other issues may soon follow. We need to stop ignoring the water scarcity issue and take action to conserve this precious resource before it is too late. "No one likes limits, particularly when it comes to water, when every rainstorm, indeed every twist of the tap, brings an illusion of abundance. If there is not enough water now, it is tempting to think, there must be a dam to be built, a glacier to be towed, an ocean to be desalted, a river to be moved—some way to harness technology and ingenuity to fill the void . . . Certainly that has been the history of the human experience with water, particularly over the past century, as the damming of rivers, the construction of aqueducts, and the mining of aquifers have defied nature to bring water where it is needed, in the United States and around the world. The idea that the future might bring more such triumphs is hard to shake, and indeed it may be possible one day that seawater can be desalinated cheaply enough to make it a greater part of the world's water equation, or that the waters of a vast river may be successfully rerouted from one part of a country to another (Jehl 2003; xvii).

In this case, the real "silver bullet" is not going to be the creation of additional supply, although that will be one part of the equation. It will be the change in behavior of riparians in international basins toward the multilateral pursuit of regional water security through the development of basin-wide cooperative management solutions and institutional frameworks to achieve more sustainable and equitable management of depleted river flows.

I propose that ultimate water security can only be achieved in such settings when sought multilaterally through the development of basin-wide cooperative management solutions and institutional frameworks.

*The Nile River Basin portion of the chapter was jointly written by Teagan E. Ward and Hillery L. Roach. The Jordan River Basin portion was exclusively written by Teagan E. Ward

REFERENCES

Abdullah Ali, Ali. 2009. "Can the Nile Waters be Thought of in a Different Way?" *Sudan Tribune*, November 30.

"Agreement betwen the Government of the United Arab Republic and the Government of Sudan." *1959 Water Agreement*. 1959 8-November. http://ocid.nacse.org/tfdd/treaties.php?page=full&origin=river&TN=230 (accessed 2010 24-October).

Al-Kharabsheh, A., and R. Ta'any. 2005. Challenges of water demand management in Jordan. *Water International*. 30(2):210–219.

Ali, Abdulla Ali. "The Egyptian role in Sudan's development and underdevelopment 1899–2010." *Sudan Tribune*, 2010 27-June.

Allan, J. A. 2002. "Hydro-Peace in the Middle East: Why No Water Wars? A Case Study of the Jordan River Basin." *SAIS Review—Geopolitics and Water Resources* :: 255–272.

Amro, R. 2006. "Historical Political Conflict of Jordan River Water Resources." In *Water in the Middle East: Cooperation and technological solutions in the Jordan Valley*, edited by K. D. Hambright, F. J. Ragep, and J. Ginat. Portland: Sussex Academic Press.

Arsano, Yacob. *Ethiopia and the Nile: Dilemmas of National and Regional Hydropolitics.* Doctoral Thesis, Center for Security Studies, Swiss Federal Institute of Technology, Zurich: ETH Zurich and Yacob Arsano, 2007.

Awiti, Alex O. "Advancing Global Sustainability." *Framework Agreemetn on Utilization and Management of the Nile Basin Waters.* 2010. www.envidevpolicy.org/2010/04/framework-agreement-on-utilization-and.html (accessed 2010 10-October).

Bedri, Kawther. "Statistical Profile and Situation Analysis of IDPs." *National Population Council*, 1998.

Bulletin, World. 2010. "Egypt's Mubarak Dismisses Ethiopia War Threat," *Worldnet*, November 25.

Bulloch, J., and A. Darwish. 1993. *Water Wars: Coming Conflicts in the Middle East.* London: Victor Gollancz.

Cascao, A. E. 2009. "Changing Power Relations in the Nile River Basin: Unilateralism vs. Cooperation?" *Water Alternatives* 2 (2): 245–268.

Chou, S., Bezark, R., and A. Wilson. 1997. Water Scarcity in River Basins as a Security Problem.

Comprehensive Peace Agreement. 2002. Agreement, The Government of the Republic of The Sudan and The Sudan People's Liberation Movement/Sudan People's Liberation Army.

Conway, Declan. 2005. "From Headwater Tributaries to International River: Observing and Adapting to Climate Variability and Change in the Nile Basin." *Global Environmental Change* 2005: 99–114.

Descheemaeker, Katrien, Tilahun Amede, and Amare Haileslassie. "Livestock and Water Interaction in Mixed Crop-Livestock Farming Systems of Sub-Saharan Africa: Interventions for Improved Productivity." *IWMI Working Paper 133* (International Water management Institute), 2009.

Dumont, H. J. 2009. "A Description of the Nile Basin, and a Synopsis of Its History, Ecology, Biogeography, Hydrology, and Natural Resources." In *The Nile: Origin, Environments, Limnology and Human Use*, edited by H. J. Dumont. 89 Monographiae Biologicae

EAC. 2010. *History of the EAC*, May 10, available at http://www.eac.int/about-eac/eac-history.html. (Accessed July 15, 2010).

Elhance, A. P. 1999. *Hydropolitics in the 3rd World.* United States Institute of Peace: Washington, D.C.

El Nur, Ibrahim. "Human Security in Sudan." In *Human Security in the Arab World*, by UNDP: Arab Human Development Report. UNDP, 2008.

El Nur, Ibrahim. "The Changing Hydraulics of Conflict and Cooperation in the Nile Basin: The Demise of Egyptian-Sudanese Bilateralism." *AUC Papers* (AUC Press), December 2010.

El Zain, Mahmoud. 2000. *Development Priorities for the Nile Basin Countries: What Difference can the Nile Basin Initiative Make.* Report, Institute of of Social Studies, The Hague, WIC.

Ethiopian Reporter. "Ethiopia Says it has Evidence that Egypt Supported Rebel Movements."

Ethiopian Reporter. 2010 November 27.

Ethiopian Reporter. 2010. "Seven Nile Basin Initiative Member Countries Agree to Sign the Cooperative Framework Agreement," April 14.

Ethiopian Reporter. 2010. "Is the Nile Cooperation Framework Agreement Doomed to be Stillborn?" April 3.

Fisher, F. M. 2006. "Water: Casus Belli or Source of Cooperation?" In *Water in the Middle East: Cooperation and Technological Solutions in the Jordan Valley*, edited by K. D. Hambright, F. J. Ragep, and J. Ginat. Portland: Sussex Academic Press.

Friends of the Earth—Middle East. 2006. World Water Monitoring Day. Available at http://www.foeme.org.

Getachew, Tarikua. "Developing New Nile Philosohpy." *Addis Fortune*, 2010 25-July.

Hadyia, Abdallah. "Contemporary Civil Conflicts in the Nile Basin States." *Digest of Middle East Studies*, Spring 2009: 17–30.

Gleick, P. H. 1993. "Water and Conflict: Fresh Water Resources and International Security." *International Security* 18 (1): 79–112.

Graves, W. 1993. "Introduction." In *Water*. Special Edition of National Geographic.

Jehl, D. 2003. "Introduction." *Whose Water is it? The Unquenchable Thirst of a Water-Hungry World*, edited by B. McDonald and D. Jehl. Washington: National Geographic.

Kagwanja, Peter. 2007. "Calming the Waters: The East African Community and Conflict over the Nile Resources." *Journal of Eastern African Studies* (Routledge) 1, no. 3 (November): 321–337.

Kung, Ruedi. "Addressing the Dimensions of Transboundary Water Use: The Nile Basin Initiative." *Mountain Research and Development* (International Mountain Society) 23, no. 1 (February 2003): 4–6.

Lowi, M. R. 1993a. *Water and Power: The Politics of a Scarce Resource in the Jordan River Basin*. Cambridge: Cambridge University Press.

Lowi, M. R. 1993b. "Bridging the Divide: Transboundary Resource Disputes and the Case of West Bank Water." *International Security* 18 (1): 113–138.

Mahmoud Pasha, Mohamed, and Lord Lloyd. "Exchange of Notes between His Majesty's Government in the United Kingdom and the Egyptian Government in Regard to the Use of the Waters of the River Nile for Irrigation Purposes." *1929 Water Agreement*. 1929 7-May. http://ocid.nacse.org/tfdd/treaties.php?page=full&origin=river&TN=92 (accessed 2010 24-October).

McDonald, B., and D. Jehl, eds. 2003. *Whose water is it? The unquenchable thirst of a water-hungry world*. National Geographic, Washington, D.C.

MENA Development Report. 2007. *Making the Most of Scarcity: Accountability for Better Water Management in the Middle East and North Africa*. Washington: The World Bank.

Milly, P. C. D., K. A. Dunne, and A. V. Vecchia. 2005. "Global Pattern of Trends in Streamflow and Water Availability in a Changing Climate." *Nature* 438: 347–350.

Minakawa, Noboru, Gorge Sonye, Gabriel O Dida, Kyoko Futami, and Satoshi Kaneko. "Recent Reduction in water level of Lake Victoria has Created more habitats for Anopheles Funestus." *Malaria Journal* (BioMed Central), July 2008: 2.

Mohamoda, Dahilon Yassin. 2003. *Nile Basin Cooperation: A Review of the Literature*. Nordic Africa Institute.

Mohsen, M. S. 2007. "Water Strategies and Potential of Desalination in Jordan." *Desalination* 203: 27–46.

"Nile Basin Initiative Website." 2010. Nile Basin Initiative Website. http://www.nilebasin.org/newsite/ (10 July)

Pearce, F. 2006. *When the Rivers Run Dry: Water—The Defining Crisis of the Twenty-First Century*. Boston: Beacon Press.

Phillips, D. J. H., Attili, S., McCaffrey, S., and J. S. Murray. 2007. "The Jordan River Basin: 1. Clarification of the Allocations in the Johnston Plan." *Water International* 32 (1): 16–38.

Phillips, D. J. H. Attili, S., McCaffrey, S., and J. S. Murray. 2007. "The Jordan River Basin: 2. Potential Future Allocations to the Co-riparians." *Water International* 32 (1): 39–62.

Phillips, D. J. H., Jagerskog, A., and A. Turton. 2009. The Jordan River Basin: 3. Options for satisfying the current and future water demand of the five riparians. *Water International*. 34(2): 170–188.

Postel, S. L. 1993. "The Politics of Water." *World Watc*. 6 (4): 10–19.

Postel, S. L. and A. T. Wolf. 2001. "Dehydrating Conflict." *Foreign Policy* 126: 60–67.

Salem, Metwali. 2011. "Ministry to Form Committee Tasked with Protecting Egypt's Nile Quota," *Al Masry Al Youm*,March 3..

Seckler, D., R. Barker, and U. Amarasinghe. 1999. "Water Scarcity in the Twenty-First Century." *Water Resources Development* 15 (1/2): 29–42.

Shuval, H. I. 2000. "Are the Conflicts between Israel and Her Neighbors over the Waters of the Jordan River Basin an Obstacle to Peace? Israel-Syria as a Case Study." *Water, Air, and Soil Pollution* 123: 605–630.

Simon, P. 1998. *Tapped Out: The Coming World Crisis in Water and What We Can Do about It*. New York: Welcome Rain.

Solomon, S. 2010. *Water: TheEepic Struggle for Wealth, Power, and Civilization*. New York: HarperCollins.

Staff. 2011. "Cairo Won't Punish Burundi for Signing Nile Pact," *Al Masry Al Youm*, March 3.

Staff, 2011. "South Sudan Backs Independence-Results" *BBC New*, February 7.,

Starr, J. R. 1991. "Water Wars." *Foreign Policy* 82: 17–36.

Sudan Tribune. 2010. "Ethiopia Signs New Nile Treaty Despite Egypt, Sudan Opposition," *Sudan Tribune*, May 14.

Swain, A. 2008. "Mission Not Yet Accomplished: Managing Water Resources in the Nile River Basin." *Journal of International Affairs* 61 (2): 201–214.

Tutwiler, Richard. *Geography of the Nile Valley* Cairo, (2010 3, January).

United Press International [UPI]. 2011. *Ethiopian Dams on Nile Stir River Rivalry*. Available at: http://www.upi.com/Science_News/Resource-Wars/2011/03/16/Ethiopian-dams-on-Nile-stir-river-rivalry/UPI-30771300295011/. (Published: March 16, 2011).

United Nations. 1997. *Convention on the Law of the Non-navigational Uses of International Watercourses*. Convention, General Assembly, United Nations, United Nations.

United Nations Department of Economic and Social Affairs, Population Devision. 2009. *World Population Prospects: 2008 Revision Population Database*, available at http://esa.un.org/unpp/. (Accessed 2010 12-August).

United Nations Department of Economic and Social Affairs, Population Division. 2009. "World Urbanizations Prospects: The 2009 Rivision." United Nations Department of Economic and Social Affairs.

UNWWAP. 2009. *Facing the Challenges*. Development Report, The United Nations World Water Development Report 3, Paris: UNESCO Publishing.

Ward, D. R. 2002. *Water Wars: Drought, Flood, Folly and the Politics of Thirst*. New York: Riverhead Books.

Waterbury, J. 1979. *Hydropolitics of the Nile Valley*. Syracuse: Syracuse University Press.

Wichelns, Dennis, John Jr. Barry, Martina Muller, Megumi Nakao, Lisa D. Philo, and Adam Zitello. 2003. "Co-operation Regarding Water and Other Resources Will Enhance Economic Development in Egypt, Sudan, Ethiopia and Eritrea." *Water Resources Development* 19 (4): 535–552.

Wolf, A. T. 2003. "Water Wars" and Other Tales of Hydromythology." In *Whose WIs It? The Unquenchable Thirst of a Water-Hungry World*, edited by B. McDonald and D. Jehl. Washington: National Geographic.

Wolf, A. T. 1998. Conflict and cooperation along international waterways. *Water Policy*. 1:251–265.

Chapter Four

Water Disputes in South Asia

Sheila Rai and Sanghamitra Patnaik

The subcontinent of South Asia consists of six independent sovereign nations: India, Bangladesh, Pakistan, Sri Lanka, Bhutan, and Nepal. These countries have a collective population of more than a billion and their peoples practice three of the world's major religions—Hinduism, Islam, and Buddhism. The region also contains several other cultural and religious minorities, and its peoples speak in thousands of dialects and belong to many racial groups. Its nations have different political systems—from monarchy to democracy—and two of them, neighbors India and Pakistan, possess nuclear arms. The region is surrounded on three sides by the Indian Ocean, and by the Himalayas in the north. According to Kaplan (2010, 135), "It is the monsoon that truly unites them." However, it should be noted that several mighty rivers—the Ganges, Indus, and Brahmaputra—crisscross the region and impact cultural, geographical, and economic spheres of people's lives. Their water is the lifeline for the subcontinent. In recent years increased demand for the water, due to rapid industrialization, agricultural development, and urbanization has produced tension and competition among these countries. It has been observed that "water is ransom," and more importantly, that "water is power," not only in South Asia but also all over the world.

By 2025, 52 countries containing two-thirds of the global population are expected to be short of water. According to the Asian Development Bank (ADB), China and India alone will have a combined shortfall of one trillion cubic meters in 2030. Bangladesh, Cambodia, Nepal, Pakistan, the Philippines, and Vietnam are at, or near, water stress conditions (The Strait Times, 18 October 2010). When water is scarce, competition for limited supplies can lead nations to view access to water as a matter of national security. History is replete with examples of competition and disputes over shared fresh water resources. Water and water-supply systems are likely to be both objectives of military action and instruments of war.

SOUTH ASIA—TRANSBOUNDARY WATER ISSUES

The location, size and contiguous borders of India with other South Asian countries, and its capacity as both upper and lower riparian, have generated conflict with most of its neighbors, except Bhutan, on cross-border water issues. Given an atmosphere of mistrust, upper riparian India has serious issues to resolve with lower riparian Pakistan and Bangladesh, and with upper riparian Nepal as well. There have been deadlocks owing to physical limitations and political apprehensions on all sides. What is, however, quite appreciable is that the countries of the subcontinent have made several efforts to resolve their differences over water distribution through bilateral agreements. India and Pakistan signed the Indus Water Treaty (IWT) in 1960, allocating three eastern rivers (the Ravi, Sutlej and Beas) to India and three western rivers (the Indus, Jehlum, Chenab) to Pakistan. The IWT has, remarkably, survived the ups and downs of Indo-Pak relations, and serious differences over various projects being undertaken by India over the Jhelum and Chenab rivers.

Similarly, the Ganges Water-Sharing Treaty (GWST) was signed between India and Bangladesh in 1996 and the dispute over Farakka Barrage has also been reasonably resolved, although differences continue on Bangladesh's share of water during lean periods. Nepal and India signed the Mahakali Treaty in 1996. The Nepalese Parliament has ratified that treaty but there are still certain unresolved issues (Treadwell and Akand 2009).

Notwithstanding these treaties, serious differences over water sharing, water management and hydropower projects continue to spoil relations between India, on the one hand, and Pakistan, Bangladesh, and Nepal, on the other. Differences between India and Pakistan continue to create ill will between them on 11 large hydroelectric projects India plans to construct on the Jehlum and Chenab Rivers.

The partition of India in 1947 redrew the political map of the subcontinent. New boundaries between India and Pakistan created various intractable and complex issues, but despite these new barriers several common features such as the transboundry rivers did not change. New arrangements and agreements were required to share the waters of several transboundary rivers.

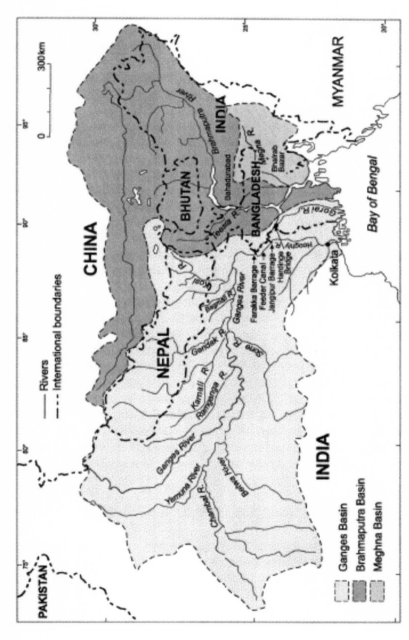

Map 4.1. Indus Ganges and Brahmaputra Rivers

THE INDUS GANGES BRAHMAPUTRA (IGB) RIVER SYSTEMS

In South Asia there is a vast network of rivers, many of which are common to the countries of the region. These rivers can be categorized into two groups:

1. Peninsular Rivers: These are rivers that are dependent on seasonal rainfall. Most of them either run dry during the summer or their water level goes down considerably.
2. The Himalayan Rivers: These rivers originate from the snow-clad Himalaya Mountains. Snow and glaciers of the Himalayan ranges feed them. An important feature of these rivers is that they flow through deep gorges and carry heavy silt due to their steep flow in the hilly terrains, and often change their courses and create problems for human settlements along the riverbeds. The Indus, the Ganges, and the Brahmaputra are the three big river systems of this region.

Besides their economic and social importance, several South Asian rivers have religious and cultural sanctity as well. There are myths about their origin and role to which people subscribe even today.

All the three river systems of South Asia—the Indus, the Ganges and the Brahmaputra—have an international character. They flow through more than one country. The Indus flows through India and Pakistan and the other two river systems through India, Bangladesh, and Nepal. In the western part of the sub-continent, the waters of the Indus basin are shared by Pakistan and India. In the North and Northeast, the basins of the Ganges, Brahmaputra, and Meghna are shared by India, Nepal, Bhutan, and Bangladesh, and in some areas by China. The sharing of water resources of these rivers by the respective co-basin countries has been obviously a matter of dispute. It has proved to be a formidable challenge for the riparian countries to devise and abide by mutually-acceptable formulas for sharing and development of river waters.

INDIA—BANGLADESH RIVER SYSTEMS

Bangladesh and India have had a long, common cultural, economic, and political history. The cultures of the two countries are similar—in particular the cultures of Bangladesh and the Indian states of West Bengal and Tripura. However, since the partition of India in 1947, Bangladesh (formerly East Bengal and East Pakistan) became part of Pakistan. The problem with India and Pakistan was that while the river regimes were the same as earlier, the British withdrawal in 1947 divided India into two separate political entities.

These political boundaries were not congruous to the river regimes. Therefore, one of the major irritants between the two countries was the sharing of the river waters. It is a known fact that the sharing of river waters of an international basin is a crucial issue to the interests of the riparian countries. If their interests are similar, or they are complementary to each other, mutual cooperation is possible for efficient use and management of water resources. But if their interests are diverse or conflicting then problems are bound to occur. Thus, the two big river systems—the Indus and the Ganges— which were shared by both India and Pakistan, generated a lot of controversies and conflicts. While the Indus dispute was solved with the conclusion of the Indus Treaty, the Ganges water controversy, which actually concerned East Pakistan, remained unresolved for several decades.

GANGES BASIN

The water issue between India and Bangladesh revolves around the Ganges. The Ganges originates from the Gangotri glacier in the Uttar Kashi district of Uttar Pradesh at an elevation of 7010 m above sea level at the southern slope of the Himalayan Range. It is interesting to note that the Ganges is not known by its name either at its place of origin or at the end (Rao 1975; 57). At its source it's called Bhagirathi and is joined at Dev Prayag by Alaknanda, which rises in the glaciers of Bhagirath—Kharak and Salo—Panth. After its confluence with Alaknanda the two streams are called Ganges. The river Ganges enters into the plains of Uttar Pradesh at Haridwar. At Nagal in the Bijnour district, it takes a wide sweep towards the southeast and flows in a wide bed, often changing the course of its streams. After leaving Uttar Pradesh, the Ganges enters Bihar in Rohtas district. As it enters West Bengal, it swings around the Rajmahal hill ranges and starts flowing south. Nearly 40 km below Farakka it is divided into two: the left arm is called Padma and flows eastwards into Bangladesh, and the right arm is called Bhagirathi and continues to flow to south in India's West Bengal. The Bhagirathi flowing west and southwest of Kalkata (formerly Calcutta) is called Hooghly. After reaching Diamond Harbor it takes a southward direction and is divided into two streams before joining the Bay of Bengal at Dhovlal. The right arm, known as the Haldi River in the Midnapur district of Bangladesh, also joins the Bay of Bengal. The river Padma, after entering Bangladesh, is joined by the Brahmaputra and the Meghna forming a huge delta, and ultimately flows into the Bay of Bengal. The total length of the river Ganges is about 1550 miles (Kay 1965). The river Ganges has highly seasonal flow. Almost 80 percent of its annual flow takes place during the four months of July to October. Nearly 82 percent of the rainfall in the Ganges plain also occurs from June to September (Abbas 1984; 1). It may

Table 4.1.   Ganges River Basin Descriptive Statistics

Geographic location	India: 62.9%
	China: 19.1%
	Nepal: 8.0%
	Bangladesh: 7.4%
	Bhutan: 2.6%
Length of Ganges River	2,525 kilometers
Basin drainage	1,080,000 square kilometers
Basin mean annual flow	525.02 cubic kilometers

Sources: Sharma et al. (2008); Singh & Arora (2007)

be relevant to mention that the Brahmaputra rises from a glacier in the Kailash Range of the Himalayas in southeast Tibet, flows through the Indian states of Arunachal Pradesh and Assam, and then enters Bangladesh.

The controversy between India and Pakistan over the Ganges began shortly after the partitioning of India in 1947. The initial problem arose because of the apparent deterioration of the river Hooghly on which lie the docks, wharves, and jetties of the Port of Calcutta, India's busiest port, providing access to international trade. The dispute was triggered by India's plan to construct the Farakka barrage in 1950–51. The declared purpose of the barrage was to divert water from the Ganges into the Bhagirathi-Hooghly River through a 38.3 km long feeder canal. This diversion was considered necessary mainly during the dry season, to improve the navigability of the Calcutta Port and to combat salinity in the greater Calcutta area from tidal ingress. It was believed that the Hooghly River was silting up, jeopardizing the normal operation of the Calcutta Port. The concern for the Calcutta Port was based on the apparent loss of business, profitability of shipping, commercial, and other industrial ventures due to the shallowing of the Hooghly. These economic and political pressures resulted in the diversion of water from the Ganges at Farakka into the Bhagirathi-Hooghly River as one of the solutions. Pakistan had objected to such construction alleging that it would affect the flow of water from the Ganges into East Pakistan (Gulati 1988, 105). India brushed off these apprehensions as being purely hypothetical, since the project was just at the stage of preliminary investigations.

Between 1951 and 1970, a series of negotiations was held at political, bureaucratic, and technical levels between Pakistan and India about the proposed construction of the Farakka Barrage. Pakistan tried several approaches to reach some concrete agreements including cooperative ventures, negotiations at higher levels, as well as the assistance of a third party like the UN.

It raised the issue at various international forums. But all such efforts proved futile. India eventually decided to construct the barrage at Farakka, a village in the Murshidabad district in West Bengal, near the Bengal-Bihar border and about 400 km north of Calcutta. The construction of the barrage actually began in 1961 and was completed in 1971, despite the absence of any agreed understanding between the two countries. It was the longest barrage of the world and cost about Rs. 170 crores (Murthi 1975, 10).

The Ganges water dispute could not be solved during the Pakistan era (1947–1971). While both the countries had agreed on Indus waters, a similar agreement on the Ganges could not be concluded. In retrospect, many doubts have been raised whether Pakistan was actually sincere about resolving the crisis (Khurshid 1987). Apparently, India too was reluctant and did not want Pakistan's influence in the implementation of the Farakka Barrage project.

Meanwhile the bloody Liberation War of 1971 helped Bangladesh (erstwhile East Pakistan) gain its independence from Pakistan with full military support from India. The "Treaty of Friendship and Peace" and the "Indo-Bangladesh Trade Pact" were signed by both countries—India and Bangladesh—which heralded cordial and intimate relations between the two neighboring countries.

JOINT RIVER WATER COMMISSION

Soon after the independence of Bangladesh, both India and Bangladesh agreed in principle to cooperate in the areas of flood control, irrigation, and power development in the Ganges-Brahmaputra basin (*The Times of India*, 30 January 1972). This was duly emphasized in the Indo-Bangladesh "Treaty of Friendship."

In March 1972, Bangladesh's Prime Minister, Sheikh Mujib, and Mrs. Indira Gandhi signed a joint declaration during her visit to Dhaka. They agreed to establish a Joint Rivers Commission (JRC) of experts from both

Table 4.2. Sharing of Lean Season Flow of Water at the Farakka (Amount in ft³/s)

10 Days Period	Dependable supplies at Farakka	Amount agreed upon for Hooghly	Remaining flow for Bangladesh
21 to 30 April, 1975	55,000	11,000	44,000
1 to 10 May, 1975	56,500	12,000	44,500
11 to 20 May, 1975	59,250	15,000	44,250
21 to 31 May, 1975	65,500	16,000	49,500

Source: Upreti 1993, 134

countries. The JRC was constituted on November 24, 1972, and it conducted joint surveys of embankments on common rivers on both sides of the boundary. It organized flood control programs and exchanged data about common river water development projects during 1972–75. The working of the JRC for mutually-acceptable solutions of the sharing of the Ganges waters was indicative of Bangladesh's reconciliation with the Farakka Barrage project. The two countries signed an agreement on April 18, 1975 (1975 Agreement), for temporary allocation of Ganges waters as follows:

1975 AGREEMENT—DIVERGENT VIEWS

Under the 1975 Agreement India was to take a smaller share than its needs. India's share had varied between 20 percent in the first ten days and 24.43 percent in last ten days, while Bangladesh received 80 percent and 75.57 percent, respectively, between April and May (Baral 1988, 41; Indian Express 17 January 1989) (Table 4.2). The 1975 Agreement was considered to be an important breakthrough and a historical development (Qureshi 1981, 238). It was indeed an outcome of the political understanding between the two countries and also a goodwill gesture on the part of India in settling the problem. It was thought that the problem of water sharing would also be resolved as the Farakka Barrage was accepted as *fait accompli*. This accord between the two countries could not be fully implemented after the assassination of Sheikh Mujib in August 1975. The assumption of power by the military regime in Bangladesh resulted in the collapse of friendly relations between the two countries. The new government in Bangladesh launched an anti-India tirade. The issue of sharing of water resources naturally became a major target of dispute. Consequently, India's attitude towards Bangladesh also hardened.

Meanwhile, the construction of the feeder canal from the Farakka Barrage to the Bhagirathi River was completed by 1974, and the barrage was ready for commissioning. India requested that Bangladesh allow for experimental operation of the Farakka Barrage project. In April 1975, Bangladesh allowed India to test run the operation at the Farakka Barrage and the feeder canal for a period of 41 days, from April 21 to May 31, 1975.

After the expiry of the 1975 Agreement on May 31, 1975, India began to unilaterally withdraw water (40,000 cusecs) at Farakka. Bangladesh viewed it as a breach of the agreement and was vociferous about it. It demanded that the issue of sharing the Ganges waters during the whole year should be discussed instead of just discussing the lean period. This proposal was not acceptable to India, who believed that during the rest of the year (outside of the lean period) there was no scarcity of waters available to either country. India instead complained that despite specific provisions in the 1975 Agreement, Bangladesh did not cooperate by supplying data and information required to prepare a joint report on the effects of withdrawal of waters at Farakka.

Bangladesh, on the other hand, accused India of causing hardship due to the shortage of water. Several opposition political parties in Bangladesh criticized India on the issue of Farakka. They were critical of the policies of the Awami League (AL) over the issue of sharing water resources and accused the party of not protecting the interests of the country. The "Farakka Peace March" was organized in Bangladesh to mobilize public opinion. Maulana Bhasani wrote a letter to Mrs. Indira Gandhi requesting her to personally intervene and resolve the issue (Asian Recorder 1976, Col. 13189). He also threatened to launch a march to Farakka to demolish the barrage. Mrs. Indira Gandhi, while emphasizing that a spirit of mutual understanding was necessary in order to resolve the crisis, reiterated strongly that: "India was open to persuasion and reasoned argument but no one should expect India to submit to threats and palpably unreasonable and unjustified demands" (Asian Recorder 1976).

The government of Bangladesh took the water sharing issue to several international forums, including the United Nations General Assembly (Upreti 1993, 136). The UN responded to Bangladesh's case with an ambivalent consensus statement, issued on September 26, 1976, urging both parties to negotiate, while recognizing that "the situation called for an urgent solution." India maintained that it was a bilateral issue and any attempt at internationalization of the issue would only jeopardize an amicable solution of the problem (Gulati 1988, 112).

In post-emergency 1975 elections in India, Mrs. Gandhi and her party were defeated. The new government, led by the Janata Party, promised to settle issues with the neighboring countries on a priority basis. Consequently, an agreement was concluded between Bangladesh and India on November 5, 1977 (1977 Agreement) (Foreign Affairs Record 1977, 215–216). The five-year 1977 Agreement fixed the quantum of water to be released to Bangladesh at Farakka for the dry season (January 1 to May 31) according to a sharing schedule on a 10-day basis. The 1977 Agreement provided a partial and temporary solution to the problem as it dealt only with the lean period. Although the 1977 Agreement did not receive a favorable response in many quarters in India, it reflected the spirit of *bonhomie* and indicated that no matter how complex a problem, it can be solved bilaterally. The 1977 Agreement faced strong criticism from the opposition parties in India and was labeled as an example of the "poor performance of the ruling Janata Party's diplomacy."

As noted above, the sharing of the Ganges water during the dry season was not a permanent solution and required augmentation of the Ganges dry season flow. The 1977 Agreement recognized the need for this augmentation, and provided a time frame of three years to finalize all augmentation proposals. Bangladesh and India had different perceptions regarding the flow augmentation and therefore prepared different proposals. Bangladesh felt that the total water requirements of the Ganges basin could be met from the resources available within the basin itself. India, however, proposed to transfer waters from the Brahmaputra to upstream of Farakka at the Ganges. Obviously, both Bangladesh and India disapproved of each other's proposals.

The return of the Congress-I party in India under Mrs. Indira Gandhi in 1980, gave rise to apprehensions in Bangladesh about the continuation of the 1977 Agreement. The Congress-I, as an opposition party in 1977, had criticized the agreement on the ground that it failed in safeguarding India's interest. Bangladesh expressed interest in bilateral negotiations on the water issue. The summit involving General Ershad of Bangladesh's government and Mrs. Indira Gandhi, in October 1982, helped in creating a congenial atmosphere for water negotiations (Upreti 1993, 139). The 1977 Agreement, however, was allowed to expire in 1982.

Variegated Bilateral Efforts

During 1982 and 1988, Bangladesh and India entered into a short-term water-sharing arrangement by signing two Memoranda of Understanding (MOUs)—one for a period of two years (1983–84) and another for three years (1986–88). The MOUs expired at the end of 1988. These MOUs, as well as accompanying negotiations, reiterated the need for linking augmentation with water-sharing arrangements.

From 1989 onwards, India continued withdrawing water from the Ganges without any mutual agreements. Meanwhile, Bangladesh continued to urge India to agree to a long-term sharing agreement as conditions in the Ganges-dependent areas in Bangladesh became critical due to upstream diversion. To cope with the situation, several levels of negotiations took place between the two countries to arrive at a permanent water-sharing arrangement at Farakka, followed by meetings between the two prime ministers in 1992 and 1993. Notwithstanding the efforts, differences persisted and the four-decade-long impasse continued.

Political changes in both countries in the middle of 1996 promised to lead to a permanent solution. In May 1996, the United Front-led coalition government came into power in India. In Bangladesh a month later the Awami League was voted back to power and Sheikh Hasina assumed the office of prime minister. These two developments, happening almost at the same

Table 4.3. Formula for Sharing the Ganges Waters between India and Bangladesh

Availability at Farakka	Share of India	Share of Bangladesh
70,000 cusecs or less	50 percent	50 percent
70,000–75,000 cusecs	Balance of flow	35,000 cusecs
75,000 cusecs or more	40,000 cusecs	Balance of flow

1 cusec = 1 cubic foot per second
Source: Annexure I of the 1996 Treaty

time, marked the turning point for both the countries. Both governments felt that there was a need to come to an agreement within the year before the onset of the next dry season. After negotiations at various levels, an agreement was reached and the prime ministers of Bangladesh and India signed a historic treaty on December 12, 1996 (the Ganges Water Sharing Treaty, referred to herein as the 1996 Treaty), for sharing the Ganges waters for a period of thirty years.

The 1996 Treaty is based on the principles of equality and fair play, taking into account the interests of both the countries. The 1996 Treaty is renewable by mutual agreement at the end of the 30-year period with a provision for review every five years or earlier. The preamble to this treaty contains provisions for water sharing (Cherian 1997, 47).

The agreement was arrived at on the basis of the average availability of water between 1949 and 1988. India and Bangladesh are each guaranteed to receive 35,000 cusecs of water in alternating three 10-day periods during the period of March 11 to May 10, as indicated in Annexure II of the 1996 Treaty. This means that Bangladesh shall receive the guaranteed amount of water during March 11–20, April 1–10, and April 21–30, while India shall receive the same amount during the periods March 21–31, April 11–20, and May 1–10.

Interestingly, the divergence over "augmentation," which had led to an impasse in the past, was sidestepped. The 1996 Treaty is essentially focused on sharing of lean-season flows. Though the present 1996 Treaty does not include a minimum guarantee, it has several provisions that provide a measure of security to Bangladesh (Iyer 2003, 132).

Institutional Mechanisms

A Joint Committee consisting of three members from each country, to monitor purposes and settle disputes, was constituted to finalize procedures for setting up teams at Farakka and Hardinge Bridge for joint observations during the period January 1 to May 31. Any difference or dispute arising in this regard, if not resolved by the Joint Committee, shall be referred to the Indo-Bangladesh Joint Rivers Commission. The unresolved issues shall be referred to the two governments, which shall meet urgently at the appropriate level to resolve it by mutual discussion. There is no provision for arbitration in the 1996 Treaty. Soon differences arose on the amount of water flow and hence the distribution.

Actualization of the Treaty: Areas of Discord

This led to a serious dispute that was extensively covered in the newspapers in both countries. Bangladesh accused India of violating the 1996 Treaty and wanted India to protect the average flows and assure 35,000 cusecs to Bangladesh irrespective of the actual flows in the river at Farakka (WASSA Project Report 2003, 54). The joint observations of flows also came under debate. The Indian view was that the 1997 lean season marked a difficult hydrological year with a late winter and subsequent overcast skies that retarded summer snowmelt.

The impact of India's Farakka Barrage on agriculture in Bangladesh is a source of dispute. Bangladeshis believe that the Farakka Barrage is respon- sible for reduced rice and other crop yields. India rejects this claim. The rainforests of Sundarbans have also shown signs of deterioration through increased salinity, chlorinity, and insufficient nutrients in the water. There are mixed conclusions as to the ecological effects of the Farakka Barrage but there is a strong view that the barrage has caused a decline in fish catches. People living in the area claim that the increased salinity is threatening their crops, industry, and animal drinking water. It is unlikely that Bangladesh will receive any compensation for losses.

However, despite several differences, the 1996 Treaty between India and Bangladesh has been working reasonably well, and neither country has asked for a review. Whether it will continue to work well will depend on the state of the political relationship between the two countries. In other words, it is politics and not water that will determine the future of the 1996 Treaty.

INDIA—PAKISTAN

The only international water sharing treaty that exists between India and Pakistan is the Indus Water Treaty, which became effective in April 1960 after eight years of arduous negotiations to resolve the dispute over the usage of the Indus waters for irrigation and hydropower.

Map 4.2.   The Indus Basin

THE INDUS BASIN

The Indus system of rivers comprises the main river Indus and its five tributaries from the east, the Jhelum, Chenab, Ravi, Sutlej, and Beas, and three tributaries from the west, the Kabul, Swat, and the Kurram Rivers (Williams 1955, 5 June).

The Indus is 2880 km long and the length of its tributaries is 5600 km (Garg 1999, 79). The complicated origins of the Indus River system play a

key role in the water debates, as the rivers originate in and pass through a
number of countries.

- The main Indus River rises in Tibet and after flowing through the Indian
  states of Jammu and Kashmir enters Pakistan.
- The river Jhelum originates in Verinag in the valley of Kashmir and enters
  Pakistan.
- The Chenab River rises in Lahaul in the Himachal Pradesh state of India
  and after flowing through Jammu province enters Pakistan.
- The Ravi River rises near Kulu in Himachal Pradesh, and flowing through
  Punjab enters Pakistan.
- The Sutlej rises in Tibet and flows through Punjab before entering
  Pakistan.
- The river Beas rises in Himachal Pradesh and flows wholly within India.

The Kabul and Kurram rivers rise in Afghanistan. The waters of the Swat in
Peshawar valley join the Kabul River.

Though the Indus basin has depended on irrigation since ancient times, it
was the British who developed an elaborate network of canals in the Indus system of rivers. However, their emphasis was that lands belonging to the Crown
should receive such irrigation as would earn revenue for the British Indian
government from water cess as well as from the sale of Crown wastelands
(Williams 1955). Thus, the Indus system waters were used gainfully to irrigate
annually about 23.4 million acres in the Indus plains and 2.6 million acres
above the rim stations before the partition in 1947 (Gulati 1973, 18–24).

PARTITION AND ITS AFTERMATH

The partitioning of India in 1947 created a new international border, which
cut the network of irrigation infrastructure and tributaries of the Indus River
system unevenly. The bulk of the irrigation canals developed on the Indus
system went to Pakistan. Out of 26 million acres of land irrigated annually
by Indus canals, 21 million acres lay in Pakistan and only five million acres
in India (Gulati 1973, 59). As per the 1941 census, the population dependent
on the Indus system waters was 25 million in Pakistan and 31 million in
India, (Gulati 1973, 59). Besides, India had "another 35 million acres of land
crying out for irrigation from the Indus basin sources"(Williams 1955). India
faced food shortages. It needed large amounts of food to feed the 310 million
people, plus those millions who migrated from the irrigated areas of West
Punjab and Bahawalpur, now in Pakistan.

The geography of the partition was such that the diversion structures of some of the irrigation systems were located in India, while the distribution network was in Pakistan. The dispute over sharing of Indus waters therefore came to the fore. The existing canal headwork of Upper Bari Doab Canal (UBDC) and the Sutlej Valley canals were in India (in the state of East Punjab), while the lands being irrigated by their waters were in Pakistan (in the West Punjab and Bahawalpur States). In order to maintain and run the systems existing pre-Partition, two Standstill Agreements were signed on December 20, 1947, by the chief engineers of East Punjab (India) and West Punjab (Pakistan). These interim arrangements were to expire on March 31, 1948, after which East Punjab started asserting its rights on its waters. On April 1, 1948, India stopped supplying water to canals that irrigated about 1.6 million acres of land in Pakistan. India's argument was that it was no longer obliged to supply water to Pakistan since the Standstill Agreements had not been extended.

According to Williams (1955), the water supplies were cut because the canal colonies served by these headworks did not pay the standard water dues. The people in charge of the headworks were applying exactly the same rules that were applied in pre-Partition India—no canal dues, no water (Williams 1955).

To work out some sort of arrangement to diffuse this international water dispute, representatives from India met their Pakistani counterparts in April 1948. On April 30, 1948, Indian Prime Minister Jawahar Lal Nehru intervened and India agreed to release water to those canals. However, the release of water to Pakistan did not end the dispute. In May 1948, a high-level inter-dominion conference was held in New Delhi that resulted in the signing of the Delhi Agreement to facilitate bilateral talks between the two countries.

Though the Delhi Agreement was not final, it did provide some basis to deal with the problem. Per the Delhi Agreement, East Punjab agreed not to withhold water from West Punjab without giving the latter time to tap alternative sources. As regards the payment of seigniorage charges to East Punjab, the West Punjab government agreed to deposit immediately in the Reserve Bank of India "such ad hoc sum as maybe specified by the Prime Minister of India" (Gulati 1973, 69). However, Pakistan did not abide by the agreement. It sought to use the Indus water dispute as a political ploy over Kashmir. Pakistan tried to create anti-India hysteria in Pakistan over this issue. It unilaterally abrogated the Delhi Agreement arguing that it was signed under duress. Pakistan also refused to pay the dues to India (Gupta 1960) and looked for third-party adjudication by referring it to the International Court of Justice for a final verdict. India opposed Pakistani moves.

INTERNATIONAL INTERVENTION

By 1951 the two sides were no longer meeting, and the situation had become intractable. The Pakistani press was calling for more drastic action. The deadlock created tension between the two countries and brought them to the brink of war. It was in this atmosphere of mutual distrust and contrived tensions that David Lilienthal, formerly the chairman of the Tennessee Valley Authority (TVA), and the U.S. Atomic Energy Commission visited India and Pakistan in February 1951 on a supposedly private visit. Lilienthal had a keen interest in the subcontinent and was eager to resolve the water-related conflict between India and Pakistan by exploring areas of possible cooperation, and to promote friendship between the two countries that might, in time, lead to the settlement of the Kashmir dispute. After his visit to the subcontinent, Lilienthal wrote a politically-charged article, titled "Another 'Korea' in the Making," in which he analyzed the Indo-Pakistan relations. He prefaced his article with the comment: "India and Pakistan are on the edge of a war over which shall possess Kashmir—a fight the United States might be forced to enter . . . The direct issue is whether the historic region of Kashmir and Jammu shall be part of India or Pakistan. On one of this disputed region's frontiers lies Red China, on another Red Tibet. Along another frontier is Soviet Russia" (Lilienthal 1951, 11).

Interestingly, Lilienthal was more concerned about the presence of communist China and the Soviet Union at the borders of Kashmir and the Cold War politics in the region. Nonetheless, explaining the importance of the Indus waters for ensuring food security to millions of people in India and Pakistan, Lilienthal proposed that the canal water dispute could be solved by India and Pakistan working out a joint program to develop and operate the Indus basin river system. He believed that with new dams and irrigation canals, the Indus and its tributaries could provide additional water needed by each country for increased food production. He suggested that the World Bank use its good offices to bring both the countries to a consensus, and help in financing of an Indus Development program. Lilienthal's idea was well received by Eugene R. Black, then-president of the World Bank and a close friend of David Lilienthal.

In September 1951, the World Bank formally offered its good offices to both India and Pakistan to work out a solution to the Indus water issue on the basis of the Lilienthal proposals. The World Bank offer was conditioned by the "essential principle" that "the problem of development and use of Indus basin water resources should be solved on a functional and not a political plan, without relations to past negotiations and past claims, and independently of political issues" (Pitman 1951, 159).

By May 1952, the first of a long series of conferences began in Washington D.C., and later moved to Karachi and New Delhi. But it soon became clear that Black's hopes for a quick resolution on the Indus water dispute were premature. Although both the World Bank and Lilienthal had expected India and Pakistan to reach an agreement on the allocation of Indus waters, neither of the countries seemed willing to compromise their positions. While the Pakistani delegates insisted on their "historical use rights" of waters from the Indus and its tributaries, the Indian side argued that the previous distribution of waters should not set the future allocation. India argued for a new basis for distribution of waters of the western tributaries going to Pakistan and the eastern tributaries to India.

THE INDUS WATERS TREATY

In 1954, after nearly two years of negotiations, the World Bank offered its own proposal, stepping beyond the limited role it had played so far, and it pressured the two sides to consider concrete plans for the future of the basin. The proposal offered three eastern tributaries of the basin to India and the three western tributaries to Pakistan. Canals and storage dams were to be constructed to divert waters from the western rivers and replace the eastern river supply lost by Pakistan. Whereas India accepted the World Bank proposals, Pakistan vacillated and accepted in principle only after the Bank pressed it for a reply. Pakistan argued that its share of waters from the Indus river system should be based on the pre-partition distribution. Further, as the World Bank proposal was more in line with the Indian plan, the Pakistani delegates were outraged. They threatened to withdraw from the negotiating table, and as a result, negotiations between the two countries virtually collapsed.

India's acceptance of the World Bank proposals was based on the hope that in five years' time India would be able to make use of the waters of the eastern rivers. This was, however, frustrated by Pakistani procrastination. Pakistan was seeking a comprehensive replacement-cum-development program in Pakistan involving a large investment of about US$1.12 billion. The World Bank, the United States,, and certain Western countries were ready to foot the bill for this huge construction program in Pakistan, so that the canal water dispute between India and Pakistan could be solved amicably. It was on March 1, 1960, that the World Bank made a public announcement of the financial plan it had evolved for the replacement and development works of the Indus systems. It was estimated to cost about 1000 million dollars (partly in foreign exchange and partly in local currencies). The Bank announced that the requisite expenditure would be contributed by Australia,

Table 4.4.   Comparison of Western and Eastern Rivers of the Indus Basin Vis-à-Vis Requirement for and Availability of Irrigation Water

Western rivers (Allocated to Pakistan)	*Eastern rivers (Allocated to India)*
• Cultivable area = 25.100 million acres	• Cultivable area = 22.856 million acres
• Water requirement (for irrigation purposes) = 50.01 MAF	• Water requirement (for irrigation purposes) = 46.37 MAF
• Mean annual supplies = 135.6 MAF	• Mean annual supplies = 32.8 MAF
• *Surplus = 85.59 MAF*	• *Deficit = 13.57 MAF*

Source: Warikoo 2001, 295

Canada, New Zealand, Germany, the United Kingdom, the United States, the World Bank, and India and Pakistan. Ironically, the bulk of this financial plan was meant to be spent in Pakistan (US$691 million out of US$747 million of grants and loans, with India getting only US$56 million as a loan for the Beas dam, as against Pakistan getting all her development underwritten by the Bank's financial plan) (Gulati 1973, 277–8). The World Bank press release did not mention the additional U.S. grant of US$235 million (in local currency) to Pakistan (Gulati 1973, 277–8). Yet India stuck to its commitment to conclude the Indus Waters Treaty based on the World Bank proposals. The Treaty was duly signed on September 19, 1960, at Karachi by Jawahar Lal Nehru, the prime minister of India, President Ayub Khan of Pakistan, and W.A.B Iliss of the World Bank (Warikoo 2001. 290).

Under the Indus Treaty, the waters of the three eastern rivers (Sutlej, Beas and Ravi) were allocated to India for her exclusive use. The waters of the three remaining western rivers (Chenab, Jhelum and Indus) were allocated to Pakistan, with the exception of certain specified uses that India could make of these waters such as hydroelectric use, non-consumptive use, and limited agricultural use in their upper catchments.

According to the Indus Treaty, Pakistan was required to construct and bring into operation a system of reservoirs and canals to transfer waters from the western rivers to feed the canals, which were dependent upon the supplies amounting to about 24 million acre feet (MAF) from the eastern rivers prior to partition. It is pertinent to remember that such a mass transfer of water from one basin to another is a distinct departure from the concept of the international law of upper and lower riparian rights. Consequently, the Tarbela and Mangla Dams on the Indus and Jhelum Rivers, five barrages, one siphon, and eight inter-river link canals were constructed. An Indus Basin Development Fund (IBDF) was established and administered by the World Bank. The replacement works were constructed using the IBDF at a cost of about US$1208 million (WASSA Project Report 2003, 48).

The Indus Treaty provided for the creation of two permanent posts of commissioners—one from each side (and each of whom was required to be a high ranking engineer, competent in the field of hydrology and water use) to monitor the implementation of matters arising out of the Treaty and to serve as the regular channel of communication between the two countries. Promotion of cooperation between the two parties, settlement of differences, and monitoring the implementation of the Indus Treaty comprised the purpose and function of the commissioners.

DIVERGENT PERSPECTIVES

The Indus Treaty faced strong criticism in India. Members of the Parliament belonging to the Congress, PSP, and other political parties pointed to the glaring mistakes committed in the conclusion of this treaty. Nehru, in his address to the Lok Sabha on November 30, said "We purchased a settlement, if you like; we purchased peace to that extent and it is good for both countries" (Indian Express 1960,). Congress MPs from Punjab and Rajasthan called the treaty disadvantageous to India, stating that their home states "had been badly let down." Another Congress MP, lamented that the "interests of India had been sacrificed to placate Pakistan." Ashok Mehta, the leader of the PSP in the Lok Sabha, described it as a "peculiar treaty under which Pakistan, already a surplus area, would be unable to make full use of her share of the Indus waters and would have to allow it to flow into the sea. On the contrary, India after the fullest development of the water resources, would still be short of supplies" (Indian Express 1960).

The Indus Treaty was signed by Nehru in the fervent hope of ushering all-round improvement in India-Pakistan relations and resolution of all outstanding problems including Kashmir. Perhaps Nehru was impressed by Ayub's offer of joint defense with India made in early 1959 in the wake of deteriorating India-China relations (Dawn 1959). Ayub's offer, however, needed to be viewed in the light of Pakistan being a member of the U.S.-sponsored military pacts SEATO and CENTO, which made him susceptible to Western prescriptions for regional peace and cooperation. At that time the United States and its friendly Western nations viewed the Communist bloc—USSR and China—as a greater threat. Although India did not accept the offer of joint defense, it sought to improve relations with Pakistan by agreeing to substantially pay for the cost of irrigation programs in Pakistan, besides surrendering the use of three western rivers. India treated the Indus water issue as a technical engineering problem. On the other hand, Pakistan exploited it as a political weapon in its Cold War against India. Pakistan also succeeded in extracting huge financial assistance of about US$1 billion from the World Bank, the United States, and other Western countries, using the geopolitical environment in the region to its advantage (Warikoo 2001, 294).

In retrospect, it is often held that India was too generous, both in terms of allowing the use of the waters in the western rivers and by making a payment of more than GB£62 million to Pakistan. It is also interesting to consider why the World Bank advanced such disproportionate proposals to India, "particularly when the eastern rivers given to India carried 20 to 25 percent of the total flow of the Indus Basin as against 75 to 80 percent in the three western rivers allocated to Pakistan" (Garg 1999. 85). Out of the total annual flow of 168.4 MAF of water in the Indus system of rivers, the total requirement of irrigation water was 96.36 MAF for the entire cultivable area of the Indus basin, thereby leaving a surplus of 72.02 MAF that would be going to the sea. Did Cold War considerations play a role in the World Bank's decision?

It is still debated in India as to why the Indian delegation agreed to a much lower share of the water available in the eastern rivers (Khosla 1958, 234–53). It has been observed that India's disadvantageous position in this Indus Treaty was due to shortsightedness of the then-existing Jammu and Kashmir government in not analyzing the existing and future water requirements for irrigation, hydro power generation, and other uses in the state. Therefore, the Indian delegation failed to ensure the necessary safeguards in the treaty for future consumption of water for hydropower purposes, except for the run-of-the-river methods.

With the backdrop of the internationally-accepted Helsinki Rules framed by the International Law Association, which postulate the equitable utilization of waters of an international drainage basin based on several factors— such as hydrology of the basin, population dependent on the waters of the basin, economic and social needs of the basin, etc. — it has been asserted that India did not get a fair deal. According to S.K. Garg, who has computed the respective entitlement of India and Pakistan on the basis of the population, drainage areas, length of rivers, and cultivable area, India should have been given a 42.8 percent share in the water, as against the actual allocation of 20 to 25 percent flowing in the three eastern rivers. (Garg 1999, 85). The fact that the underlying parameter of distribution in the Indus Treaty was based on the number of rivers rather than the quantum of water exposes a major flaw in the treaty. Had the quantum of water been the criterion, the Kabul, Kurram and Swat Rivers of the Indus basin could have been included in the calculations for requirements and availability of water in Pakistan. According to Indian critics of the treaty, India was simply hoodwinked by Pakistan and the Americans.

It has been pointed out that Pakistan's Indus basin has acute problems of water logging and salinity due to excessive availability of Indus waters and consequent canal seepage and percolation of an excess amount of water (Warikoo 2001, 298). According to a study, in Pakistan Punjab alone, five million ha have already gone out of cultivation due to salinity caused by water logging, 6,90,000 ha are in an advanced stage of deterioration, and two million ha are affected to a lesser degree' (Murakami 1995, 52).

Despite all these alleged flaws and biases, the Indus Treaty has been hailed as one of the most successful and long lasting international water-sharing treaties. The Indus Commission has survived the wars of 1965, 1971, and 1999, a border confrontation during 2001–02, and the Mumbai terrorist attack in 2009. It has provided ongoing machinery for consultation and conflict resolution through inspection, exchange of data, and visits. The treaty also refers to the mediation and arbitration by "Neutral Experts," jointly appointed by both governments, in case of disputes arising between the two. The Indus Treaty has thus defiantly stood the test of time, consistently remaining one of the few common meeting platforms for the two traditional enemies; however, it has not been completely free from problems. The first dispute post-Indus Treaty revolved around the construction of the Salal Dam by India on the Chenab River to irrigate Punjab's agricultural lands. Pakistan objected to its design. After much negotiating, India agreed to reduce the height of the dam and also to the permanent closure of the diversion canal. The agreement was signed in April 1978.

Nonetheless, the increasing needs for water and power in both India and Pakistan have exposed the Indus Treaty to tensions in recent decades. In contrast to Bangladesh and Nepal, India and Pakistan are essentially independent of each other in managing their water supplies under the Indus Treaty. As a result, concerns related to water security have not been very acute in the past, but recently the situation has changed. Both India and Pakistan have various proposed projects that are sparking controversies and posing serious challenges to the already-fragile peace in the region. Extreme radical elements in Pakistan even talk about using nuclear options against India to protect Pakistan's water rights (Suba 2009).

SOURCES OF POLITICAL DISPUTES/TENSIONS:

i. Wullar Barrage (The Tulbul Navigation Lock)

The Indus Treaty allows India limited existing and new water uses from the western rivers in J&K as well as restrictive, non-consumptive uses on the Chenab and the tributaries of the Jhelum, for hydropower.

In 1985, India started construction of a barrage some 439 feet long with a lock at the mouth of Wullar Lake, the largest fresh water lake in J&K. The barrage was built to facilitate navigation in the 22 km stretch between the towns of Sopore and Baramula by regulating the flow of Jhelum in the lean winter season. Needless to mention, this would bring economic benefits to the people living in the valley. The Wullar Barrage would also regulate the flow of water into Jhelum, control the floods, and moderate the silt flows into Pakistan, thereby improving the efficiency of the Mangla dam. However, Pakistan raised strong objections to this project, contending that India cannot store water in excess of .01MAF as "incidental storage" on the river Jhelum. The construction work was stopped in 1987 due to this opposition. Pakistan also pointed out that the Wullar Barrage might cause damage to its project of linking Jhelum and Chenab with the Upper Bari Doab Canal. One important concern of Pakistan, which is extraneous to the IWT but squarely a security issue, is that in case of war between the two countries, India could control the flow of water and access through the river route (Sridhar 2005, 5).

India argues that the Tulbul scheme as envisaged is only a control structure (barrage) to regulate the natural storage of Wullar without any additional storage and rise in water level in the lake. The objective is only to improve the navigable draft in the river after the floods, over a period of four months during the winter season. India has also highlighted the additional power benefits that would accrue from all the hydroelectric projects downstream, to both India and Pakistan due to increased regulated lean-season flow downstream of the lake. According to India, the objection of Pakistan is therefore, less technical and more political. The project's impact, India asserts, would be beneficial to the Mangla Dam in power generation and to Pakistan's triple canal system due to regulated flow of water. The matter remains unresolved.

ii. Kishanganga Project

Pakistan has opposed another Indian project on the Kishanganga (known as the Neelum in Pakistan-administered Kashmir). It involves diversion of water from the Neelum to another tributary of the Jhelum, called Bunar Mandhumati, near Bandipur in the Baramula District that Pakistan believes is not allowed under the Indus Treaty. The contention is that the Jhelum will consequently face a 27 percent water deficit at the completion of the project, which envisages construction of a channel, a tunnel, and a dam near the Line of Control. On the other hand, Pakistan plans to construct the 969 MW-capacity Neelum-Jhelum Power Plant with Chinese assistance. This Pakistani project is scheduled to be completed in 2017. Pakistan is genuinely concerned and fears that India's Kishanganga project would lead to a shortfall of water flow into the Neelum, reducing its power generation by an estimated nine percent (Agriculture Corner 2010).

India intends to complete the Kishanganga project by 2016 by diverting Kishangangas'a water to Wullar Lake before Pakistan is able to invoke the provision of prior appropriation. India also claims that Pakistan need not worry because the water diverted by the Kishanganga project would reach Pakistan through the river Jhelum.

iii. Baglihar Hydro Electric Power Project

The Baglihar project has been on the drawing boards of Indian planners since 1992, invoking intense public debate and fueling an Indo-Pakistani dispute related to the project. The Baglihar Hydropower Project (BHP) is located on the river Chenab in Ramban tehsil of Doda district of Jammu and Kashmir. Its construction began in 1999.

The dispute over the 470-feet-high, 317-meter-wide BHP centers on the design specifications. Pakistan has raised several technical objections, and contends that it violates the Indus Treaty, which lays down the rights and obligations of India and Pakistan for the use of waters of the Indus system of rivers. India disagreed with Pakistani objections. Pakistan approached the World Bank, which had brokered the Indus Treaty, to appoint a Neutral Expert (NE) to resolve the differences. The World Bank has appointed a NE to resolve the differences.

Politicians and Islamic groups in Pakistan accuse India of stealing upstream Indus system waters, threatening Pakistan's very existence. More sober Pakistanis complain that numerous new Indian projects on the Jhelum and Chenab will create substantial live storage even in run-of-the-river hydro dams, and will enable India to drastically reduce flows to Pakistan during the crucial sowing season, something they allege actually happened for a couple of days when the Baglihar reservoir was filled by India after the dam's completion.

During the past few years the noise about the Indian water projects in J&K has been raised by Islamic fundamentalists. Pakistani leaders describe India as an eternal enemy and accuse it of planning a "water bomb" strategy to strangle Pakistan's economic development (Ahmad 2009, 5).

The extremists in India have talked about the abrogation of the Indus Treaty. The extremists on both sides, in a worst-case scenario, may pressure for such abrogation. Such actions will only hamper the water relations further and negate whatever has been achieved so far. In fact, Article VII of the Indus Treaty, on "Future Cooperation," leaves open the possibility of newer avenues of cooperation without the need for the signatories to renegotiate or abandon the treaty. Water is a common, increasingly scarce resource that needs to be shared for the mutual benefit of both countries. The time is ripe to

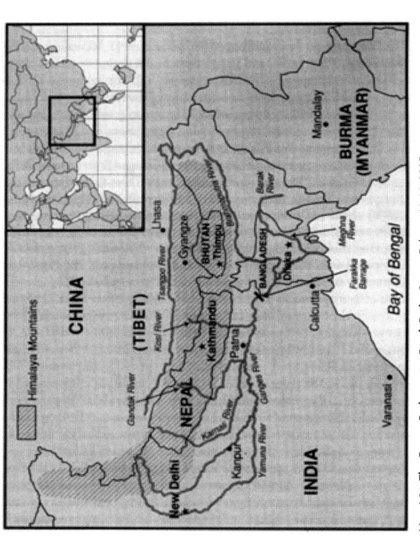

Map 4.3   The Ganges Brahmaputra Barak Basin *Source*: Rahman M. M. 2005a.

build on this cooperation (Mattoo 2010). Clearly, the only option is to engage with each other to effectively harness the Indus waters jointly.

INDIA AND NEPAL

Nepal and India share one of the largest geo-hydrological regions, called the "Ganges Brahmaputra Basin." Nepal covers a large part of the upper catchment of the sub-basin of the Ganges River. Major rivers of the sub-basin, such as the Mahakali, Karnali, Sapt Gandaki, and Sapt Kosi, originate from Trans-Himalaya region, cross Nepal, and flow southwards to join the Ganges in India. They therefore are international or transboundary in nature. Though Nepal occupies 13 percent of the total drainage of the Ganges basin, its contribution to the flow of the Ganges River is much more significant, amounting to about 45 percent of its average annual flow. In the dry seasons, Nepal's contribution to the total run-off is as much as 70 percent. These hydrological features bind India and Nepal in a relationship of geographical interdependence and economic complementarities on issues of water resource development.

Although the potential for joint endeavors between India and Nepal is considerable, their relationship on water resource development has not been easy and forthcoming. Their efforts have been heavily influenced by geopolitics and are marked by an emphasis on historical wrongs (real and perceived), big-versus-small-country syndrome, failure to understand each other's sensitivities, an aggressive posture, and a negative approach.

As discussed earlier, the Indo-Bangladesh dispute over the Ganges water emerged because of the Farakka barrage project in West Bengal. Similarly, projects on the Kosi and Gandak have generated riparian conflicts between India and Nepal, especially over the Tanakpur Barrage project. Misunderstanding between the parties based on principles, sensitivity, ignorance, indifference to information-sharing relating to water disasters, and politicization for electoral benefits have contributed to some of these tensions.

The importance of water resources development for Nepal lies in the fact that it not only facilitates Nepal's agricultural and industrial growth, provides hydro-power, and accelerates fishery development, but also generates capital because Nepel sells surplus energy to other countries. However, Nepal's major problem has been lack of capital and technological knowhow to develop its water resources (Upreti 1993, 93). Both countries needed electricity and water to improve their agricultural and industrial sectors. India was also willing to purchase unused power from Nepal.

All types of water development projects undertaken by India have been multi-purpose in nature, providing hydropower generation, irrigation, and other facilities. It should also be noted that India has provided both capital and technological assistance for these water resource development projects. The technological aid includes machinery, equipment, and technical expertise (Upreti 1993, 95–96).

THE SARADA AGREEMENT

The efforts to exploit Himalayan river water began before India's independence. The British Indian government contemplated building a barrage in Nepal to provide irrigation to western United Provinces in India. After a series of negotiations with its Nepalese counterpart, the British India government signed the Sarada Agreement in 1920 (Sarada Agreement or 1920 Agreement) for the construction of a barrage on the river Mahakali at Banbasa, bordering the present Mahendranagar in Nepal, and a power station at Khatima. According to the Sarada Agreement, 4000 acres of land on the eastern banks of the Mahakali River were transferred to India to build the Sarada barrage, and in exchange Nepal received 4000 acres of forested land in areas to the east as well as Rs. 50,000. Furthermore, the Sarada Agreement allowed Nepal to withdraw a minimum of 400 cusecs and a maximum of 1000 cusecs of water from the Sarada Canal in dry and wet seasons, respectively, for irrigation (Upreti 1993, 95). The Sarada Agreement, however, did not clearly stipulate how much water India could withdraw. This vagueness left room for critics of the 1920 Agreement to call it an "unequal treaty" (Gyawali and Dixit 1999, 553–564). The 1920 Agreement was to provide much-needed irrigation water and power to develop the Terai region in both countries. The Sarada Agreement still regulates the diversion of waters of the Mahakali River exclusively for irrigation and power to Uttar Pradesh in India (World Bank 1987). The 1920 Agreement allowed India to construct a barrage at her own expense on the Mahakali River, on the parts of land that Nepal had transferred.

THE KOSI PROJECT

Several other mutually-beneficial water resources projects have been undertaken by Nepal and India, largely financed by the government of India. The Nepalese government has cooperated by providing land and the raw materials. One of the first such river-water development projects undertaken by India and Nepal was the Kosi project. It was a multipurpose scheme including hydropower generation, irrigation, and flood control. After a long, drawn-out process of negotiation between the governments of India and Nepal, the Agreement of 1954 (1954 Agreement) was signed in 1960, and later amended that same year.

The River Kosi is known as the "river of sorrow" in India due to its floods. It originates at an altitude of over 7000 m above MSL in the Himalayas. The upper catchments are 62,620 sq km (85 percent of the total length) that lie in Tibet and Nepal. The remaining 11,410 sq km falls in India and mainly passes through the north of the state of Bihar. It originates in Tibet and flows through India and Nepal. Annual floods result in a loss of life, damage to agricultural crops and property, and cause enormous miseries to people in the region. The Kosi also carries enormous silt during the monsoon season and spills into the plains of the Indo-Nepal border. The meandering flow of the Kosi has rendered about 1295 sq km of land useless in Nepal, and 7,770 sq km of land useless in India, because of deposition of sand: hence, the desire to tame the river.

The Kosi scheme consists of a canal system, flowing channels on both sides, a barrage across the river, and a hydro station (Joshi 1951, 60).

In the 1980s India presented a proposal to construct an alternative to the Kosi barrage. The proposal ran into difficulties at its very inception. Nepal was unhappy with the 1954 Agreement on issues of compensation. India was to compensate for the land acquired in Nepal as well as all damages done in the course of the construction of the barrage. India was also responsible for the design, construction, and operation of the project. Nepal contended that the 1954 Agreement was skewed in terms of the benefits that accrued to the two countries. In terms of irrigation, for instance, only 29,000 acres in Nepal benefited, whereas the barrage had the capacity to irrigate 1.5 million acres. Some groups in Nepal also expressed their displeasure at the submergence of territory and the resultant displacement of people, none of whom received any compensation. India's control and management of the barrage was also considered to be an infringement on Nepal's territorial sovereignty. After prolonged discussions, Nepal's bruised sensitivities were smoothed and the second phase of the project began with Prime Minister Lal Bahadur Shastri's visit to Nepal in 1965. The 1954 Agreement was amended in 1965 but the amendment still did not solve several issues. The main points of contention between India and Nepal were about the length of the lease to India in Nepal and the issue of mutuality of power pricing and sharing. Power generated was to be shared between the two countries, and the rates were to be on concessional basis and decided by mutual agreement. But India brought down the capacity of the power plant from 20,000 kW to 13600 kW, to which Nepal had strong objections as both countries were supposed to inform the other if their power consumption exceeded 6800 kW. In 1991, secretary-level talks were held on the issue of building the Sapt Kosi High Dam. But the feasibility of this project was questioned from social and environmental perspectives. The issue of power-sharing and generation was taken up in the subsequent talks, and in 2006 a "concessional power tariff" was finally agreed upon; yet, the Agreement has not solved two major spheres of disagreement between the two countries.

THE GANDAK TREATY

After about three years of negotiation the Gandak Agreement between Nepal and India was signed on 4th December 1959 to construct a barrage, canal head regulator, and other appurtenant structure and canal systems for purpose of irrigation, flood control, and development of power in Nepal and India. Unlike the Kosi barrage, which is on the Nepal-India border, this barrage was built inside Nepalese territory. Moreover, unlike the 1954 Agreement, the Gandak Treaty included detailed descriptions of the irrigation facilities to be provided from the project to Nepal, and also provided for construction of a powerhouse with an installed capacity of 15,000 kW in the Nepalese territory on the main western canal (NICOH 2006). The Gandak Treaty specifically addressed the issue of management and control of the facility.

THE MAHAKALI TREATY

The Mahakali River is a major transboundary river basin between India and Nepal. It forms the western international border of Nepal with India. Starting from Apihimal, the river flows in a gorge section in the upper region. The Mahakali, after it flows into India, is known as the Sharda, which meets the Karnali (Ghaghra) in Indian territory. The river basin has a total drainage area of 15,640 sq km, about 34 percent of which lies in Nepal.

Conflicts between India and Nepal over sharing the benefits of the Mahakali River started shortly after India's unilateral decision in 1983 to construct the Tanakpur Barrage about 18 km upstream of the Sharada Barrage. India started building this barrage at Tanakpur to divert water from the Mahakali River to generate electricity and provide irrigation. The left afflux bund of this barrage was to be connected to Nepalese territory, and a few sectors of Nepalese land were also to be submerged. The project raised tension over the following issues:

- Reservoir submergence of a small area at the border in Nepal territory due to construction of the Tanakpur Barrage and power project in Indian territory.
- Power benefits to be shared with additional water allocation for irrigation in Nepal areas of the barrage.
- Equal sharing of water was demanded by Nepal on the basis that the river forms a common border in certain stretches, as against equitable sharing suggested by India.
- The prescriptive rights of irrigation established in India, which according to Nepal were to be treated as an additional benefit from the proposed dam.
- Incidental benefits of flood control in India should also be assessed in working out benefits and apportioning the costs of the dam.
- Nepal desired all hydropower projects to be designed as peaking stations and a separate tariff to be worked out based on the costs of alternative energy from fossil/nuclear/gas-based generation, in order to decide the rate of sale of power to India.

The dispute and differences were finally resolved on February 12, 1996, when a treaty was signed between Nepal and India (the Mahakali Treaty) concerning the Integrated Development of the Mahakali River, including the Sharada Barrage, Tanakpur Barrage and Pancheswar project. Nepal ratified the Mahakali Treaty on September 20, 1996, while India ratified it on November 27, 1996. The treaty specified the quantum of water and hydropower that Nepal is to receive from the Mahakali in the pre-Pancheswar scenario (WASSA Project Report 2003, 20–21).

The Mahakali Treaty subsumes all other Indo-Nepalese agreements relating to downstream projects on the river; thus, it absorbs the regime established by the Sarada Agreement. It also validates the Tanakpur Agreement (1991), and endorses the idea of a multipurpose Pancheswar project.

The scope of the preamble of Mahakali Treaty is quite comprehensive. The treaty aims at "integrated development of the Mahakali River." It emphasizes the determination of India and Nepal to promote and strengthen their relation of friendship and close neighborliness for cooperation in the development of water resources. The preamble recognizes the river as a boundary river on major stretches in-between the two countries as well as the desire of the two countries to enter into the treaty, as equal partners, to define their obligations and corresponding rights and duties with regard to utilization of Mahakali River waters.

The Mahakali Treaty has a life of 75 years. It has been welcomed by a large number of people on both sides of the border. Many Nepalese experts say that the Mahakali Treaty has successfully broken the impasse created by a legacy of entrenched views along national lines on both sides, and leaves both sides as winners. Despite several unclear provisions and incomplete arrangements, the Mahakali Treaty has undoubtedly provided a mechanism for reinforced legal collaboration between India and Nepal on the Mahakali River.

In the past, relations between the two countries have suffered for two reasons. Firstly, the Indian policy makers have failed to understand the sensitivities of the smaller neighbor. Nepal, a small kingdom sandwiched between two Asian giants—India and China—has its own worldview. India took Nepal for granted on many occasions. Secondly, Nepal overemphasized sovereignty issues and nursed the grudge and mistrust against India. The influence of geopolitics in Indo-Nepal water resource development has been disproportionate and troublesome. The Nepalese have long viewed India as a hegemonic power that arm-twists neighbors to enter into unfair arrangements. While Nepal showed disenchantment over joint water resource projects, irritants also arose in bilateral relations due to Nepal's balancing act with China, and turbulent domestic politics of the kingdom. India, in turn, accuses Nepal of suffering from small-country syndrome, imagining non-existent conspiracies and ignoring India's contribution in different sectors of the economy of Nepal. Further, fragile and unstable political uncertainties in Nepal also play a role in fueling anti-Indian sentiments.

CONCLUSION

The sharing of water resources of an international river basin has been a matter of contention in various parts of the world. While many of the disputes have been resolved, some of them exist even today. Water politics is therefore not a new phenomenon; however, a new politics of water scarcity is emerging at local, regional, national, and international levels—as tensions rise over limited supplies in the face of growing demands. The awareness regarding the development potential of water makes the issues all the more pertinent.

South Asia has emerged as the new focal point of water-related conflicts given the rapid growth of the region—which is putting immense pressure on water resources. This pressure is coupled with the concentration of unending internal and international tensions and countries plagued by historical animosities and internal instabilities. Water disputes and tensions have the potential to destabilize the region. While a full-scale war (India-Pakistan) on water is only a distant possibility, still-prevailing tensions could prevent cooperation and retard economic growth.

The genesis of politics around water resources in South Asia could be traced to the period of colonial rule and the British withdrawal thereafter. Actually, the creation of political boundaries in the existing socioeconomic, political, and geographical realities disturbed the river systems of the region and their uses. Like many other issues, the sharing of water resources also acquired disputable dimensions. The proclivity of each country to view the problem through the prism of national interest has precluded amicable, long-lasting solutions. Issues of national pride and interest, political differences among the co-basin countries, attitudes of the ruling elites, domestic compulsions of the riparian countries, and big-power-small-power complexities, have further obscured appropriate resolutions.

Mutual cooperation for the development of natural resources on a bilateral or trilateral or multilateral basis is generally successful where the countries aspiring to cooperate share certain commonalities in terms of size, population, natural resources, level of economic development and economic capabilities, nature of political systems, etc. It becomes rather difficult where such commonalities are absent and vast differences exist. In such cases the issue of big-versus-small power becomes pertinent and the smaller states generally develop a fear psychosis towards the bigger state. This obviously impedes bilateral cooperation. The geographical and economic superiority of India instills apprehension amongst its smaller neighbors of being dwarfed in the power equation, thus breeding distrust and suspicion between the states of the region. India's actions, policies, and perceptions have always been viewed with a large amount of suspicion. This fear psychosis is reflected in the issue of sharing water resources between India and her contiguous small neighbors—Pakistan, Bangladesh, and Nepal.

Notwithstanding the above, the fact remains that the political situation in the Indus water basin today is not what it was fifty years ago. Initially, regional pulls/pressures within the South Asian neighbors were fewer, if not totally non-existent; hence, none of them had to take into account the regional political demands for "their share" of water on a particular river system. The national governments in India and Pakistan were strong in relation to the provincial governments. In India, the towering personality of Jawaharlal Nehru and the dominance of the Congress Party partly played an important role in this process, while in Pakistan the pressure at the national level between the military and polity kept the regional politics at a low-key level. Today the situation is different. The relations between the federal governments and provinces/states, and between regional politics and parties, play a larger role at the national level, and the federal governments have to take into account the regional aspirations. Given the political alterations in the preceding decades, one is likely to see more problems in the coming decades.

Domestic and foreign policy compulsions have also aggravated the issue of water resources in South Asia. Due to political instability the process of structural development has not been adequate in Pakistan, Nepal, or Bangladesh. The authoritarian nature of the political systems in these countries allows a minimal role for public opinion. The ruling elites of these countries have displayed more interest in preserving their own authority than in resolving problems and issues of importance such as water resource management. On the contrary, the creation of "external enemies" has proved expedient as a diversionary tactic for preservation of authoritarian regimes.

As water does not respect territorial boundaries and flows from one state to another, this gives rise to questions of equity, share, and benefits. This obviously necessitates the evolution of mechanisms to solve these issues. Transboundary cooperation around water issues, which stems from a drive for sustainable development in the face of shared stress, has a long and successful history. This development imperative—not the fear of conflict per se— motivates countries to pursue tough, protracted negotiations such as the IWT, the Mahakali Treaty and the Indo-Bangladesh Accord of 1996, examples that could prove to be a cementing factor rather than reason for wars.

The Indus Treaty of 1960 illustrates that despite several armed conflicts fought between India and Pakistan over a variety of issues, water is one issue where the two countries have accommodated each other. In fact, according to the "water wars rationale," which forecasts war between countries "dependent upon a shared water resource if there is water scarcity, competitive use and the countries are enemies due to a wider conflict," India and Pakistan, by this logic, are prime candidates to go to war. Political experts were quick in predicting "hydrological warfare" in the South Asian region. But fortunately the successful negotiations translated into treaties like the IWT have promoted cooperation rather than conflict. It can thus be argued that the countries of South Asia have cooperated because they are "water-rational," realizing that cooperation is needed to safeguard the countries' long term access to shared water.

The challenge now is to ensure that cooperation is not derailed but strengthened. The following suggestions could prove fruitful in this context:

- Reversing the usual approach of demand to supply, one should now proceed from limited availability to the response of demand management and resource conservation. Water resource management coupled with development should become the path for the future.
- Comprehensive water laws need to be formulated to govern the relative priorities of different demands and sharing of water by different users.

- A basin-wide development approach to water resources of common rivers could inject a new consciousness of community among the people of the region, which could pave the way for regenerating the dented spirit of a common cultural and political identity, thus building the base for a common South Asian destiny.
- Participatory people-centric water management solutions rather than centralized, bureaucratic planning of water projects are a key to many of the water scarcity problems confronting this region.
- Aggressively pursuing a water peacemaking strategy can provide dividends beyond water for stakeholders. It can build trust and serve as an avenue for dialogue when parties are stalemated on other issues. Transnational networks of organizations including media, research bodies, and NGOs could help in organizing, publicizing, and strengthening the beneficial aspects of a community approach in water resource development.
- Water use efficiency needs no emphasis. Mismanagement in use of water by using antiquated techniques and heavy cropping of water-intensive varieties of farm products need to be transformed. Measures to efficiently use water in irrigation should be adopted, including drainage water recycling, rotational irrigation, adoption of water-conserving crop technology, conjunctive use of surface and ground water, switching from canal based irrigation to pipe based irrigation, and better management of canals to reduce wastage, etc.
- Given the low (or zero) price, many consumers in India, Pakistan, Bangladesh, and Nepal, especially in the agricultural sector, pay a very low fee. Pricing water at or near its true market value would help water management and reduce demand for water, thereby resolving water shortage problems. But it is a politically sensitive issue and can be tackled only by political courage.
- Regional cooperation is an important instrument for collective self-reliance and ecologically-sustainable development. Such cooperation in water management could help mitigate the disastrous effects of flood and would promote development activities ensuring prosperity, progress, and peace.

REFERENCES

Abbas, B. M. 1984. *The Ganges Water Dispute.* Dhaka:

Ahmad Tufail. July 31, 2009. *Pakistan's Water Concerns: Water Disputes between India and Pakistan- A Potential Casus Belli,* (eds.) Noor Ul Haq and Muhammad Nawaz Khan, http://www.henryjacksonsociety.org/stories.asp?id=1230, 4–5.

Ahmed, Q. K, Biswas, A. K., and Rangachari, R. 2001, Ganges Brahmaputra Meghna Region: A Framework for Sustainable Development, Dhaka, The University Press Limited.

Aiyar Anklesaria Swaminathan S, 2010. News International (Rawalpindi), April 13.

Author. 1976. "Title of Article."*Asian Recorder* XII (23): Col 13189.

Baral Lok Raj. 1988. *The Politics of Balanced Interdependence: Nepal and SSARC.* New Delhi: 41.

Cherian, John. 1997. "A Historic Accord." *Frontline* January 10: 47.

Author. 1977. "Article title." *Foreign Affairs Record* XXIII (11): 215–216.

Garg, S. K. 1999, *International and Interstate River Water Dispute.* New Delhi: Manoher.

Gulati, Chandrika J. 1988. *Bangladesh: Liberalism to Fundamentalism.* New Delhi: Manoher

Gulhati, N. D. 1973. *Indus Waters Treaty: An Exercise in International Mediation.* Bombay: Allied.

Gupta, Sisir. 1960. "The Indus Water Treaty." *Foreign Affairs Reports* 9 (12):

Gyawali, Dipak, and Dixit Ajaya. 1999. "Mahakali Impasse and Indo-Nepal Water Conflict." *Economic and Political Weekly* 34 (9): 553–564.

NICOH Nepal India Cooperation on Hydropower, Independent Power Producers' Association Nepal Confederation of Indian Industry, January 2006

Iyer, R. Ramaswamy. 2003. "Dispute and Resolution: The Ganges Water Treaty." *Indian Foreign Policy Agenda for the 21st Century* (Vol. 2). New Delhi: Foreign Service Institute.

Joshi, Bhuvan Lal. 1951. *Indo-Nepal Economic Cooperation.* Kathmandu: Indian Cooperation Mission.

Kaplan, Robert. 2010. *Monsoon- The Indian Ocean and the Future of American Power.* New York: Random House.

Karim, Ahmed Tariq 1998, "The Bangladesh—India Treaty on sharing of the Ganges Waters: Genersis and Significance," BISS Journal, Vol. 19, No. 2 216

Kay, R. 1965. "Article title." In *Standard Encyclopedia of the World's Rivers and Lakes*, edited by Gresswell and Anthony Huxley, X–XX. London: Weidenfield & Nickelson Ltd.

Khadka, Narayan 1991, Foreign Aid, Poverty and Stagnation in Nepal, New Delhi, Vikas.

Khosla, A. N. 1958. "Development of the Indus River System: An Engineering Approach." *India Quarterly* 14 (3): 234–53

Khurshid, Begum. 1987. *Tension Over the Farakka Barrage, A Techno-Political Tangle in South Asia.* Dhaka: Calcutta Port Trust.

Lilienthal, David. 1951. "Another 'Korea' in the Making." *Colliers Magazine* 4 August: X–XX.

Mattoo, Amitabh. 2010. "Pakistan's Water Concerns," *News International (Rawalpindi)*, May 11.

Murakami, Masahiro. 1995. *Managing Water for Peace in the Middle East: Alternative Strategies.* Tokyo: United Nations University Press.

Nepal, B. H, ed. Imtiaz Alam 2001, "Water Resources Strategy—Nepal," Kathmandu: Ministry of Water Resources.

Pitman, G. T. Keith. 1951. "The Role of the World Bank in Enhancing Cooperation and Resolving Conflicts on International Water Courses: The Case of the Indus Basin." In *International Water Courses: Enhancing Cooperation and Managing Conflict*, edited by M. A. Salman and Laurence Boisson deChazournes, page info. Washington: World Bank Technical Paper, no. 414, 159.

Qureshi, M. L. 1981. *Survey of Economy: Resources and Prospects of South Asia.* Colombo: Marga Institute.

Rao, K. L. 1975. *India's Water Wealth, Its Assessment, Uses and Projections.* New Delhi: Orient Longman.

Sinha, Rajesh 2006, "Two Neighbors and a Treaty: Baglihar Project in Hot Waters," *Economic and Political Weekly*, February 18.

Sridhar. 2005. "Indus Water Treaty." *Security Research Review*

Suba, Chandran D. 2009. *India Pakistan Dialogue on Conflict Resolution and Peace Building.* New Delhi: Institute of Peace and Conflict Studies, Issue Brief 122.

Upreti, B. C. 1993. *Politics of Himalayan River Waters.* New Delhi: Nirmala Publications.

Verma, NMP, Conflict Resolution and Institutional Arrangements for Flood Disaster. Management on Indo-Nepal Fringe: Focus on Kosi Basin, http://repository.unm.edu/

Warikoo, I. K. 2001. "Peace as Process: Reconciliation and Conflict Resolution in South Asia." In *Perspectives of the Indus Water Treaty,* edited by Samaddar Ranabir and Reifeld Helmut, X–XX. New Delhi: Manohar.

WASSA Project Report. 2003. Miah Maniruzzaman, Khalilur Rahman, Hamid Shahid, Mukherjee Somnath, and Verghese George. "Water Sharing Conflicts Between Countries, And Approaches to Resolving Them." *Project on 'Water and Security in South Asia.* Coordinated by Siddiqi, Toufiq A., and Tahir-Kheli Shirin, Sponsored by the Carnegie Corporation of New York, Vol. 3, Honolulu, Hawaii, 17

Williams, Rushbrook. 1955. "The Indus Canals Water Dispute." *Leader* Allahabad, 5 June

Chapter Five

Sino-Indian Water Wars?

Pia Malhotra-Arora

INTRODUCTION

"Prognosticators state that the next big crisis in the world is going to be caused by a damned shortage of water. The 20th century wars were about oil but the wars of the 21st century will be about water" (Ismail Serageldin 1995).

In regions of the world like South Asia, which are mainly agricultural and depend heavily on irrigated water for their livelihoods, water takes on an existential role. Water can bring countries to the warring playground, where logic is easily drowned in the din of pure competition for resources. India and Pakistan have been involved in altercations over shared water resources since their independence almost half a century ago. India and Bangladesh, India and Nepal, and India and China are the latest to quibble over water. Water woes are slowly gravitating towards a looming crisis, which if not handled at the right time, holds the potential to create widespread instability in the region.

Even as India and Pakistan tussle over shared river waters and even as water threatens to become the next core issue between the two countries, another region in the vicinity is emerging as an area of contention: India-China. When it comes to water issues, what India is to Pakistan, China is to India. China is the upper riparian and holds the potential power to disrupt water flows into the lower riparian, India.

A report by the Strategic Foresight Group (June 28, 2010), titled "The Himalayan Challenge," outlines Indian and Chinese plans to construct over 200 big and small dams on the Himalayan rivers the Yangtze, Brahmaputra, and Ganges to meet their escalating water needs. Asia is a region that is home to two of the fastest-growing economies of the world, India and China, and as reserves of oil dwindle, pressure on alternative power sources like hydro-power is expected to mount. The report also mentions that as water shortages increase, friction between the countries could increase and potentially lead to a conflict between India and China.

Moreover, rising water shortages, decline in food availability, reduction in opportunities in rural areas, soil erosion, desertification, and construction of dams all combine to create a threatening environment which could lead to the displacement of about 50 to 70 million people in India, China, Nepal, and Bangladesh by 2050 (Strategic Foresight Group 2011, 2).

One of the biggest areas of water usage in both India and China, besides agriculture and urbanization, is increasing industrialization. China is the world's largest producer of steel and its water consumption is twice that of developed nations to produce one ton of steel. The Indian steel sector, which ranks amongst the top ten producers in the world in terms of output, is much worse. On average, the integrated iron and steel plants in India consume 20–25 m of water per ton of finished product, as opposed to the global stan-dard of 5 m^3 (Strategic Foresight Group 2011, 4).

The twenty-first century is unique in a way because we no longer have an assumption of a river system (Brahmaputra) being stable, due to melting Himalayan glaciers; this in turn affects the relationship between the countries that share this river system.

Earlier the diplomacy between such countries was fairly straightforward, but now this is changing because melting glaciers and climatic changes are challenging these assumptions (Crow and Nirvikar 2009, 306–307).

A very important aspect which colors the water debate in the region is the political relationship between the countries in the region. Relations between India and Pakistan, India and Bangladesh, India and Nepal, and India and China are volatile. Water only adds to the plethora of problems that these countries already face such as border issues, issue of migrants, cross border infiltration, and drug trafficking.

Leading economies and contenders of political influence in the region both are likely to dispute over the water issue, especially over the Brahmaputra which originates in Tibet. India and China's positions on Tibet are murky at best. The water issue adds another potential area of confrontation between the two.

Analysts have gone as far as attributing China's intransigence on Tibet to its need for securing water resources (Sinha 2010). The Tibetan Plateau is the headwaters for many of Asia's rivers including the Yellow, Yangtze, Brahmaputra, Indus, and Sutlej. China's water resources are dwindling and it is expected to fall short of its water demands by 25 percent by 2030 (Washington Post 2010).

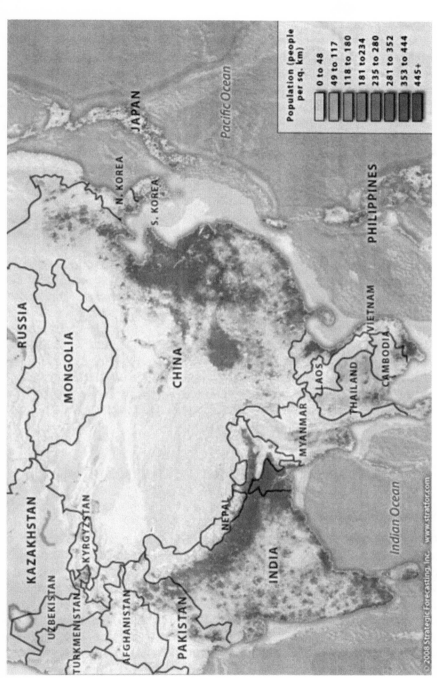

Figure 5.1. Population Density Map of Asia

Both India and China are industrializing at a very fast pace and one of the consequences of this industrialization has been the unsustainable use of water by the two countries. Since the agricultural revolution in Asia, the amount of land under irrigation has tripled. The water resources, however, have decreased. The Indian Ganges River and the Chinese Yellow River no longer flow easily due to much silting and upstream extraction of the water. They have become pretty stagnant.

The World Bank (2009) issued a statement on water and climate change in South Asia: "will amplify current levels of variability and may fundamentally change most hydrological systems." Climate-induced changes and changing seasonal patterns could have significant impact on lives and livelihoods of northern South Asia (World Bank 2009).

Glaciers in South Asia and China feed 47 percent of the world's people (Brown 1995, 23). In the past both India and China had extensively relied on groundwater to support their industrialization; however, excessive use of groundwater has left a very small amount of available water for future use. Both countries are looking for new sources of water, especially in the Himalayas. They are planning to build megaprojects to harness this water. Several rivers such as the Bramhaputra and Indus are international rivers originating in Chinese Tibet prior to entering India and Pakistan. An upper-stream riparian, China has several advantages over India. First, it controls the rivers. Secondly, Chinese technical know-how is superior. Lastly, financially it can afford ambitious projects. India plans to develop its northeastern states and needs water from the same rivers. Hence, a fiercely competitive, suspicious, and oftentimes combative relationship between the two giants of Asia has made the region a prime candidate for conflict.

GROWING DEMAND FOR WATER IN CHINA

Surface Water Shortage

One of the most basic water problems in China is the lack of availability of surface water. Surface water in China is around one-quarter of the global average and it is also distributed very unevenly. The north and the northwest, which has a population of about 380 million people or around 30 percent of the national population, has over half of the country's arable land but it has only seven percent of its surface water. Its per capita resources are roughly 20–25 percent of the average for China as a whole, and five to six percent of the global average. The North China plain has only 10–15 percent of the per capita supply for the country as a whole, or less than four percent of the global average (Pommeranz 2009, 2–3). Northern waters also carry far more sediment than the southern ones and also more industrial pollutants per cubic meter. On top of that the North China plain has high seasonal fluctuations in water supply. Thus, China's dams, though used mainly for hydro-power, are also used for storing water for the dry parts in China.

The Chinese Ministry of Water Resources estimates that water consumption in China will increase by one percent annually. Its water resources are dwindling, making it progressively drier. In 2009, total freshwater reserves dropped to 2.42 trillion cubic meters, 353 billion cubic meters less than in 2000, which represents a 13 percent decline (Jaffe and Schneider 2011).

According to Chinese experts, these declining water resources and severe droughts in 2000, 2007, 2009, and 2010 are mainly due to climate changes. The Chinese planners have relied heavily on deep wells using electrically-powered pumps to bring up underground water. Extraction of water by these means is, however, only a short-term solution. Large-scale exploitation of groundwater in North China at times has been almost ten times greater, which is not sustainable in the long run. Water tables in North China have been falling by about five feet every year and even 10 feet in some places. It is estimated that this unsustainable extraction will lead aquifers to completely dry in 30 to 40 years. "In Southwestern Shanxi province over-pumping has dropped the water tables by some seventy meters or nearly 230 feet. As aquifers are depleted, land levels often fall. This process known as subsidence now affects an area in Northern China the size of Hungary" (Brown 1995, 70).

GROWING DEMAND FOR WATER IN INDIA

Lack of Power Supply

There are very serious water shortages in several regions of India, resulting in these areas being unable to meet their domestic and irrigational requirements. Inefficient and unreliable supply of power makes water pumping difficult from deep wells. In India and China the per capita water availability is about one-fourth of the global average.

India relies heavily on the vagaries of its monsoon. Rains are irregular. Almost 90 percent of monsoon rains occur in a short period of four months. India has a network of canals build by the British in selected parts of India. Most of them are not well-maintained, and people with political connections and rich farmers take more than their share of water, depriving the small land holders of adequate water. Also, India is away behind China in storage capacity. India has only one-fourth of the storage capacity of China, and one-fifth of the storage capacity of each of the United States and Australia. Hence, India's heavy reliance on groundwater. India has made huge strides in enhancing its agricultural production over the last few decades. Improvements in hybrid seeds and chemical fertilizers have made India self-reliant in food production, but these hybrid seeds and fertilizers require more water. Thus, groundwater has become the major source of water—about 70 percent of it is used for irrigation and 80 percent for domestic use.

India's federal structure, domestic politics, and lack of proper coordination between various levels of government also impact water distribution. The federal government's failure to enforce water sharing arrangements between the states has allowed several upstream states to build extra water storage, denying much-needed water to downstream states (Vajpeyi and Zhang 1998, 93–106).

The Major Water Issues between India and China

Tibet

Since the 1959 annexation of Tibet by China it has been under the total control of the Chinese. Ninety percent of Tibetan water flows downstream to the South, and Tibetan rivers supply over 30 percent of China's freshwater. China is planning several projects to exploit these rivers by diverting their water. It plans to tap the Tsangpo River to divert its water to the North. The proposal was first mooted by a Chinese hydrologist Guo Kai, and later by Li Ling (1998). In 1998 Jian Zemin issued a memorandum detailing the proposal in support of exploiting Tibet's immense water resources for the Chinese economy. China's quest for more water from these rivers has recently created much diplomatic activity and tension between India and China at their (Sino-Tibet-India) border. Several sharp verbal exchanges have taken place in diplomatic and public statements between the two countries.

Climatologist Isabel Hilton (2010) observes that 15,000 glaciers across the Tibetan plateau are melting "at an accelerated rate," raising concerns for harvests and river flows in China and India. The whole Tibetan region is "a climate change hot spot." She and other Western scientists have claimed that "the majority of the glaciers across this region are in retreat. The continued research on these glaciers suggests that they will be gone by 2050" (Walker 2009). Climate change is further aggravating water flows in these rivers, which are as crucial to China as they are to India.

Figure 5.2.   South to North Water Diversion Plans

Zangmu Hydroelectric Project

The second water issue between India and China is China's Zangmu project. Zangmu is a "run of the river" hydel generation dam on the Brahmaputra (called the Tsang-Po in China). In 2009, *Asia Times Online* had reported that China would go ahead with the construction of this dam. The dam is expected to be completed in 2015. It is being constructed at Namcha Barwa on the eastern plateau of Tibet and is going to be the world's largest dam with 26 turbines equipped to generate 40 million kilowatts per hour of hydroelectricity. The power output could be twice the output of the Three Gorges Dam.

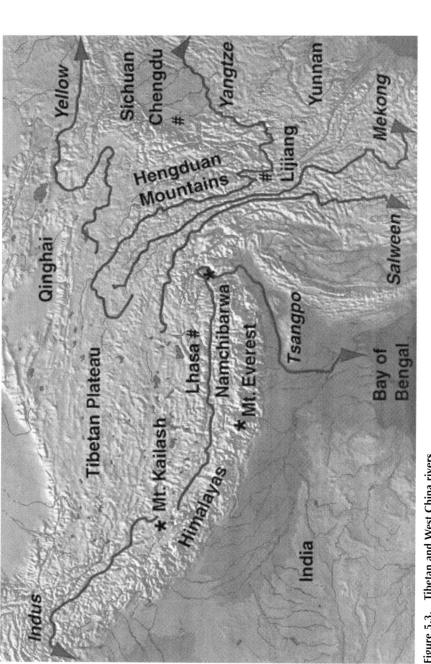

Figure 5.3.   Tibetan and West China rivers

India has expressed its reservations about the project. It fears that the dam would reduce the flow of waters from the Brahmaputra. The Chinese government, however, has assured India that the dam does not have storage capabilities and would not lead to a reduction in the flow of the Brahmaputra to India. Some Chinese engineers have suggested that the dam could provide cheap electricity for India, Nepal, and Bangladesh, and could facilitate flood control in the Brahmaputra-Ganges basin. A lingering issue that still persists in India, though, is the lack of information from China on the project. Until 2009 China had denied its intentions to build the dam.

South to North Water Diversion Project

The most important and divisive issue between India and China is the Indian concerns about China's ambitious plans to divert water from its south to the arid north, a very real concern. The "South to North Water Diversion Project" (also referred to herein as the South-North Project) was first proposed by Mao Zedong in the 1950s and involves diversion along three main routes (Figure 5.2).

On December 9, 2008, *Asia Times Online* reported that China was planning to go ahead with a major hydroelectric dam and water diversion scheme on the great bend of the Yalong Zangbo River in Tibet. The Indian Prime Minister Manmohan Singh reportedly raised the issue during his January 2008 visit to Beijing, but a December 2008 report from *Asia Times Online* observed that China had refused to provide any assurances on the nature of the project, and is going ahead with diverting the river. No firm statements were issued by the Chinese government except denials by low-level or out-of-office former officials, such as former water minister Wang Schu Chang (Pommeranz 2009, 7).

The idea behind this US$65 billion plan is simple: to take water from the Yangtze and its tributaries and move it to North China, where water is much scarcer. But implementing the scheme is extraordinarily difficult for technological reasons.

Once this project is completed, it will be the largest construction project in history. It would carry almost 45 billion cubic meters of water per year, which is roughly the annual average flow of the Yellow River (Pommeranz 2009, 4). China wants to transfer around 36 billion cubic meters of water every single year from the Yangtze River basin and ship it to north (Jaffe and Schneider 2011). According to Wang Hao, Director of the Water Resources Department at the state-run China Institute of Water Resources and Hydropower Research in Beijing, "Transferring water from the south to north makes perfect sense."

In 2010, Wei Zhimin, a water expert in the ministry of water resources in Hebei Province, stated in an interview with Xiaoxiang Evening News that the South-North Project would not solve north China's water crisis, but was nevertheless essential. "Lifeline is one word to describe it," Wei said. "And by lifeline, I mean a lifeline for north China, Beijing, Tianjin, and Hebei included" (Jaffe and Schneider 2011).

As mentioned above, the South-North Project has been in the pipeline for many years. On October 14, 2008, Chinese engineers began digging a tunnel through Tibet's Galung La Mountain in Nyingchi Prefecture in order to build a highway to China's last road-less county, Medog County, located 30 kilometers from India's border. The road construction, to be completed by 2010, is linked to the proposed dam construction at the Great Bend of the Brahmaputra. China's increased infrastructure activities near the Great Bend were even visible on Google Maps (Stobdan 2009).

The diversion of the River would have three routes. The project is the largest water transport system in the world. The first two lines, the eastern and central, are principally intended to supply water to Tianjin and Beijing, two of China's largest and most economically important metropolitan regions, as well as to smaller cities and some industries in the eastern provinces—Jiangsu, Anhui, Shandong, Hebei, Hubei, and Henan.The western line, which is in the planning stages, will draw water from three tributaries of the Yangtze and channel it more than 500 kilometers to the headwaters of the Yellow River.

The eastern line is slated to be finished by 2013. The completion of the central line, originally scheduled for 2010, has been pushed back to 2014. According to the *Xinhua News Agency* (May 9, 2011), China had already invested US$ 17.45 billion by the end of 2010. E Jingping, vice minister the Ministry of Water Resources and the director of the South-North Project, said in February 2010 that China would spend nearly US$ eight billion more in 2010.

The central and western lines will rely solely on gravity to move water. Water from the eastern line must be raised about 45 meters, consuming 1225 kilowatt hours per cubic meter, or 2.8 billion kWh per year. This is about the same amount of energy generated in a year by a 400-megawatt coal-fired power plant. The eastern route would take water from the Lower Yangzi in Jiangsu province up to Tianjin and on to the Shandong peninsula. This route was the least complicated of the three routes and parts of it became operational in 2008.

The second is the central route that runs from the Three Gorges Dam in Sichuan to Beijing. The work on this route was suspended due to ecological and environmental problems. However, it is expected that water from this route would reach Beijing around 2014.

The most complicated of the three routes, and the one that has the potential to affect countries other than China, is the western route. Work on this route was scheduled to begin in 2010 but was postponed due to technical difficulties and environmental concerns. The route would take water from the Yarlong-Tsangpo (also known as the Brahmputra in India), Dadu , Tongtian, and Jinsha Rivers in Tibet (Pommeranz 2009, 4). There are various issues related to this project but the major issues are relating to its size and cost. A diversion of this scale impacts flow speeds and sedimentation rates. Conveyance canals passing through poorly-drained areas may also raise the water table and add excess salts to the soil. This route is nevertheless the one that holds the maximum potential by tapping the enormous water resources in China's southwest.

The repercussions of this Project are immense. Any construction in the proposed location would definitely affect the lives of many minority groups like the Tibetans, the Yi, and Miao.

The South-North Project would also have immense environmental problems, especially its western route which would affect the lives of millions in India's northeast and in Bangladesh. One major concern for people outside China is that the plan envisages not only impounding huge quantities of water behind a dam, but more importantly, changing the direction of the water flow beyond the dam. Presently, the water that would be diverted flows into Assam (India) and forms the Brahmputra and then it joins the Ganges to form the world's largest river delta. This river delta is very important. It provides water to over 300 million people. The western route will involve drawing water from several rivers that originate in Tibet including the Tsangpo and would result in a drastic shortage of water for India. This western route project envisages building a dam on the great bend of the Brahmaputra before it enters India. India depends on the waters of the Brahmaputra for its own hydroelectric projects. Taking out about half of the river's water, which flows through the centre of India's northeastern state of Assam, "would make the River a seasonal ditch" (Ranjan 2009).

Of India's hydropower potential of 150,000 megawatts (MW), 50,000 MW is in the northeast and Arunachal Pradesh, which is mainly fed by the Brahmaputra's tributaries—Siang, Subansiri, and Lohit—and supports development of 28,500 MW of hydro projects. The Brahmaputra accounts for 29 percent of the total run-off all India's rivers and its waters are also central to India's own "National River Linking Project," which envisages diverting waters from the water-surplus Himalayas to the water-scarce river basins of South and Peninsular India. The project is currently in limbo due to concerns and reservations within the country, but if and when initiated, the project would be heavily dependent on the waters of the Brahmaputra.

Opinions on the impact of diverting water from the Bramhaputra differ. Even some Indian analysts believe that Indian fears are uniformed. According to them, the Brahmaputra in reality is a "smallish" river before it enters India and it picks up the bulk of its water in India itself. "When the Brahmaputra enters India, it picks up considerable waters from the Yangsang Chu at Jidu, the Siyom and the Sipi at Yembung and several others before it leaves the hills at Passighat. Around this place, it more than doubles its size with the waters from the Lohit and Dibang" (Mehta 2006, 113). BG Verghese, a leading water expert in India, claims that India's hullabaloo over the water diversion project is unfounded, and excessive claims only increase the mistrust between the two countries. He states that China's Zangmu project should not be a concern for India as it is only a run-of-the-river project and every country has the right to build hydroelectric projects to generate electricity for its people. Instead of arguing over speculated projects, he suggests that India and China should find ways of cooperating in the Brahmaputra basin (Verghese 2010).

On the other hand, there are experts who believe that even though the Brahmaputra picks up more water from the Indian side, the fact remains that the headwaters of the Brahmaputra are in Tibet. If the origin itself is controlled, the scope of any water reaching India is indubitably at risk (Kondapalli 2010). China, for its part, claims that it has no plans of diverting the Brahmaputra and that the Zangmu dam is not a storage dam and is intended only for the generation of hydroelectricity. It would not result in water shortages in India.

The Ministry of Water Resources in China has also presented conflicting opinions over this issue. China's former Minister for Water Resources, Wang Shucheng, has said that the water diversion proposal is "unnecessary, unfeasible and unscientific," and has no government backing (The Hindu 2009). Engineers in China are skeptical about the project since it would involve building a 300-meter-high dam at an elevation of about 4000 meters, which is technically impossible (Mehta 2006, 119). Moreover, it would be built in an earthquake-prone zone. The delays and costs that were associated with the other two routes have already generated reservations about the third route. These routes led to displacement of millions and are running behind schedule. Work on the western route has not started as yet, and China has not even conducted technical and feasibility studies on this route. At this state the plans are clearly nebulous. The Chinese officials and people are anxious about the displacement of a large number of people, as well as about the technical and ecological costs of the project.

In his visit to Beijing in 2010, Indian External Affairs Minister SM Krishna was given assurances by his Chinese counterpart that the dam China was building on the Tsang Po would not affect the flow of water of the Brahmaputra. However, considering China's usual reluctance to share information and the absence of a water-sharing treaty between the two countries, this becomes a major concern for India. Beijing had even denied the Zangmu project for a long time, before finally admitting its existence in 2010. India should continue to insist on regular hydrological data sharing and satellite imaging to avoid any confrontation later.

Besides technical and political factors there are several other practical reasons which have slowed down the project, listed below.

High Water Price

Transferring water from one part of the country to the other is going to be expensive. Some provinces like Tianjin are looking into alternative options such as desalinating sea water.

Timing and Destination

The main line that would serve water to northern and western provinces will not be completed for at least a few decades.

Pollution

Analysts predict that the water to be transported in the eastern line, from the Yangtze, would probably be too polluted and fouled with industrial and municipal pollutants for domestic and agricultural use (Jaffe and Schneider 2011).

Dwindling Supply of Water

This decrease in water in the south has also prompted southern states in China, or the "transfer provinces," to resent the transfer to the north, anticipating a shortage of water for themselves (Jaffe and Schneider 2011). Despite these reservations the Chinese authorities have continued with the western line because the northern provinces are important for them and need more water. "The Yellow River Basin has very little water, but this area has to supply 70 to 80 percent of the energy in the country," said Shaofeng Jia, vice director of the Center for Water Resources Research at the Chinese Academy of Sciences. "Developing this requires the west line of the transfer," (Jaffe and Schneider 2011).

ABSENCE OF AN INSTITUTIONALIZED WATER SHARING MECHANISM

In 2006, India's external affairs minister stated in the Indian Parliament that issues relating to trans-border rivers flowing from Tibet into India were discussed during the recent visit of the Chinese president to India."In the Joint Declaration issued on November 21, 2006 during the visit, the two sides agreed to set up an expert-level mechanism to discuss interaction and cooperation on the provision of flood-season hydrological data, emergency management, and other issues regarding trans-border rivers." He further observed that there were reports that China planned to build a 40,000 MW hydroelectric power plant and a dam on the Yarlung Zangbo river and divert 200 billion cubic meters of water to the Yellow river. "If this project fructifies, it is bound to have repercussions (on India). "We have taken it up with the Chinese authorities who have said there are no plans to that effect." India has learned from several sources that actual construction had not started (Arabia 2009).

The absence of a water-sharing mechanism or water treaty between the two countries makes a resolution of a potential problem highly complex. For instance, India and Pakistan have recently quibbled over water issues, but since their issues are within the framework of the Indus Water Treaty, the countries have institutionalized mechanisms like the Indus Water Commission, third party arbitration, and neutral expert intervention, to help mitigate any problems. China and India do not have a similar arrangement. As a result, being the upper riparian, China has more leverage on the issue. India feels that it would be at China's mercy during the dry season, and for protection from floods during the rainy season.

The only agreements between India and China are two Memorandums of Understanding, but these are limited to readings of water levels and do not include agreements on river diversion. Annually, China and India share hydrological data for three stations (Nugesha, Yangcun, and Nuxia) on the Brahmaputra River, from June 1 to October 15 (Ranjan 2009). It was also agreed that the upper riparian, China, would provide hydro-data in times of crisis. There were flash floods in Assam in 2004 and India requested from China data on the quantity of water being released by it. Initially this information was being provided, but later China demanded that India would have to pay a high fee for the water readings (Kondapalli 2010).

In 2006 a mechanism of consultation over water and rivers between New Delhi and Beijing was set. The expert-level mechanism was designed to discuss trans-border river issues in an institutional manner. There were three meetings after its inception. At these meetings, however, China denied that it had any plans to divert waters on a large scale from the Brahmaputra (Walker 2009).

In 2008, India's prime minister had a long discussion with Chinese President Hu Jinato on this issue. India-China water disputes are further complicated by their serious conflict over the demarcation of disputed borders in
the India-Tibet, and India-Laddakh, sectors, and the Chinese claim on India's
Arunachal state. China even protested a visit to this area by the Indian prime
minister in 2010, and unsuccessfully tried to block a development loan to
India by the Asian Development Bank. India is not convinced by Chinese
assurances. In the past China has broken several private assurances given
to India. In fact, China started preliminary work on the Zangmu Project on
April 2, 2009 (Walker 2009, 12). The proposed dam would be the first of the
planned five. It would be 118 meters high and would produce about 540 MW
of power. The Tibetan sources have told India that the project has been under
construction for several years and the Nanshah regional administration had
moved people from the area beginning in about 2007. Such secret actions of
the Chinese do not give much comfort to India and create a hostile environment, which could lead to   conflict. Weak international legal frameworks
and the absence of robust water-sharing agreements only magnify these
breakdowns.

The absence of information adds fuel to the fire in this very volatile
relationship between India and China. According to Kondipalli (2010), the
chances for a water treaty between the two countries seem quite remote due to
the long-simmering border dispute. A water treaty will have to accommodate
other issues such as land boundaries and borders. Neither India nor China
seem to be ready for such an accommodation. It should also be noted here
that China has been very reluctant to reach any agreement on water with other
lower riparian neighbors, for example on the Irtysh River between China and
Kazakhstan, or on the rivers between Russia and China. On the Mekong there
is no formal agreement between China and Vietnam. China is not part of the
Mekong commission. Similarly, China and India have no agreements on the
Indus or Bramhaputra. In their public and private discourses Chinese agree
to discuss water issues with lower riparians provided that the lower riparians
use the water only for irrigation and not for industrial purposes. Such offers
have been made to Bangladesh and Pakistan (Kondipally 2010).

Even though the chances for a treaty at present are slim, there are certain
options that India could exercise. It could take this issue to the World Water
Council or the International Court of Justice and ask them to resolve it. Some
West Asian countries have taken their water issues to the World Water Council and their issues have been successfully resolved. An intervention like this,
however, might stiffen the stance of China, instead of relaxing it (Kondipally
2010). It is difficult to say that China will bend on its core national issues.
Several countries that are downstream have apprehensions about China's

planned projects. Water diversions of the Mekong have already drawn the ire of countries like Vietnam and environmental groups.

Sino-India Cooperation: Promises and Prospects

According to Verghese (1997), India must focus more on ways to cooperate with China, and keep water issue separate from its border disputes. In practical, political terms the above opinion would invite tremendous opposition and uproar in India. The present Indian government is not strong enough to compromise on issues related to "national honor." There is no doubt that cooperation, and a more cordial relationship, would benefit both countries. They realize that climate change in the Himalayas would create ecological havoc in the region. The melting of glaciers will trigger droughts, cause desertification, increase sandstorms, and disrupt water supply from major Himalayan Rivers (Patel 2006). Water is emerging as a banner issue between India-Pakistan, India-Bangladesh, India-Nepal, and India-China. Any conflict, even if it is short of military confrontation, will be disastrous for the region. The only way to mitigate this insecurity is by initiating joint projects to better manage this vital resource. India and China are the two largest emerging economies in the region, maybe even in the world. They have to provide leadership to their neighbors by being more flexible and accommodating in water conservation and sharing, energy swaps, and in improving irrigation methods.

It is important to bear in mind that any solution to the water issue will have to be regional and cut across the different countries in Asia. The countries in the region must have a stake in the decision; otherwise, no arrangement will be sustainable. Greater attention and importance should be given to basin-wide cooperation on water management. Protection of water sources, improving and maintaining water quality, issues of drainage, flood control, water harvesting, and watershed management are some potential areas where cooperation can be envisioned.

A blanket refusal by the Chinese to allay Indian claims of an impending water crisis should be avoided. Instead, India and China need to seriously engage themselves on water sharing issues. This engagement should not be open-ended and should be carried forward with the final goal of an institutionalized water-sharing mechanism or a water treaty between the two. India also needs to strengthen its intelligence and information capabilities, in both ground- and satellite-based imagery, about China's water-related projects in Tibet.

Both China and India could work on substitutes to big hydroelectric projects, which have a negative ecological impact, and instead focus on water conservation and water management. In the absence of these, India and China risk turning the now seemingly-excessive claims of water crisis, into an actual disaster.

China needs to be more transparent about its projects. In the past China has never consulted riparian states prior to undertaking dam constructions upstream. None of the downstream countries have legal arrangements or provisions of international law to deal with China's river manipulation. China has not joined the Mekong River Commission, and has also not ratified the UN convention on Non-Navigable Use of International Watercourses (1997). Environmentalists have been protesting China's diversion of over 20 transborder rivers in Central Asia. Still worse, projects in Tibet are undertaken by China's biggest construction companies like Gezhouba Corporation and Huaneng Group, which are known for their secrecy and lack of accountability (Stobdan 2009).

Progressive water management programs in India and China could save a massive quantity of water. Big dams do provide water and power but they also create long-term ecological and human displacement and suffering (Vajpeyi and Zhang 1998, 93–106). Smaller projects could be more effective. According to Iyer there are many areas of water cooperation among nations like "protection of the water sources (rivers, lakes, mountains, forests, aquifers) from pollution, degradation or denudation; the preservation and regeneration of deteriorating wetlands (e.g., the Sunderbans in India); improving and maintaining water quality; dealing with common problems such as drainage in the Indus basin in both India and Pakistan, or the occurrence of arsenic in aquifers in both India and Bangladesh; coping with floods: and minimizing damage, water harvesting, and watershed development (Iyer 2003).

India and China are neighbors, and whether they like it or not destiny and geography—rivers, mountains, borders, cultures, and history—have placed them very close to each other. They are also two of the biggest economies, with different political systems but common aspirations to improve the quality of human lives in their respective nations. The wisest course for both will be to cooperate under the already-existing "Panchsheel" framework to avoid ecological conflicts and endangering the lives of billions of their people.

REFERENCES

Briscoe, John, et al., 2005. *India's Water Economy: Bracing for a Turbulent Future.* World Bank, 4.

Brown, Lester R. 1995. *Who Will Feed China.* New York: Norton and Co.

Crow, Ben, and Nirvikar Singh. 2009. "The Management of International Rivers as Demands Grow and Supplies Tighten: India, China, Nepal, Bangladesh." *India Review* 8 (3): 306–339.

Claude, Arpi. 2008. "Himalayan Rivers: Geopolitics and Strategic Perspectives," *Issue*: Vol 23.2. June 23.

"China denies report on diversion of Brahmaputra," *Arabia* 2000; 11/30/2006

Dutta Suvrokamal. 2008. "Watershed Management-India's Crying Need," *Mainstream*. XLVI(6): http://www.mainstreamweekly.net/article516.html

Hilton, Isabel. 2011. "Glaciers Across Asia," Speech at the Woodrow Wilson Center, Washington, DC.

Himalayan Solutions: Cooperation and Security in River Basins. 2011. Strategic Foresight Group. http://www.strategicforesight.com/HimalayanSolutions.pdf.

Hirji Rafik, and Richard Davis. 2009. "Environmental Flows in Water Resources Policies," *Plans and Projects*. World Bank Publications. 49–51.

Iyer, Ramaswamy. 2003. "Relations with Neighbours." In *Water: Perspectives, Issues, Concerns*. New Delhi: Sage Publications.

Jaffe, Aaron, and Keith Schneider. 2011. "A Dry and Anxious North Awaits China's Giant, Unproven Water Transport Scheme." *Circle of Blue* 1 March. http://www.circleofblue.org/waternews/2011/world/a-dry-and-anxious-northawaits-china%E2%80%99s-giant-unproven-water-transport-scheme/.

Jain, P. C. 2004. "Permanent Solutions for Water Scarcity: Watershed Management." *Kerela Calling*. July. http://www.kerala.gov.in/keralcalljuly04/p17–19.pdf.

Li Ling. 1990 *How Tibet's Water Will Save China*. Beijing, Ministry of Water Development.

Mehta, Raj. 2010. "Re-plumbing China: Leading to the World's First Water." *Center for Land Warfare Studies Journal* Summer 113:

"Melting Of Glaciers, India Takes Up Matter With China," 2007 *Arabia*, 30 August.

Patel, Shri Premji Bhai. 2006. *Success Story of Community Participation for Groundwater Recharge- An Initiative by Vruksha Prem Seva Trust*. Upeta, District Rajkot, Gujarat.

Pomerantz, Kenneth. 2009. "The Great Himalayan Watershed: Water Shortages, Mega Projects and Environmental Politics in China, India, and Southeast Asia." *Asia Pacific Journal* 30–2-09, July 27:

Rajiv, Gandhi Mission for Watershed Management. MP. http://www.watermissionmp.com/

Ramesh Randeep. 2007. "China and India warned their water is running out," *The Guardian*. 23 January. New Delhi.

Ranjan, Rajiv. 2009. Copenhagen Accord: China's Role in Climate Diplomacy. *World Focus*.

Sharon La Franiere. 2009. Possible Link Between Dam and China Quake, *The New York Times*. February 6

Ramachandran, Sudha. 2008. "Greater China: India Quakes Over China's Water Plan," *Asia Times Online*. December 9.

Sinha, Uttam Kumar. 2010. "Tibet's Watershed Challenge," *Washington Post*, June 14.

Stobdan, P. 2009. "China should not use water as a threat multiplier," New Delhi: *Institute for Defense Studies and Analysis*.

Telephonic interview by author with Srikanth Kondipally (Associate Professor of Chinese studies at Jawaharlal University, New Delhi), January 15, 2010.

Telephonic interview by author with BG Verghese (leading water expert and author of many books on water in India), .

The Hindu. 2009, 20 Oct.

The Himalayan Challenge: Water Security in Emerging Asia. 2010. Strategic Foresight Group. http://www.strategicforesight.com/Himalayan%20Challenge%20ES.pdf.

United Nations. 2009. "Asia and the Pacific. Facing the Challenges," *World Water Development Report 3.* Case Study. 19.

Vajpeyi, Dhirendra, and Tingting Zhang. 1998. "To Dam or Not to Dam: India's Narmada River Basin Project." In *Water Resource Management, A Comparative Perspective,* edited by Dhirendra Vajpeyi, London: Praeges.

Verghese, B. G. 1990. *Waters of Hope, Himalaya-Ganga Cooperation for a Billion People.* Oxford-IBH.

Walker, Martin. 2009. "Walker's World: China's new enemies," Oct 19.

World Bank Annual Report 2009. Washington: World Bank.

Chapter Six

Conflict and Cooperation

The Aral Sea Basin

Dhirendra K. Vajpeyi and Brittany Brannon

INTRODUCTION

The swift disappearance of the Aral Sea has been regarded as one of the worst man-made disasters of the twentieth century. The consequences resulting from the sea's swift decline span multiple borders and have affected the lives of the 48 million people currently living in the region (Lauener 2010). The significant degradation of environmental quality, serious deterioration of the health of the population, reduction in the efficiency of the regional economy, and significant desiccation of the sea itself are just a few of the growing problems facing the area.

Following the collapse of the Soviet Union in December 1991, the Central Asian republics gained full independence, and with it, full responsibility for the devastating water crisis. Since then, very little progress has been made in tackling various environmental problems, including water resources. Rampant corruption and authoritarian leadership within the region have further complicated and adversely affected all spheres of governance and cooperative efforts among countries in the area (Table 6.1). While multiple water-related treaties and agreements have been made among the regional nations, adherence to the treaties has been marginal and failure to honestly cooperate has resulted in additional tension within the region. Help from outside institutions has adequately addressed these problems and suggested viable solutions, but their influence on the corrupt regimes has fallen on deaf ears. The leaders of these Central Asian countries prefer the economic status quo over adopting the proposed innovations, and are reluctant to accept them even at the risk of a deteriorating quality of life.

Table 6.1.   Central Asia: Basic Facts

Country	Total Area	Total Population	Total GDP
Kazakhstan	1.1 m. sq miles	15.5 million	$182.3 billion
Tajikistan	55,800 sq miles	7.5 million	$13.8 billion
Kyrgyzstan	77,000 sq miles	5.5 million	$11.7 billion
Turkmenistan	190,000 sq miles	4.9 million	$33.6 billion
Uzbekistan	174,500 sq miles	27.9 million	$77.6 billion

Source: Nichol 2010

As the situation within the Aral Sea basin remains critical, the countries of Uzbekistan, Tajikistan, Turkmenistan, Kazakhstan, and Kyrgyzstan are on a potential collision course. The possibility of an open and armed conflict is unlikely, but prevailing tensions hamper the economic and political growth of the region. By examining the past and current geographic nature of the Aral Sea basin, explaining the history behind the crisis, and taking note of the current power struggle within the region, a proper assessment can be made to determine whether the predicament is indeed solvable through nonviolent means.

GEOGRAPHIC BACKGROUND

In the last thirty years a dramatic decrease in the size of the Aral Sea, once the fourth-largest body of freshwater in the world, has gravely endangered the region's environment in general and water availability in particular. Between the years of 1967 and 1997, the water level fell by more than 14 m, its area shrunk by more than 40 percent, and its volume decreased by 60 percent (Elhance 1997, 210). While the Aral Sea itself touches only Uzbekistan and Kazakhstan, the two major rivers that flow into the sea, the Amu Darya and Syr Darya wind through multiple countries (Figure 6.1). Thus, the condition of the Aral Sea is greatly affected by the treatment and usage of the two rivers by the upstream nations.

According to Vinogradov (1996) the Amu Darya, 1,415 km long, has the highest water-bearing capacity of the region, with an average perennial runoff of roughly 69 km^3 and a basin area of 465,500 km^2. In contrast, the Syr Darya carries less water than the Amu Darya, but is the longest river in Central Asia at 2,212 km. Both rivers flow out of the Tien Shan and Pamir Mountain ranges of the Himalayas, northward through their alluvial valleys onto the flat expanse of the Qoraqum (Kara Kum) and Qyzlqum (Kyzl Kum) Deserts before forming large deltas and emptying into the Aral Sea. However, the annual inflow to the Aral Sea has dropped from 50 km^3 from both rivers

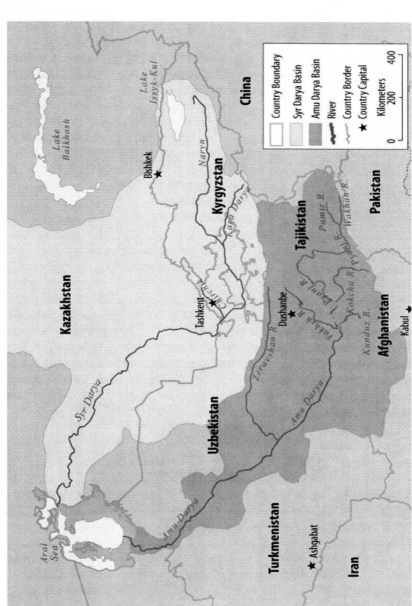

Figure 6.1.   Aral Sea Basin   *Source:* U.S. Senate 2011.

to just 5 km³ from the Amu Darya only, with the flow of the Syr Darya being nonexistent since 1978 (Vinogradov 1996, 399–400).

In 1987, the Aral Sea split into two, becoming the Large (Bol'shoi) Sea and the Small (Maloi) Sea (Peachey 2004, 4). To restore the Aral Sea to its original boundaries would require the flow of 1,000 cubic kilometers of water per year, or ten years of full flow from both the Amu Darya and Syr Darya rivers (Wegerich 2001, 11). This requirement, however, is almost impossible to achieve without economic and political coordination and cooperation between the countries of Central Asia. Given the current fiscal and political situation in the region, the possibility of complete recovery in the Aral Sea is unlikely.

THE RAPID DISAPPEARANCE

Elhance (1997) cites three major factors that have brought about the increasing environmental degradation in the Aral Sea Basin: (1) water-intensive cash-crop production (mainly cotton); (2) poor water and land management practices; and (3) pollution of water and land from intensive use of agrochemicals (Figure 6.2). All three factors are a legacy of Soviet-era control over Central Asia and continue to plague current policies. Yet it was not until the mid-1980s, under Mikhail Gorbachev's policy of *glasnost*, that the international community realized the full extent of damage to the Aral Sea. The Soviet Union was aware of this major catastrophe, and referred to it as a "Quiet Chernobyl" (Kobori 1998, 26). However, the Soviets still neglected to take any action to reverse their policies and prevent further ruin. Still today, the Soviet footprints are apparent all over the region, adversely affecting the environment, water resource policies, and other sectors of Central Asian economies.

THE RISE OF "WHITE GOLD"

Cotton was "king" in the region even before the Russian conquest, and was a major trade product with Russia and other nations (Wegerich 2008, 73). The Soviet occupation of the region in the 1930s introduced Moscow-approved grand solutions to agricultural production, ignoring the region's water and other environmental concerns. Soviet planners emphasized agricultural products rather than finished products or other crops appropriate for the climate. Because cotton is a water-dependent crop and was traditionally not grown year round, heavy irrigation was needed in order to sustain the industry.

Beginning in 1956 under Khrushchev's "Virgin Lands" campaign, 88.6 million hectares were devoted within Central Asia to promote the "cotton first" concept,

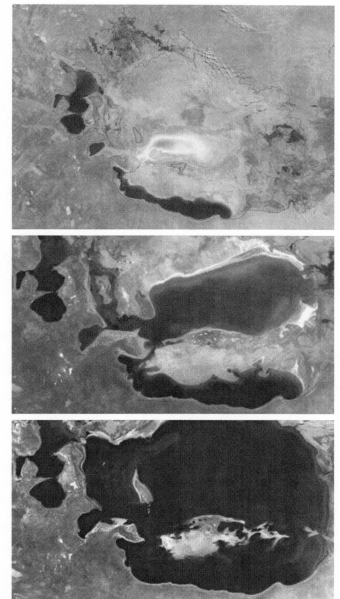

Figure 6.2. Aral Sea Basin: 1989, 2003, and 2009

assuming that specializing in cotton would provide the greatest monetary return and create economies of scale. To create a system of farming with the intention of maximizing production, Soviet planners moved a large numbers of people to *kolkhozi* (collective farms) and *sovkhozi* (state owned farms) (Peachey 2004, 2–3). As a result of this campaign the Central Asian regional cotton production reached 9 million tonnes, making it the world's fourth largest producer of cotton (Grabish 1999, 39). In Uzbekistan alone, tonnage of cotton per hectare rose from 1.2 in 1913, to 2.0 in 1960, and peaked at 2.7 in 1980, doubling what it had been 65 years earlier (Peachey 2004, 3).

Because cotton can produce valuable hard currency in export markets, the Central Asian nations believed cotton to be the most economically feasible choice. It has been observed that the power, and ultimately the fate, of quite a few Soviet political elites depended on the success or failure of the program (Spoor and Krutov 2003, 596). These elites were under pressure to succeed, hence corruption, the over- and underreporting of the cotton output, and the forced organization of labor during peak periods became the structural features of the economies of Uzbekistan, Turkmenistan, and Tajikistan in particular (Spoor and Krutov 2003, 596–597). It created an administrative political organization which encouraged "report-padding" to conceal the harvest shortfalls, embezzlement, bribery, greed, abuse of power purely for private aggrandizement, a lack of supervision, nepotism, and further environmental degradation and tension among the republics (Tsukatani 1998, 58). Hence, the obsession with mass production of cotton set the stage for the current crisis and corruption within the region. To feed this obsession, massive irrigation and chemicals were used to increase the production of cotton, while the environmental factors and impending impact on the water resources were essentially ignored.

POOR PLANNING

Along with the need of irrigation networks, canals, and reservoirs to supply the cotton fields was inefficient and poor management of the infrastructure. The first Soviet irrigation project was the development of the Fergana Basin in the upper and midstream areas of the Syr Darya (Kubo et al. 2009, 469). The Soviets initiated the building of the current irrigation system in Central Asia and began the establishment of a collective farming monocropping system that called for more water than ever before. Thus, as the cotton acreage in Central Asia expanded rapidly, the need for irrigation from the Amu and Syr Darya Rivers was heightened. To meet this need, the two rivers were diverted with around 20 medium and large-sized reservoirs, 60 diversion canals, and 50 dams of varying sizes (Murray-Rust 2003, 3). Thus, the total irrigated

Table 6.2.   Land under Irrigation, 1950–1986 (Thousand Hectares)

Country	1950	1960	1965	1970	1975	1980	1985	1986
Uzbekistan	2,276	2,571	2,639	2,697	3,006	3,476	3,930	4,020
Tajikistan	361	427	468	518	567	617	653	662
Turkmenistan	454	496	514	643	819	927	1,107	1,185

Source: Critchlow 1991, 63, and Glantz 1998, 42

area in Central Asia increased from 4.5 million hectares in 1965, to 7 million hectares in 1991 (Wegerich 2008, 73).

The new Soviet plan discarded the aging, traditional irrigation and farming systems despite their efficiency and sustainability during the pre-Soviet era. A fine example of the traditional irrigation practices could be found in Uzbekistan, where a highly successful crop rotation system was used to grow cotton one year, alfalfa the next, herd livestock on the fallow fields the third year, and then repeat the cycle. Because of these sustainable farming practices, soil and fertility levels remained stable until the 194's (Peachy 2004, 3). The older canals did not divert the region's major rivers, thereby allowing the rivers to properly flow into and maintain the Aral Sea.

However, given the unquenchable thirst for cotton, the "outdated" practice of crop rotation and sustainable farming was replaced with techniques that inefficiently distributed resources and sapped the rivers of water (Table 6.2). For example, the 1,200 kilometer-long Kara-Kum canal, which was started in 1954 and completed in 1988, did not utilize water-saving techniques to improve irrigation efficiency. Seepage became enormous due largely to the unlined, open, and exposed canals (Peachey 2004, 7). Because of these massive canals, water from the Syr Darya failed to reach the Aral Sea and the Amu Darya supplied a minimal amount by the late 1970s (Glantz 1998, 38).

Despite the building of unsustainable canals and discarding of traditional practices, the "modern" technology introduced by the USSR was not efficient. Of the 19 million hectares of irrigated land in the former USSR, slightly over 7 million hectares were equipped with sprinklers, with the rest relying on surface irrigation (Tsukatani 1998, 55). The outdated irrigation system, waiting to be updated, led to an inadequate drainage system, resulting in an annual loss of about $1 billion (UNEP 2005, 32).

According to O'Hara, the building of dams and upstream reservoirs was a political strategy used by Moscow planners to "divide and rule" Central Asia. O'Hara asserts that "disputes over water reinforced the national distinctiveness of the republics," and the "competition for water increased, forcing the Republics to ask Moscow to intervene" (O'Hara 2000, 430). To tighten their

Table 6.3.   Changing Pattern of Land Use from Food to Cotton

Country	Population (million)	Rural Population	Population Under-nourished	External Ag. Assistance ('000)	% Arable Land Under Cotton
Kazakhstan	15	45%	6%	46	6%
Kyrgyzstan	5.2	65%	4%	19	3%
Tajikistan	6.3	75%	56%	47	35%
Turkmenistan	4.9	55%	7%	37	31
Uzbekistan	26	65%	25%	62	36%

Source: UNDP 2010, 23

administrative control, Soviet planners created River Basin Organizations in 1986 (BVOs), which were responsible for managing the water according to the limits set by the Scientific-Technical Council of the Soviet Ministry of Land Reclamation and Water Management (Wegerich 2008, 76). These organizations were later incorporated into the current water-management infrastructure.

Thus, the Soviet Union developed an inefficient and wasteful framework irrigation system for the agricultural sector in Central Asia, which still permeates the region's policies. Considering that irrigated land is now responsible for producing 90 percent of the region's crops (Peachey 2004, 7), and 50 percent of the region's GDP (UNEP 2004, 30), the economic investment and labor required to update the system is large and daunting. Additionally, the problem becomes even more overwhelming considering that roughly 60 percent of the population of Central Asia lives in rural areas and practices irrigated farming. Any change to the system will affect, and will require massive efforts from, millions of people (Table 6.4) (Lauener 2010).

CHEMICAL IMBALANCE

Excessive usage of chemicals further led to the pollution of the land and air. As the Soviet approach required over-irrigation, soil fertility declined significantly, thus requiring an increase in the quantity of fertilizers, herbicides, and pesticides used to maintain and expand cotton productivity and production (Glantz 1998, 46). In the region, around 202–205 kilograms of pesticides per hectare were used, in comparison to only 3 kilograms per hectare in other parts of the Soviet Union (Peachey 2004, 4). The pesticides used were of inferior quality, more contaminating than those available on the world market, and highly subsidized to allow for no incentives for efficient use (Spoor 1998, 421). As a result, the over-use of agrochemicals has caused more than 3 billion m^3 of contaminated water to be discharged annually into the Amu Darya River (UNEP 2005, 34).

Table 6.4. Agricultural Sector (2010)

Countries	Employment in Agriculture	Agriculture as % of GDP	Major Exports (Agriculture)
Kazakhstan	<10%	<10%	Grains
Kyrgyzstan	55%	35%	Cotton, Horticulture
Tajikistan	n/a	25%	Cotton
Turkmenistan	n/a	30%	Cotton
Uzbekistan	40%	20%	Cotton, grain

Source: Granit et al. 2010

Pesticide use, along with an improper water discharge system, has slowly added to salinization in the region. Between 1990 and 1999 alone, the area of salinized soils increased in the Amu Darya basin from 1.16 to 1.82 million ha (57%), and from 0.34 to 0.61 ha (79%) in the Syr Darya basin (UNEP 2005, 31), and this can be largely attributed to the problem of water being used to flush out existing salts in the soil, carrying with it more salts in the process and continuing the cycle of salinization (Spoor 1998, 421). The Soviet-designed drainage infrastructure forced the conveyance system discharge to back into the two main rivers, thus further aggravating the downstream water quality and increasing salinity (Murray-Rust 2003, 4).

The water quality resulting from chemical use and salinization has affected not only the agricultural sector of society, but also has had a stark effect on human livelihood. The most prominent health impacts are found in the lower reaches of the Amu Darya and Syr Darya, where the highest concentration of pollutants can be found (UNEP 2005, 37). As a downstream riparian, Uzbekistan suffers from poor air and water quality: 11 percent of all babies die before reaching the age of one, 83 percent of children have serious illnesses, and two-thirds of people suffer from hepatitis, typhoid, or throat cancer (Tsukatani 1998, 61). Uzbekistan is not alone, however, as during the last 15 years of Soviet Union control, incidents of typhoid fever increased to a level 30 times greater than the world average, hepatitis grew to seven times the world average, and esophageal cancer increased to a level 50 times greater than the world average, over the entire Central Asian region (Peachey 2004, 6). The "King Cotton" era not only affected health but has been one of the major factors in impeding socioeconomic development of the region since its independence. The following data (UNDP Regional Water Intelligence Report) illustrates how the Soviet policies influenced land use by replacing land once used for food with cotton-exclusive fields, creating food scarcity and hindering socio-economic growth (Table 6.3).

While Soviet planning and control started the cycle of degradation and laid the foundation for current woes, the problem continues to plague the region despite the countries' independence and concern expressed by international organizations. The following section explains the actions in the post-Soviet period and the reasons for their limited success.

POST-INDEPENDENCE REALITIES

The demise of the USSR in December 1991 brought significant political and economic changes in Central Asia. Politically, the people within the region took on the challenge of forming legitimate governing institutions. In the economic realm, the people realized that for the first time since the 1930s they were free to adopt their own course and not the dictates from Moscow in all spheres of national policymaking, including the management of their water resources. Now, the cooperation and coordination of these policies became their responsibility in the absence of a central Moscow-driven framework. However, without one central authority to coordinate, cooperation between the states became problematic to the detriment of economic and agricultural development in the region.

Also, access to vital water was not distributed equally. The new national boundaries allocated unequal amounts of water resources to the states. Uzbekistan had to import 91 percent of its water, while Turkmenistan imported 98 percent (Weinthal 2003, 270). Conversely, the upstream nations of Kyrgyzstan and Tajikistan possess 90 percent of all Aral basin water resources, leaving the downstream nations dependent on their water-rich neighbors (Peachey 2004, 9). It is to be noted that over 90 percent of the Aral Sea basin surface water is used mainly for irrigation in the downstream nations of Uzbekistan and Turkmenistan (Granit et al. 2010, 7). Based on water alone, the downstream riparians appear to be economically vulnerable to their upstream neighbors. Yet the situation becomes more complicated. Tajikistan and Kyrgyzstan are poorer, carry less political weight, are more rural and agriculturally reliant, have fewer resources to develop than the other Central Asian states, and are heavily dependent upon Uzbekistan for energy in the winter. Besides water, these two countries in the region face multiple socioeconomic problems in modernizing their infrastructures and reducing conflicts with their more prosperous and powerful neighbors.

WATER RESOURCE GOVERNANCE

Since a large portion of the economy within Central Asia is reliant upon its agricultural industries, the desire to keep water usage at the current "zero sum" policy is strong (Granit et al. 2010, 8). As each nation vies for regional economic dominance, the control over scarce water resources becomes increasingly important. Hence, the economic and political stability of the region hinges upon the treatment and distribution of the regional water.

I. DOMESTIC

At the time of independence from the Soviets, it seemed that these Central Asian countries would enter into a new cooperative spirit in the economic and political spheres, including the management of water resources. On February 18, 1992, all Central Asian countries signed the "Cooperation in the Management, Utilization, and Protection of Water Resources in Interstate Sources" agreement (Weinthal 2003, 274). Under Article 3 of the Agreement, these states promised to "commit themselves to refrain from any activities within their respective territories which, entailing a deviation from the agreed water shares or bringing about water pollution, are likely to affect the interest of, and cause damage to the co-basin states" (Weinthal 2003, 274). The Interstate Commission for Water Coordination (ICWC) was established as the executive organization for implementing the tenets of the Agreement. The ICWC was entrusted with responsibilities of policy formation and allocating water to the five states, replacing Soviet control and at the same time attempting to foster strong relationships amongst the Central Asian governments. Under the ICWC, high-level government representatives of these states met annually to discuss preliminary plans and agreements for the following year's water supply (Murray-Rust 2003, 5).

The ICWC remains responsible for water management in both the Amu Darya and Syr Darya basins. Decisions of the ICWC are by consensus, with each state having equal votes in decisions (McKinney 2003, 7). Basin Water Management Organizations (BVOs) execute these decisions and serve as organs of the ICWC along the Amu Darya and Syr Darya rivers. As previously mentioned, the BVOs were initially established under Soviet planners in 1986, and were responsible for managing water according to the set limits determined by the Scientific-Technical Council of the Soviet Ministry of Land Reclamation and Water Management (Wegerich 2008, 76). Under the current management of the ICWC, the five water ministers meet on a quarterly basis to prepare water allocation plans for the ICWC's approval. The regional BVOs then implement the plans and additionally perform executive functions regarding the operation of hydraulic works, structures, and installations on the rivers (Weinthal 2003, 274).

II. INTERNATIONAL

The international community became involved in the region even before the Soviet collapse. Following public outcries in several countries about the Aral Sea in the 1980s, an agreement was made between the Soviet Union and the United Nations Environmental Program (UNEP) to develop a rehabilitation plan for the Aral Sea (Weinthal 2003, 276). Unfortunately this program was cut short due to the Soviet collapse despite strong UNEP commitment to the problem. Its involvement picked up again in 1992, when the UNEP and the World Bank began preparing proposals for long-term solutions to the problem. The following proposal, aptly named the Aral Sea Basin Program (ASBP), was presented to the Central Asian states in January 1994: (1) to stabilize the environment of the Aral Sea Basin; (2) to rehabilitate the disaster zone around the sea; (3) to improve the management of the international waters of the basin; and (4) to build the capacity of regional institutions to plan and manage these programs (de Chazournes 2006, 150).

The Central Asian states approved the ASBP proposal and created three additional intergovernmental institutions between 1993 and 1995: (1) the Instate Council on the Aral Sea Basin (ICAS) to coordinate policies of the ASBS; (2) the Sustainable Development Commission (SDC) to rehabilitate economic, social, and environmental conditions in the region; and (3) the International Fund for Saving the Aral Sea (IFAS) which was originally established to collect contributions for the ICAS from the five states and other donors (de Chazournes 2006, 152–153).

In 1997 an agreement was made among the five riparian states to merge the ICWC into the IFAS and make the IFAS the highest regional authority for water management (McKinney 2004, 197). The presidency of the IFAS is rotated among the five heads of state of the Central Asian region. The primary activities of the IFAS include raising funds for joint measures to conserve the air, water, and land resources of the Aral Sea basin; determining financing; establishing a regional monitoring system; and implementing international programs on saving the Aral Sea and improving the ecology of the basin (McKinney 2004, 197).

The Executive Committee of the IFAS (EC IFAS) serves as the regular decision-making body and is made up of the deputy prime ministers of the respective nations (Granit et al. 2010, 11). While the IFAS operates on the macro-level through environmental management, funding administration, and political decisions, the BVOs in the Amu Darya and Syr Darya, under the leadership of the ICWC, deal with the technical aspects of water regulation among the states (Murray Rust 2003, 5).

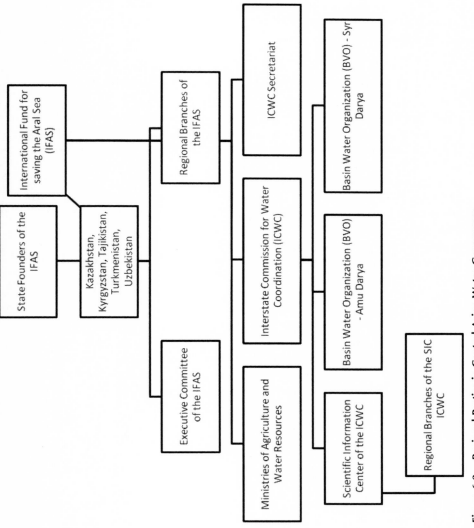

Figure 6.3. Regional Parties in Central Asian Water Governance

On December 15, 2010, the IFAS began to finalize the process for the Third Aral Sea Basin Program (ASBP-3), with the assistance of the United Nations Economic Commission for Europe (UNECE), and financed by the German government. The ASBP-3's four strategic areas include integrated water resource management, environmental protection, socioeconomic issues, and institutional and legal strengthening of water management in the region (UNECE 2010).

COLLABORATION WITHOUT IMPROVEMENT

After the Soviet departure, all these steps towards multinational cooperation were envisaged and most of them have been less than effective. Both the IFAS and UNECE have been trying hard to solve the water problems within the Aral Sea basin. However, they have met with a lot of frustrations and little success. As Marton Krasznai , regional advisor for the UNECE, has observed, "All Central Asian countries agree that the effectiveness of the utilization of water resources in the region is insufficient and complicated because of poor management. The relative weakness of regional institutions is part of the problem. As a result we have seen recurrent disputes over water release regimes and water distribution in recent years. The effects of these disputes go far beyond the sector itself. Water (and related energy) issues are arguably the most stubborn stumbling blocks that hinder much-needed regional political, economic and environmental cooperation and integration" (Krasznai 2008). Krasznai (2008) further points out that the roots of failure to properly deal with the water problems are as follows: lack of sufficient political support; structural problems in implementing decisions; a missing legal framework for regional cooperation; and a lack of modern technological methods and knowledge management. The multiple causes listed by Krasznai shed light on the complicated nature of the intertwined problems, and how difficult it is to overcome them.

I. INTRASTATE PROBLEMS AND INTERSTATE TENSIONS

According to Transparency International's Annual Index, the countries within the Aral Sea basin rank among the most corrupt in the world (Granit et al. 2010, 10). Following the Soviet departure, a political vacuum was created allowing authoritarian regimes to take control of power and resources, and create a competitive, rather than cooperative, environment within the region. As in many regions of the world, the desire to keep the status quo economy and increase production of exportable goods took precedence over environmental concerns. Despite some movements towards a free and open society in the region, most of the power elites have used oppressive methods and corrupt means to hold onto power. One movement away from the former corruption can be found in Kyrgyzstan, when in 2010 it elected the first woman President, Roza Otunbayeva, to lead in a male-dominated Muslim country. President Otunbayeva has helped to turn Kyrgyzstan into the region's first parliamentary democracy. It won her the U.S. Department of State's prestigious Woman of Courage award, and praise from U.S. Secretary of State Hillary Clinton for her "tremendous courage, leadership, and tenacity" (BBC 2011). However, President Otunbayeva's election to the presidency and international recognition has not been without controversy or ethnic disputes.

Shortly after Otunbayeva was elected into office, ethnic tensions between Uzbek and Kyrgyz nationalities living in the Fergana Valley region flared up, causing Kyrgyz nationals to resort to violent measures against the Uzbeks. The Fergana Valley, the most fertile and densely populated area in the Aral Sea basin, is home to both Kyrgyz and Uzbek ethnic groups. One possible cause of the 2010 conflict stems from Kyrgyz fear that the Uzbeks in the area may try to seize power and merge the Kyrgyz territory with Uzbekistan (BBC 2010). Twenty years prior to the 2010 incident, another dispute between the ethnic Kyrgyz and Uzbeks over access to land and water within the same region had left 300 people dead (Spoor 1998, 425). The important difference between the 1990 and 2010 violence is that the earlier related significantly to water resources, while the latter was exclusively ethnic and political. However, the 1990 conflict shows how resource-based conflicts can spark deeper ethnic issues within the region and lead to serious acts of violence. Thus, the likelihood of tension and conflict resulting from improper and unfair resource use is considerable, especially given the vested national and ethnic interests.

Despite Kyrgyzstan's appearance of making progress under President Otunbayeva, the International Crisis Group (ICG) ranks it, and Tajikistan, as the two most backward states in the region. The report, submitted in February of 2011, sheds light on how lack of basic resources in the region erodes allegiance to the state and fuels public discontent, supported and exploited by populists, militants, and religious extremists whose messages are well received by uneducated populations (ICG 2011, 6). Uzbekistan and Turkmenistan are also criticized by the report: "The façade of reform and prosperity conceals a deep corrosion of human and physical infrastructure" (ICG 2011, 19). Lastly, the report states that Kazakhstan's attempts to reform its economic and political infrastructures have also been disappointing, and any success thus far is attributable to the country's oil money, and not due to the state's broader policy initiatives (ICG 2011, 36).

Most of these regimes are corrupt with weak political and economic infrastructure, thereby preventing full and honest cooperation. The 2011 ICG report observes that the problems related to corruption and weak governance can be overcome only if public resources are not used for private enrichment. Systematic reforms along with donor assistance to compliment (not substitute) for state goals must be accepted and immediately utilized if progress is to be made. To do so would provide a cushion of support in solving the water woes, and prevent disputes over water and resources similar to the disputes in 1990 and 2010. The International Crisis Group lastly calls for the international community to realize that "tolerating the status quo will bring about the very problems they fear most—further impoverishment and instability, radicalization, and latent state collapse" (ICG 2011, 36).

II. LACK OF STRUCTURE, ABUNDANCE OF CONFUSION

With the corruption and shady authoritarian governments in Central Asia, the structures set up by the regional treaties thus far lack sincerity and are inadequately enforced. Quite often states have broken their commitments on distribution of water, usually whenever they felt that they had greater economic-political leverage in negotiating deals (Karaev 2005, 66). It is to be noted that the downstream countries of Uzbekistan and Kazakhstan are stronger both militarily and economically. Accordingly, their relationship with the upstream countries is asymmetrical, allowing these downstream nations to use relatively harsh threats. For example, Uzbekistan has repeatedly threatened not to keep its commitment of supplying power to Tajikistan after Tajikistan built additional capacities to become less dependent on Uzbekistan (ICG 2011, 11). Such disagreements and lack of cooperation in complying with water consumption agreements strain relationships and constructive policy implementation.

Several regional and international organizations such as IFAS and UNECE have attempted to improve these relationships, but an absence of trust and leadership in the region has resulted in contradictory and unclear policy mandates and goals. Suggested policies by inter-governmental organizations and bilateral aid agencies overlap and duplicate each other and are not implemented, while local leaders compete among themselves to access international resources. These local groups have learned to play international agencies against one another to reap the largest amount of aid (Weinthal 2003, 286). According to the UNEP's Global International Waters Assessment (2005), irrational use of funds, lack of support, and the style of decision making at higher administrative and political levels further contribute to inefficient use of local technical-scientific resources. As a result about 50 percent of the projects initiated by donor groups—mainly international—have failed (Severskiy et al. 2005).

However, serious attempts are being made by ASBP-3 to address these problems. On May 21, 2010, a Donors' Coordination Meeting was held to strengthen cooperation between EC IFAS, the community of donors, and international organizations active in the region. The meeting called for more active cooperation and efforts in enforcing environmental and sustainable development goals, and participation in the development of ASBP-3. A later Donors' Coordination Conference held on December 9, 2010, in Almaty, Kazakhstan, observed that "raising donor coordination to a new level is necessary to ensure the most effective use of available resources and attraction of additional funding" (UNECE 2010). A new umbrella organization was formed to improve coordination among international donors. This group, the Central Asia Water Sector Coordination Initiative (CAWSCI), hopes to map projects and interventions, and support the identification of innovative and commonly agreed-upon strategic approaches and implementation mechanisms (Granit et al. 2010, 14). Some of the participating partners in CAWSCI include the EU Water Initiative, UNDP, UNECE, the World Bank, Germany, the Organization for Security and Co-operation in Europe (OSCE), and others (CAWSCI 2010). Hopefully, through this organization the management and structural problems that have prevented greater resolutions might be solved.

III. TECHNOLOGY-STARVED REGION

The Soviets made almost no effort to introduce and invest in technical expertise in Central Asia, and as a result the Central Asian states are still stuck with pre-independence lifestyles and outdated technologies. This problem spans multiple sectors, including energy, education, water, and transportation, and is important to the cooperation and development of the region.

Energy-related problems faced by Tajikistan and Kyrgyzstan are a direct result of decades of under-investment and the inadequacies of measures to reform and modernize energy regulatory frameworks (UNDP 2008). Currently Tajikistan and Kyrgyzstan rely upon their regionally-abundant water resources to provide for half of their electricity needs (Peachey 2004, 10). As discussed earlier the upstream nations of Tajikistan and Kyrgyzstan rely upon their downstream neighbors for electricity during the winter months. However, in exceptionally cold winters, as in 2008, breakdowns in energy infrastructure led to little or no reliable heating and electricity services. Besides human discomfort their economies were also adversely affected. Part of the blame should be shared by Tajikistan and Kyrgyzstan. They fail to utilize their own hydroelectric resources, which would significantly reduce their energy needs and dependence on their downstream neighbors.

Inefficiencies within the various non-agricultural industries also contribute to waste and loss. According to the ICG report, the energy sector in both Tajikistan and Kyrgyzstan loses around 45 percent of the total output due to technical and commercial mismanagement (UNDP 2011, 13). As a result, Tajikistan and Kyrgyzstan lose large amounts of money, and are unable to invest in state-of-the-art technology to modernize their economies.

Tajikistan unsuccessfully attempted to modernize its water resource management procedures to achieve greater self-sufficiency by constructing the Rogun Dam. The idea for this project was initially conceived by Soviet planners, but was abandoned after Tajik independence. However, in January 2010, Tajikistan launched a public campaign to raise money and investments for the Rogun Dam and hydropower plant. It eventually collected a total of $187 million. According to the International Crisis Group, once the government collected the money, it had no clear plans for its utilization. Eventually $35.8 million was deposited in private banks, $16.5–17.3 million was spent on ongoing construction works at Rogun, and the remaining is unaccounted for (ICG 2011, 14).

It is interesting to note that the desire to improve self-efficiency within Tajikistan and Kyrgyzstan does not come without political ramifications. Uzbekistan felt betrayed by Tajikistan's attempt to diminish dependence on Uzbek energy, and an increasingly-strained relationship between the two countries continues (ICG 2011, 11). Since Uzbekistan and Turkmenistan serve as the regional suppliers of natural gas they are able to control prices. They manipulate power to increase the rates and even refuse to supply gas (Granit et al. 2010, 20). Uzbekistan also believes the dam will allow Tajikistan to control the flow of water used by Uzbek agriculture (ICG 2011, 14). The president of Tajikistan responded to Uzbek concern by arguing that "certain" Central Asian countries were striving "to distort the reality and divert the world community's attention away from the real causes of the disaster" (BBC 2010). Such behavior among neighbors points out the difficult and sensitive situation around sharing water resources and production of hydroelectric power. There is tremendous mistrust among the leaders of the region, who jockey for greater power and prestige for their countries and themselves.

In the energy sector both Uzbekistan and Turkmenistan are like their neighbors in their inability to modernize. Both Uzbekistan and Turkmenistan have been living off the energy-generating capacity built in the 1960s and 1970s by the Soviets. Failure to improve the infrastructure is contributing to a bleak energy future for both countries (ICG 2011, 25).

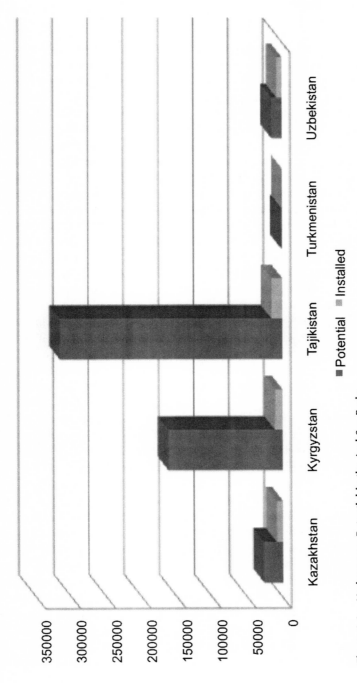

Figure 6.4. Hydropower Potential in the Aral Sea Basin

IV. AGRICULTURAL SOLUTIONS

Improvements within the agricultural sector have been marginal and under-funded, as the Central Asian states have neither incentive nor capital to invest in cleaner and more efficient technology (Spoor 1998, 412). Since neither the Central Asian governments nor the farmers within the region can afford to update their irrigation systems, reconstruction remains a difficult and seem-ingly impossible task. According to Kubo et al. there are two possible strate-gies for reforming water use. The first is to depart from the cotton monoculture by replacing cotton with a crop that consumes less water, thereby reducing water usage. The second strategy involves improving efficiency while main-taining the cotton monoculture. Yet neither of these strategies is without large complications and economic pushback from the parties involved.

It may be logical for the Central Asian nations to revert away from cotton and back to old farming practices of crop rotation to enhance water efficiency. However, fear of losing the status quo is apparent, and has kept these nations from diversifying crops. This belief is found among central authorities, elites, and ordinary people, who fear monetary losses and weakened economic systems if they reduce cotton production (Peachey 2004, 9). The degree of dependency on "white gold," water-heavy food crops, and the rural employ-ment they provide, makes it difficult to realize that fundamental changes in crop mix and land utilization are needed (Spoor 1998, 427). Irrigated farm-ing accounts for 50% of GDP within the Aral Sea region. The agricultural sector receives top priority in economic development plans, dwarfing other sectors of the economies (UNEP 2005, 30). In the words of the former ICAS/IFAS chairman, Almabek Nurushev, "Who will have the braveness to tell the farmers: 'reduce production and perish'? It will take quite some time to have rational production systems, where instead of cotton and rice, in some places the farms will produce wine and other production . . . The question is a very important one, and has to be faced in the very near future" (Spoor 1998, 427).

Kubo's second strategy of maintaining the current agrarian system is also hindered for the following reasons. First, in order to maintain current agricultural production while decreasing water use, investments must be made at the local level for new, smaller-scale, and more efficient irrigation systems. However, estimates indicate that such improvements will be out of reach for most farm enterprises (Spoor 1998, 431). Also, farmers are unaware of the benefits of water-efficient technologies, thereby reducing the possibility of major changes to the agricultural system happening from the bottom up (Severskiy et al. 2005, 12). McKinney (2004) accurately asserts that improvements in efficiency will require regional cooperation as opposed to each country or local farm updating their own systems. Without regional coordination and open sharing of information, "A drop saved by an Aral Sea Basin nation is viewed as another drop for expanding the nation's agricultural production, not for the Aral Sea. Improvements in irrigation efficiency in upstream areas will not necessarily result in more water flowing to the Aral Sea, rather the saved water will be diverted to new irrigated areas" (McKinney 2004, 215). Sadly, this is already happening throughout the basin. In Turkmenistan, for example, there has been a sharp increase in the amount of irrigated land. An additional 42,000 hectares of land has been developed between 1991 and 1996 (O'Hara & Hannan 1999, 33). Had Turkmenistan consulted with other regional partners and international parties, its efforts would have been criticized.

Improved efficiency and technology within the current system is hard to achieve without proper funding and adopting recommendations by the EC IFAS. Agreements for funding reached earlier within the IFAS framework have also changed over time. Initially, each country contributed one percent of its GNP. Later this was reduced to 0.3% for Kazakhstan, Turkmenistan, and Uzbekistan, and 0.1% for Kyrgyzstan and Tajikistan. Given the reduced overall funding and slow payments, the ability of the IFAS to update technology and repair existing water allocation systems is severely impaired (Spoor and Krutov 2003).

Another area which requires serious attention is the issue of water pricing. It is recommended by experts to use efficient and fair water pricing for sustainable use of water without reducing the size of crops. The current water-pricing policy allows farmers to operate on a "use it or lose it" philosophy. However, the government subsidies are dysfunctional and thus the farmers do not have much incentive to use the water efficiently. This system operates though the centralized system handed down by the Soviet era, and with it the practice of squandering natural resources without giving adequate thought to the consequences. The Global International Water Assessment, a report by the UN Environmental Program on transboundry water conditions, also strongly recommends that a change in the water-pricing system is necessary. It believes that the best solution is to "introduce market prices for water, taking into account the ecological health, water quality, and reliability of its delivery to the consumer . . . This will encourage a more efficient use of water by human activities" (GIWA 2005, 58).

Michael Goldman (2007) points out that the majority of the world's water consumers have inefficient water supplies because of their government's history of indifference and failure to charge people adequately for its use. Within the Aral Sea in particular, the Soviet legacy of subsidized water has allowed for the price of water to go unchanged and the use of water to remain consistent. Thus in order to solve the problem, governments need to "adopt international accounting methods for water services, submit to grading by international credit agencies, and most importantly, place a market price on water" (Goldman 2007, 794). The UNDP Regional Water Intelligence report on Central Asia also suggested market mechanisms and regulation for water and resources (Granit et al. 2010, 25).

POTENTIAL FOR CONFLICT

While there is high potential for conflict within Central Asia over water resources due to failure to honestly implement agreed-upon arrangements, there is yet a very small chance for armed confrontation. Despite occasional tensions, nations in the region have learned to cooperate with each other through international mediation and depend upon that mediation for continued financial relief and support. However, after two decades of international efforts to rehabilitate the Aral Sea and implement sustainable changes in the area, the problems associated with the desiccation of the Aral Sea still persist, and do not seem to have a sound solution in the near future (Weinthal and Watters 2010, 790). The depressing realization that the Aral Sea will never be what it once was will continue to upset the Central Asian people and outside observers, but will not cause an all-out war amongst the nations.

Most likely, conflicts may originate from local and small-scale disputes, such as the conflicts within the Osh region in 1990 and 2010, as a byproduct of both ethnic tensions and environmental woes. This assumption is the most realistic, since these conflicts on the local level may be the most difficult for the international community to monitor and prevent. These situations may escalate due to ethnic and other issues such as boundaries, national pride, and new identities. Oftentimes, local conflicts spread and seriously jeopardize state and national stability and tranquility, without outside groups being able to contain the spread of anger and instability. The water situation may spark the initial conflict, but will surely not be the sole motivation of those involved.

It should also be noted that several Central Asian countries have Islamic radical movements. These are led by populists, militants, and/or religious extremists who could use the water issue as a political vehicle to gain followers and initiate conflict at the local level. Following the June 2010 violence in Kyrgyzstan, Dennis Blair, the U.S. director of national intelligence, in his testimony to the U.S. Congress, pointed out this possibility in the region. He warned that the regional states might not be able to "manage the challenges if Islamic extremism spreads to the region from Pakistan and Afghanistan. The risks are compounded by the economic crisis . . . and by perennial food and energy shortages in some parts of Central Asia. Competition over water, cultivable land, and ethnic tensions could serve as sparks for conflict" (US Congress 2011). It should be noted here that the general consensus among policy makers and researchers is that the water-related issues could be easily exploited if there are other economic and political problems that threaten and challenge the system.

CURRENT MEASURES TO PREVENT CONFLICT: ONE STEP FORWARD, TWO STEPS BACK

Steps have been taken by the United Nations Regional Center for Preventive Diplomacy for Central Asia (UNRCCA), the OSCE, and the United States to reduce the potential conflict and terrorism resulting from localized tensions, factionalism, and environmental problems. These international efforts have the potential to increase cooperation and modernization within Central Asia. These international bodies have invested monetary resources and made a political commitment to strengthen political and economic infrastructures in the region, so that past mistakes do not haunt the future.

The UNRCCA was created in late 2007, is headed by a special representative of the UN secretary-general, and has held several regional conferences on such issues as the Aral Sea desiccation, water-sharing, and Afghanistan (US Congress 2011). According to the UNRCCA's mission statement, their goal is to "support the governments of Kazakhstan, Kyrgyzstan, Tajikistan, Turkmenistan and Uzbekistan in building their prevention capacities through enhanced dialogue, confidence building measures, and establishing genuine partnership in order to respond to existing threats and emerging challenges in the Central Asian region" (UNRCCA). In December 2010, UNRCCA and EC IFAC jointly sponsored a conference entitled, "Best Practices and International Experience with Transboundry Water Dispute Resolution," which was held to promote cooperation and efficient management of water resource related disputes and potential conflicts.

The OSCE has also emphasized the need for cooperation with the IFAS, and had gained an influential role in the Central Asian region by the time Kazakhstan took chairmanship of the OSCE in 2010 (US Congress 2011). It was hoped that Kazakhstan's position would facilitate better coordination in policymaking, and mitigate potential tensions. Unfortunately, at the OSCE Heads of State and Government Summit on December 1–2, 2010, in Almaty, these hopes were diminished due to diplomatic conflict and bickering among the states. Uzbekistan harshly criticized Kazakhstan for its reaction to the April 2010 Kyrgyz crisis, which in turn made policy making difficult and hindered cooperation efforts (Lillis 2010).

The tense water relationship between Tajikistan and Uzbekistan surfaced at the Almaty Conference. The Tajik President Imomali Rahmon complained about Uzbekistan's de facto blockade of Tajikistan-bound rail freight to the proposed hydropower stations (Lillis 2010). One observer to the conference noted: "This lack of willingness to cooperate effectively to solve some of these wider regional issues may be down to a perceived clash of interests between states and the zero-sum attitude of some of the governing elites. It seems the OSCE chairmanship has tended to crystallize these fault lines— especially with regards to Uzbekistan's lack of willingness to cooperate with its neighbors" (Lillis 2010).

A U.S. Senate Committee on Foreign Relations' report on avoiding water wars observed that "Statistically, the likelihood of conflictual interactions over water appears slightly higher in areas of high dam density. But this propensity disappears where institutional arrangements such as treaties or river commissions exist to mitigate those pressures" (US Senate 2011, 20). As discussed above, the Central Asian nations have established several mechanisms and organizations that have reduced the possibility of armed economic conflicts. While the environmental and political situation is far from ideal, the fact is that one of the most water-scarce regions in the world has avoided serious conflicts.

The U. S. Senate Committee on Foreign Relations has also expressed concern over the growing water problems in Central Asia. In its report, submitted on February 22, 2011, the Committee outlined the problem and emphasized the strategic importance of Central Asia and its proximity to Afghanistan. The report stated that "By neglecting the interconnectivity of water issues between Central and South Asia, the U.S. approach could exacerbate regional tensions . . . The United States must be cautious and recognize that, while regional stability will not be determined solely by our efforts to support water cooperation, regional stability can be strongly undermined by misguided support" (US Congress 2011, 1–2).

CONCLUSION

According to the International Crisis Group (2011), the most viable solution for Central Asia is to first purge the government corruption, especially the corrupt leaders who use their countries' resources as a source of personal wealth. The region needs to improve the governance by instituting a merit-based bureaucracy, providing adequate compensation to civil servants, and ensuring sufficient funding to other functioning arms of the state. The ICG realizes that the efforts made by outside donors thus far have yet to address the corruption out of fear of upsetting regional leaders. Without the necessary political intervention, the fragile regimes and economies of Central Asia could create enormous uncertainties and problematic scenarios not only for the region but for the rest of the world.

Additionally, it would be in Central Asia's best interest to provide employment opportunities to the young, modernize the economic and technological sectors, and support democracy by using American "soft/smart" power in the region. The United States will be wise to seek cooperation with Russia in its attempts to foster environmental and human security in Central Asia. This region's vulnerability to future conflict is relatively high; however, if the right precautions are taken and necessary collaborative arrangements are made, such vulnerability can be reduced and conflict can be averted.

REFERENCES

BBC News: Asia-Pacific. 2010. "Plight of Kyrgyzstan's Ethnic Uzbek Refugees." June 15.http://www.bbc.co.uk/news/10317138. (Accessed March 9, 2011).

BBC News: Asia-Pacific. 2011. "Kyrgyzstan President Roza Otunbayeva Given U.S. Honor." March 8. http://www.bbc.co.uk/news/world-asia-pacific-12677394. (Accessed March 11, 2011).

CAWSCI. (2010, July 1). Retrieved March 9, 2011, from Waterwiki.net: http://waterwiki.net/index.php/CAWSCI.

de Chazournes, L. B. 2006. "The Aral Sea Basin: Legal and Institutional Aspects of Governance." In *The Multi-Governance of Water: Four Case Studies*, edited by L. Tamiotti, J. Allouche, and M. Finger, 147–171. New York: State University of New York Press.

Elhance, Arun P. 1997. "Conflict and Cooperation over Water in the Aral Sea Basin." *Studies in Conflict & Terrorism* 20 (2): 207–218.

Glantz, Michael H. 1998. "Creeping Environmental Problems in the Aral Sea Basin." In *Central Eurasian Water Crisis: Caspian, Aral, and Dead Seas*, edited by Iwao Kobori and Michael H. Glantz, 25–52. New York: United Nations University Press.

Goldman, Michael. 2007. "How "Water for All!" Policy Became Hegemonic: The Power of the World Bank and its Transnational Policy Networks." *Geoforum*

Grabish, Beatrice. 1999. "Dry Tears of the Aral." *UN Chronicle* 1: 38–44.

Granit, Jakob, et al. 2010. "Regional Water Intelligence Report Central Asia. Baseline Report."*Regional Water Intelligence Reports*. Water Governance Facility. UNDP.

(ICG) International Crisis Group. 2011. "Central Asia: Decay and Decline." Crisis Group Asia Report no. 201. Bishkek/Brussels: International Crisis Group.

Karaev, Zainiddin. 2005. "Water Diplomacy in Central Asia." *Middle East Review of International Affairs* 63–69.

Krasznai, Marton. December 7, 2010. "Water Convention." *UNECE: Activities: Project* "Regional dialogue and cooperation on water resource management in Central Asia." http://www.unece.org/env/water/cadialogue/cadwelcome.htm. (Accessed March 17, 2011).

Lauener, Paul. 2010. "A Sea Returns to Life, a Sea Slowly Dies." *New Internationalist* November 1, 2010: 16–19.

Lillis, Joanna. April 28, 2009. "Central Asian Leaders Clash over Water at Aral Sea Summit." Centre for Strategic Research & Analysis: Regional Studies: Central Asian, Russian and Caucasus Articles and Reports. http://www.cesran.org/index.php?option=com_content&view=article&id=340%3Acentral-asian-leaders-clash-over-water-at-aral-sea-summit&catid=57%3Amakale-ve-raporlar&Itemid=63&lang=en. (Accessed March 17, 2011).

McKinney, Daene C. 2004. "Cooperative Management of Transboundary Water Resources in Central Asia." In *The Tracks of Tamerlane-Central Asia's Path into the 21st Century*, edited by D. and Sabonis-Helf, T., Burghart: National Defense University Press.

O'Hara, S. 2000. "Central Asia's Water Resources: Contemporary and Future Management Issues." *Water Resources Development* 423–441.

Peachey, Everett J. 2004. "The Aral Sea Basin Crisis and Sustainable Water Management in Central Asia." *Journal of Public and International Affairs* 15: 1–20.

Severskiy, I., etal. 2005. *Aral Sea—GIWA Regional Assessment 24.* Global International Waters Assessment, University of Kalmar on behalf of United Nations Environment Program.

Spoor, Max. 1998. "The Aral Sea Basin Crisis: Transition and Environment in Former Soviet Central Asia." *Development and Change* 29: 409–435.

Spoor, Max, and Anatoly Krutov. 2003. "XI. The 'Power of Water' in a Divided Central Asia." *Perspectives on Global Development & Technology* 593–614.

Tsukatani, Tsuneo. 1998. "The Aral Sea and Socioeconomic Development." In *Central Eurasian Water Crisis: Caspian, Aral, and Dead Seas*, edited by Iwao Kobori and Michael H Glantz, 53–74. New York: United Nations University Press.

UNECE (United Nations Economic Commission for Europe). December 17, 2010. "Information: United Nations Economic Commission for Europe" http://www.unece.org/press/pr2010/10env_p43e.htm. (Accessed March 7, 2011).

UNECE. 2008. "Programs: Activities." Water Unites—Strengthening Regional Cooperation on Water Management in Central Asia: Central Asian Regional Risk Assessment, Executive Summary. November 17–18. http://www.unece.org/env/water/meetings/Almaty_conference.htm. (Accessed March 7, 2011).

U.S. Congress. Senate. Committee on Foreign Relations. "Avoiding Water Wars: Water Scarcity and Central Asia's Growing Importance for Stability in Afghanistan and Pakistan." 112th Congress. 1st sess., 2011. Committee Print, 1–22.

UNEP (United Nations Environment Program). Regional Assessment 24: Aral Sea. GIWA Regional Assessment, Kalmar: University of Kalmar on behalf of UNEP, 2005.

Vinogradov, Sergei. 1996. "Transboundry Water Resources in the Former Soviet Union: Between Conflict and Cooperation." *Natural Resources Journal* 393–415.

Wegerich, Kai. 2008. "Hydro-hegemony in the Amu Darya Basin." *Water Policy* 71–88.

Weinthal, Erika, and Kate Watters. 2010. "Transnational Environmental Activism in Central Asia: The Coupling of Domestic Law and International Conventions." *Environmental Politics* 782–807.

Weinthal, Erika. 2003. 'Making Waves: Third Parties and International Mediation in the Aral Sea Basin.' In *Words over War: Mediation and Arbitration to Prevent Deadly Conflict*, edited by M. Greenberg. Lanham: Roman and Littlefield.

Chapter Seven

Conflict and Cooperation among the Riparian Countries of the Volta River Basin in West Africa

A Geographic Perspective

J. Henry Owusu

INTRODUCTION

Water is basic to life. It is indispensable for our very existence, sustenance, and survival as humans, and consequently, our access to, and use of water for a variety of purposes such as drinking and agriculture, are critically important. Water in its own right is thus a critical resource in national development. As a resource without an alternate option, a resource that quite often must be shared by different peoples and nations with common water sources or river basins, issues of conflict or cooperation necessarily arise, especially when access is constrained or scarcity increases—situations that inevitably generate tensions. As noted by Vlek, this is because there is a clear inter-dependency of water allocation across sectors and nations, which calls for policy co-ordination and the strengthening of legal and regulatory arrangements. The following analysis discusses the areas of current and potential cooperation and conflict among the six riparian countries of the Volta River in West Africa. Until recently, the Volta River basin, which is the ninth largest in Africa, remained one of the few transboundary basins without any formal legal and institutional arrangements for its water and other resources (Odame-Ababio, 2008). This chapter focuses primarily but not exclusively on such transboundary cooperation and conflict between the river's upstream country of Burkina Faso, and downstream country of Ghana, which together constitute the main countries the bulk of whose territories are drained by the Volta River network. Approximately three-quarters of Ghana and two-thirds of Burkina Faso fall within the Volta basin, with the two countries' drainage

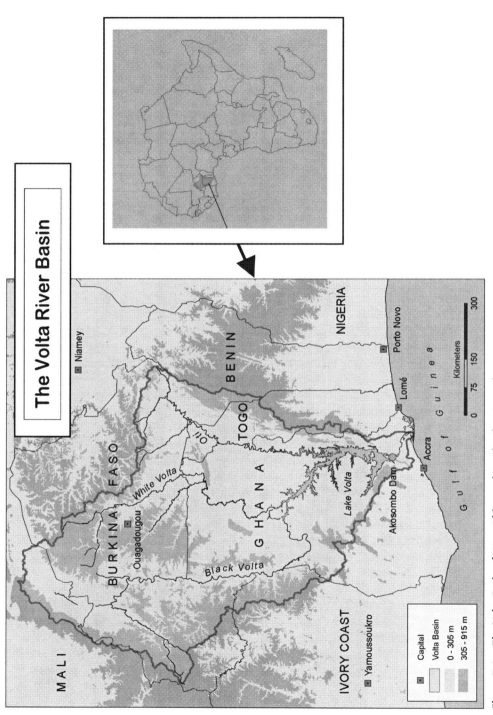

Figure 7.1. The Volta Basin of West Africa and Its Riparian Countries

areas comprising some 85 percent of the whole basin. The discussions begin with the geography of the Volta basin, followed by the basis for the focus on Ghana and Burkina Faso. Next, the basis and history of conflict between the two countries are discussed, followed by those of cooperation. The basis for further cooperation between these two and the other riparian countries, which could benefit from conscious efforts among those countries to avoid boiling conflicts, are then discussed, followed by our conclusions.

THE VOLTA RIVER BASIN

The Volta River basin (Figure 7.1) covers an area of 417,000 km^2 and generates more than 32,000 million m^3 in mean annual runoff (Lautze, Barry, and Youkhana 2006). It occupies some 28 percent of the West African region and is shared by six riparian countries, namely Mali, Burkina Faso, Benin, Togo, Côte d'Ivoire, and Ghana (Table 7.1). This basin is the ninth largest in Africa, and is drained by the Volta River and its tributaries into the Gulf of Guinea in West Africa at an estimated annual rate of about 38 km^3 (FAO 1997).

Upstream, the northernmost source of the basin's Volta River system is in Mali, where it occupies about one percent of the land area; however, it is from Burkina Faso, which constitutes about 40 percent of the basin (Table 7.1), that the most significant tributaries of the drainage network originate. These are the Mouhoun River or Black Volta, which flows northwards before turning southwards to form a small part of the northwestern boundary of Ghana with Burkina Faso, and the Nankanbé River or White Volta, which flows southeastwards from northern Burkina Faso to Ghana's northern border and then makes its way southwestwards to join the Black Volta after the latter

Table 7.1. Spatial Distribution of the Volta Basin between the Riparian Countries

Country	Country Area within Basin (Km²)	% of Basin in Country	% of Country within Basin
Burkina Faso	178,000	42.65	63.0
Ghana	167,692	40.18	70.0
Togo	26,700	6.40	47.0
Benin	17,098	4.10	15.2
Mali	15,392	3.69	1.2
Côte d'Ivoire	12,500	2.99	3.9
Total	417,382	100.00	

Source: Andah and Gichuki 2003.

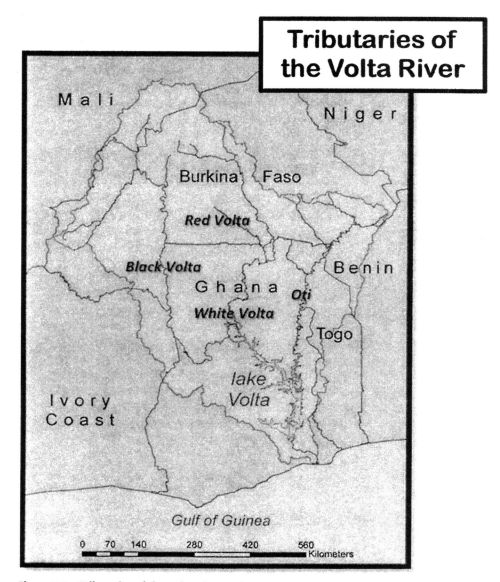

Figure 7.2   Tributaries of the Volta River and Associated Riparian Countries

has southeastern course northeastwards. The Black Volta also briefly marks a small part of the boundary between Côte d'Ivoire and Ghana.

It is in Ghana that the Red Volta, which also originates from the central part of Burkina Faso near the capital city of Ouagadougou, flows southeastwards into Ghana and joins the White Volta. It is estimated that the total annual discharge from Burkina Faso via the Red and White Volta Rivers is some 3.7 km³/year. The other major tributary is the Oti River, which originates in northwestern Benin as the Pendjari River, and flows northeast and then westward to delimit the boundary first between Burkina Faso and Benin, then between Togo and Benin for a short distance before entering Togo, where it becomes the Oti River, with a total annual discharge of some 2.2 km³. Downstream, it then demarcates the boundary between Togo and Ghana, entering Ghana further south with an estimated annual discharge of some 11 km³. There are many other minor tributaries with sources within Ghana's savannah zone but they generally dry up after the rainy season (FAO 1997).

The most significant feature in the Volta River basin is one of the world's largest artificial lakes, Lake Volta, with a capacity of some 148 km³ and a surface area of some 8,500 km². This lake is the result of the Akosombo Dam built across the narrow Akosombo Gorge in southern Ghana to "supply electric power from the Volta River for industry and for lighting our towns and villages" (Government of Ghana 1961). From Akosombo, the Volta River then flows some 100 km into the sea (Andreini et al. 2002).

In terms of climate and vegetation, the basin is located in the sub-humid to semiarid West African Savannah zone, where annual areal precipitation averages around 1000 mm with a steep south-north gradient ranging from more than 2000 mm to less than 500 mm respectively, with patterns of high spatial and temporal variability (Leemhuis et al. 2009). The climate in this region is largely influenced by the north-south movement of the Inter Tropical Convergence Zone (ITCZ). This movement makes rainfall seasonal, unpredictable, and unreliable; thus rain-fed agriculture is risky in the basin. Seventy percent of the annual total rainfall occurs in July through September, with little rainfall from November through March. Mean annual temperatures hover around 30°C, with humidity varying between 90 percent in the coastal areas to below 20 percent in the north during the harmattan and the dry season (MoWH 1998; Andah and Gichuki 2003; Gao and Margolies 2009).

With an estimated population of 18.6 million (Gao and Margolies 2009), the Volta basin is relatively densely settled, by African standards, with Ghana having 90 inhabitants per km². This is approximately three times the average population density of Sub-Saharan Africa (SSA). The six riparian countries of the Volta basin are among the poorest in the world, with some 31 percent of the population living below US$1.00 a day (Gao and Margolies 2009). Overall, the per capita income in the largely rural riparian countries is lower than the SSA average. Consequently, some 70–90 percent of the population depends largely on farming for subsistence. In fact, agricultural productivity in the basin is very low as compared with other regions in the world. This necessitates investments in irrigation to increase agricultural productivity in the basin, especially in the drier regions of Ghana and Burkina Faso. Small-scale irrigation schemes by small- and medium-scale farmers have been developing rapidly (Youkhana, Rodgers, and Korth 2006).

As noted by Odame-Ababio (2008), the basin is a complex ecosystem with varied water resources management challenges, including the absence of a framework for managing information and data sharing; risks of conflicts resulting from increasing competition among various water users and usage; soil and land degradation leading to silting of river channels and reservoirs; and increase in the growth of aquatic weeds, especially in the lower reaches of the basin. Access to safe drinking water in the basin varies from 50–84 percent, but generally, access to safe drinking water is lower in rural areas than in urban areas (GLOWA 2008). Thus, water plays a critical role in the development of the riparian countries in the Volta basin, and the demand for water resources among these countries constitutes a potential source of conflict. However, at the same time, it provides an opportunity for cooperation among them. Such potential for conflict and opportunity for cooperation in the basin are exemplified by relations between Ghana and Burkina Faso, which serve as a good proxy for a discussion of the issues of conflict and cooperation among the basin's riparian countries. This is more so since the basin largely remained, until recently, one of the few transboundary river basins in Africa without formal legal and institutional arrangements for the management of its water and other natural resources (Odame-Ababio 2008).

IMPORTANCE OF GHANA AND BURKINA FASO IN THE VOLTA RIVER BASIN

Youkhana, Rodgers, and Korth (2006) rightly point out that the management of watercourses, rivers, dams, and lakes falling within international or inter-state basins can have transboundary impacts, and within such basins, water resources management requires cross-boundary cooperation in order to realize effective joint water management and to avoid future conflicts. In the case of Africa, while most transboundary watercourses are already regulated by international agreements, the riparian states of the Volta basin have yet to conclude such a protocol for regulating the management at the international level (van Edig et al 2003; Lautze et al. 2005), and the attributes of Burkina Faso and Ghana and their relations provide an excellent case for examining issues of conflict and cooperation within the Volta basin.

The focus on the relations between Ghana and Burkina Faso is based on the relative importance of these two riparian countries in the basin (Table 7.1).

These two countries are also of particular significance given that even though both countries are largely agrarian, Ghana's main use of the Volta River is tied to the generation of hydroelectric power primarily for urban and industrial use, while Burkina Faso's is tied to agricultural irrigation. Consequently, the use and management of the Volta in the upstream and land-locked country of Burkina Faso have a lot of implications for the Ghanaian economy downstream. The associated tension generated can therefore be seen generally as a conflict between rural and urban communities in Burkina Faso and Ghana, respectively. Despite the tensions and concerns felt in urban Ghana regarding irrigation and drinking water development upstream of Lake Volta in general and in Burkina Faso in particular, there has not been any major conflict between the two countries. This suggests that there exists some limited degree of informal and formal cooperation like the recent establishment of the Volta Basin Authority (VBA). This provides the basis for further cooperation between these two and the other riparian countries, which could benefit from conscious efforts among those countries to avoid boiling conflicts, and also from the assistance of international communities and organizations like the International Union for the Conservation of Nature (IUCN), Green Cross International (GCI), and Global Water Partnership (GWP).

Historically, Ghana and Burkina Faso both shared similar, traditional water-management structures prior to the arrival of the British and the French as part of the European colonial process in the region. Until its independence from Britain in 1957 Ghana was known as the Gold Coast, and Burkina Faso was known as the Republic of Upper Volta or République de Haute-Volta until it was renamed in 1984 by President Thomas Sankara. Traditionally, for peoples of both countries surface water in general was deemed both a private good and public property and individuals and families had rights to it. It was treated as a resource that belonged to the entire community, but could be used for personal benefit as long as the collective good was not harmed (Ramatou 2002). This was a traditional cultural adaptation to the environment and associated resources enshrined in a traditional, religious belief that such waters were sacred and must be protected. Essentially, this belief was a mechanism for environmental conservation and resource sustainability. In other words, as a cultural adaptation, the community was organized in relation to a religious ideology that ensured a sound relationship between the people and their environment in terms of how they accessed and used the water resources. This form of adaptation is rooted in the people's environmental perception in which they saw themselves as stewards or custodians of their environment.

Over the years, the people of the two countries, like other traditional societies, have built a body of indigenous knowledge through generations of living close to nature, which shaped their environmental perception. Such perception has also been influenced by their experience, values, emotions, and even their ignorance with respect to the environment. It is the knowledge associated with this environmental perception that is expressed, inter alia, in the norms, taboos, and system of self management that govern resource use. In other words, in terms of this traditional environmental perception, the peoples of the two countries have traditionally had an organic rather than a mechanistic view of nature, which is largely a holistic view that conceptualizes people as being part of nature and sees the environment as being infused with spirits or gods who must not be offended. Consequently, they have traditionally deemed the environment as sacred and have as a result established a reverential "I-Thou" relationship with nature (Buber 1958). This form of reverential environmental relationship eschewed or minimized conflict. As a common traditional practice among the peoples of Ghana and Burkina Faso, this type of environmental perception has been a centripetal force—a unifying factor that ensured cooperation between them with respect to the use of the waters of the Volta River, rather than conflict with each other. For the Akan people of Ghana, who share part of the basin, all activities in rivers, streams, and the like, such as washing clothes, abstraction, or fishing, were prohibited on certain days of the week (MoWH 1998b; Odame-Ababio 2002; Lautze and Youkhana 2006)—a prohibition geared at conservation rooted in religion. For the Mossi people, who constitute some 40 percent of the population of Burkina Faso, water is considered sacred too, with regulatory functions played by the traditional chiefs and priests to maintain sanitation in villages and promote a certain degree of conservation. Sustainable water management practices were thus achieved through measures similar to the Volta's downstream portions in Ghana.

For these two peoples, cooperation was tied to the common belief that the deity expected of them some specific behavior for their own good and survival. If they conformed to such precepts, the environment and associated resources remained in good shape, and society or the community thrived as a blessing. If they violated such precepts, the environment and associated resources would deteriorate as a punishment. Also, the two societies traditionally embraced the "chain of life" philosophy in terms of their commitment to their responsibility to ancestral spirits to maintain the precepts and legacies bequeathed to the present generations; commitment to their responsibility to the members of the present generation to ensure that current needs are met adequately; and finally, commitment to their responsibility to future generations to not jeopardize their access to the resources bequeathed to them by misusing or destroying such resources. Such resources include water, access to which and use of which for a variety of purposes like drinking and agriculture, are a sine qua non of life for the future generations, their sustenance, and national development. Lautze and Youkhana

(2006) succinctly put it this way: "According to Akan beliefs, the earth was accorded a spirit of its own, which could be helpful if propitiated or harmful if degraded. Land was inherited from the ancestors. Chiefs and priests, entrusted with ensuring that ancestors and gods received proper respect, exercised control over the land and its resources to promote conditions which were beneficial to the environment and sustainable for communities" (Opoku-Agyemang 2001a; Opoku-Agyemang 2001b; Ministry of Works and Housing 1998).

Lautze and Youkhana(2006) further note that: "To achieve their goals, chiefs and priests enforced a set of rules which were intended to protect the earth and regulate use of natural resources. Most importantly, a river's waters were considered holy. Desecration in or around them was therefore prohibited as was farming on river banks (as these areas were considered resting abodes for river gods and their children). Further, beliefs concerning tree deities entailed demarcation of certain forest areas as sacred groves (in which no human activities were permitted), thereby minimizing deforestation and soil erosion. In addition, certain areas were usually designated for gathering water and these areas were generally (and logically) situated upstream from areas of other activities which may harm the water. Finally, certain days of the week entire activities such as washing clothes, water abstraction, or fishing were prohibited—helping to make use of water and exploitation of resources therein more sustainable" (Ministry of Works and Housing 1998b; Ministry of Works and Housing 1998d; Odame-Ababio 2002).

It must, however, be noted, as pointed out by Lautze and Youkhana (2006), that in the Burkinabe regions of the Volta basin, the traditional religious beliefs on which customary water management is based, and which serve as a centripetal force in terms of cooperation, may have been altered to a degree by the significantly large Muslim population in the region. By the same token, the religious syncretism that pervades in the region allows traditional practices and institutions to persist in altered forms.

As noted earlier, issues of conflict or cooperation necessarily arise with water use and management, especially when access is constrained or scarcity increases—situations that inevitably generate tensions that can be addressed either by cooperation or conflict. Before examining the water use and management in these two countries as a basis for conflict and cooperation, however, it must be noted that the Volta basin actually became transboundary as a consequence of an artificial boundary imposed by the British, French, and Germans. The new boundary replaced the pre-existing hydrologic, as well as the anthropogeographic or cultural, boundaries that separated ethnic groups in the region prior to the colonization of Africa by European countries, following the Berlin Conference of 1885 to negotiate European territorial claims in Africa. In order to establish this colonial boundary and to regulate the use of the waters from one side of the boundary to the other, the British and the French signed two agreements in 1906. The first was the "Exchange of Notes between France and Great Britain relative to the Boundary between the Gold Coast and French Soudan," an agreement that effectively stated that traditional "native" practices relating to water withdrawal and use should be allowed to continue despite the imposition of a new border (TFDD 2004; Lautze and Youkhana 2006). The second was the "Agreement between France and Great Britain relative to the frontier between French and British possessions from the Gulf of Guinea to the Niger (Southern Nigeria and Dahomey)." These two agreements both involved the Volta River basin, with their primary goal as cross-border native access. This was important because in many cases, the establishment of colonial boundaries separated people from the water resources they had traditionally used. These agreements generally allowed for a continuation of pre-colonial cross-border movement by "natives" to access water resources (The African Transboundary Water Law 2008; Gao and Margolies 2009). It must be noted that the colonial impact in terms of water use and management was somewhat minimal largely because of the inconsistency of French policies in Burkina Faso, then Upper Volta. This was because the Upper Volta was not established as a distinct territory until 1919. In fact, even as a colony, it was dissolved in 1933 and reconfigured in 1947 (Oxfam 2000). Even during its first decade of independence, it did not have a formulated or written policy related to water—meaning the colonial government made little headway in imposing any national water policy in the territory (Lautze and Youkhana 2006).

Unlike colonial Upper Volta, Ghana, then the British colony of Gold Coast, was subject to a common law legal system relating to water management, a colonial imposition on the pre-existing traditional laws. This meant that (at least) two systems of water management—state-sponsored and community-regulated—were concurrently practiced (Lund 2006). These systems appeared to exist more in parallel than in conflict, because British colonial policies allowed for the persistence of certain levels of tradition (Lund 2006; Odame-Ababio 2002). The colonial legislation relating to water in the Gold Coast colony essentially comprised two key documents, namely the 1903 River Ordinance and the 1949 Forests Ordinance (Lund 2006; Opoku-Agyemang 2001b; Ministry of Works and Housing 1998b). The River Ordinance, which applied to several rivers including the Volta, was essentially concerned with river navigation. It regulated use of water by requiring that the colonial government approve water use for irrigation, mines, and power generation (Opoku-Agyemang 2004; Ministry of Works and Housing 1998b). The 1949 Forests Ordinance was primarily designed to regulate the protection of forests. However, it stipulated that the forest authority must approve all dam or weir construction on any river and that any such construction should not obstruct the flow of water in any forest reserve (Opoku-Agyemang 2001b). With the varying degrees of colonial meddling in the traditional water use and management practices in upstream Burkina Faso, and in downstream Ghana, we can now examine the resultant water use and management practices in each of the two countries as a basis for conflict and cooperation in the Volta basin.

WATER USE AND MANAGEMENT IN BURKINA FASO

Burkina Faso, as a product of colonialism, is a land-locked country to the north of Ghana, and this makes it dependent on Ghana as a transit neighbor, a situation that elicits cooperation rather than conflict. On the other hand, any crisis in Ghana's economy affects Burkina Faso directly or indirectly. Burkina Faso has essentially an agrarian economy with minimal industrial development. Consequently, in terms of economic development, about 90 percent of the population is active in agriculture, largely because there are no alternatives. Much of their staple crops like sorghum, millet, and corn, are cultivated under rain-fed conditions, hence inadequate or failing rains tend to reduce yields with substantial financial losses to the farmers. Generally, yields tend to be low, averaging 800 kg and 100 kg of grain/ha, and this makes it necessary for farmers to invest in more labor, improved seed, and chemical inputs to boost yields. However, such investments tend to be very risky without irrigation to reduce the risk of inadequate or failing rains (Andreini et al. 2002).

Burkina Faso's demand for irrigation water jumped from 43 million cubic meters (m^3) to 203 million m^3 in the decade of 1990–2000, and to 384 million m^3 by 2010. This is expected to rise steadily over the next two decades to 638 million m^3 by 639 million m^3 (Rodgers et al. 2007), with water supply implications for Ghana downstream. According to Obeng-Asiedu (2004), the size of the irrigated area in the basin is currently small, estimated officially at about 20,000 hectares out of a potential of 165,000 hectares in Burkina Faso, and 8000 hectares out of a potential 20,000 hectares in Ghana. However, in the case of Burkina Faso, the figure almost certainly excludes much of the farmer-developed small scale irrigation. The actual irrigated area in Burkina Faso may be closer to 50,000 hectares (Rodgers et al. 2007).

An interesting aspect of water demand in Burkina Faso is that it is characterized by high access to water supply in urban areas, while access to improved water sources in rural areas—where three-quarters of the population live—remains relatively low. In the rural areas, the demand for water is tied to the fact that important irrigated crops like rice must receive supplemental irrigation during the rainy season, and tomatoes, onions, and corn during the dry season (Rodgers et al. 2007). Burkina Faso cannot meet its irrigation needs by large-scale dams. As noted by Andreini et al. (2002), it lacks economically attractive and environmentally acceptable large-scale dam sites. Consequently, the most significant irrigation schemes that have been developed are few, and the main ones are the Bagré Dam and the Vallée du Sourou. The Bagré Dam is located on the Nankanbé River at 150 km from the Burkinabe capital of Ouagadougou in the central east province of the country. It was built in 1994 and has a storage capacity of 1.7 million cubic hectometers (hm^3). The dam had several objectives, such as the generation of some 45 GWh of electricity for villages along the transmission line and Ouagadougou; the development of some 30,000 ha of irrigated lands; improvement of the regulation of the river's flows to mitigate floods, which often result in problems for the downstream neighbors in Ghana; and to sustain the flow in the dry season. In addition, it supplies water to the city of Ouagadougou and also aims at facilitating the production of some 10,000 tons of fish per annum (Berga et al. 2006). Ouagadougou also benefits from the Ziga reservoir, which is about 50 km away. This reservoir with a 200 million m^3 storage capacity started providing water to the capital in 2004. By 2008, it was supplying about 70 percent of Ouagadougou's needs.

The Sourou Valley Irrigation Project, the most important of its kind in Burkina Faso, is on the approximately 120 kilometer-long Sourou River, which has its source in Mali and flows into the Black Volta in western Burkina Faso. It was initiated in 1985 by the government in order to improve the nutritional situation of the regional population. Subsequently, it has been supported by various foreign donors including the European Union among others. The project is located north of the confluence, immediately on the border between the two countries. By the year 2000, some 3,200 hectares of land were irrigated, and it is anticipated that in the future the irrigated area to the east of the Sourou will grow to as much as 30,000 hectares. Similar projects are also planned to the west of the river. The project includes a dam to control the flow of water between the Black Volta and the Sourou. In the rainy period the cyclically flowing Sourou grows into a reservoir. In the dry period, from December onwards, the dam is opened so that the direction of flow of the Sourou then changes. As a result of this project, wet rice has become the main product and is grown on two-thirds of the land. Maize, potatoes, and sugar cane, among other crops, are also cultivated. A special feature is the growing of specialized crops including tomatoes and onions. The project also enables the cultivation of wheat as well (Falk and Attfield). However, most irrigation development in Burkina Faso is in the form of village-level schemes with imperfect hydraulic

Table 7.2.   Water Demand: Burkina Faso, Ghana and the Volta Basin Riparian Countries in General

Country	Sector	Demand: Millions Cubic Meters per Year				
		1990	*2000*	*2010*	*2020*	*2025*
Burkina Faso	Domestic	67	85	106	132	149
	Irrigation	43	203	384	554	639
	Livestock	37	46	61	78	88
	Total	147	334	551	764	876
Ghana	Domestic	82	138	192	272	284
	Irrigation	75	565	1,871	3,605	3,733
	Livestock	18	26	41	63	67
	Total	175	729	2,104	3,940	4,084
All Riparian States	Domestic	-	360	604	891	1,058
	Irrigation	-	1,169	3,170	5,974	6,730
	Livestock	-	166	294	430	511
	Total	-	1,695	4,068	7,295	8,299

Source: Rodgers et al. 2007.

control (Andreini et al. 2002). Based on Burkina Faso's emphasis on irrigation and livestock, in terms of its water demand (Table 7.2), it can be said that water use in the country is mainly rural rather than urban, especially since irrigation is seen as the primary non-domestic water use.

WATER USE AND MANAGEMENT IN GHANA

Like Burkina Faso, Ghana was largely an agrarian economy prior to its independence in 1957 from the British. However, a major difference between the two countries is that unlike Burkina Faso, with minimal industrial development and a landlocked geographic situation, Ghana has had a long history of mining, along with its largely agricultural economy. It also has direct access to the Atlantic Ocean into which the Volta River finally discharges its waters. Gold production was significant in the Ashanti region of Ghana prior to and during the colonial period, and in fact, the most significant project on the Volta River in Ghana, the Akosombo Dam, is tied to mining. The original motivation to construct this dam was to provide electricity for the production of aluminum from the locally mined bauxite as an integrated industry. As noted by Andreini et al. (2002), the initial post-colonial leadership was convinced that the construction of the Akosombo Dam on the Volta River "was the most important way of bringing Ghana forward to a more balanced economy," and that the dam would supply "electric power from the Volta River for industry and for lighting our towns and villages" (Government of Ghana 1961). Kwame Nkrumah, Ghana's first president, in fact wanted to use the dam as a nucleus around which Ghana could begin a program of industrialization (Diemer 2008).

For the people of Ghana, and with implications for the Burkinabe peoples upstream, the proposal to construct the Akosombo Dam by the post-colonial leadership marked a significant turning point in the cooperation between the two countries based on the common traditional environmental perception and associated use of the waters of the Volta River as a common resource. It marked the beginnings of a shift from the traditional, organic environmental perception, to a rather mechanistic view of nature, whereby people are perceived to be separate, and to in fact have dominion over nature, and for that matter, the environment and resources. This is largely because, as traditional societies change as they modernize or develop, the traditional "I-Thou" relationship with the environment weakens. Both Ghana and Burkina Faso have implemented programs of economic development, albeit with varying degrees of success, since their independence in 1957and 1960, respectively. The changes associated with the economic development programs have been compounded by changing demographics and resource realities, combined with changing international development strategies like Structural Adjustment Programs implemented at the behest of the World Bank and the International Monetary Fund (Owusu 1998). Consequently, this new mechanistic view of nature now began to replace the traditional, reverential "I-Thou" relationship with a rather secular, mundane, and exploitative "I-It" relationship, which tends to generate conflict since user groups now perceive the resource as an object—or prey— that can be exploited to meet economic desires. This shift to the non-traditional "I-It" human-environmental relationship is not surprising because the damming of the Volta River was initially proposed in the 1920s by a westerner, Sir Albert Kitson, the British then-director of the Gold Coast Geological Survey, who had a different environmental perception (Hart 1980). The shift then began to crystallize from 1951, when the Gold Coast government and subsequently the Ghana government under Ghana's first leader, Kwame Nkrumah, pursued negotiations with the British and the U. S. governments, aluminum producers and financiers, the World Bank, and others, to arrange for construction of what became the Volta River Project (Andreini et al. 2000).

This basic theme of development via industrial expansion has been maintained to date. It is also important to note that whilst Ghana's use of the Volta River is primarily tied to hydroelectric power production (Table 7.1), 48 percent of it is sold to an aluminum production company, Volta Aluminum Company (VALCO). Water demand from the Volta for irrigation purposes has dramatically increased since 1990, when the demand was 75 million m^3. It increased to 565 million m^3 in the year 2000, and to 1,871 million m^3, just over a period of two decades, and it is projected to reach 3,605 million m^3 in the year 2020 and 3,733 million m^3 in just five years after that. These numbers are relative to Burkina Faso's demand and those of all the riparian countries (Table 7.2). Ghana's demand for water in the basin is largely urban. To meet such urban needs, Ghana exports electricity even to the co-riparian and neighboring countries of Côte d'Ivoire to the west, and Togo and Benin to the east, which consume seven percent of the power (Andreini et al. 2000). The Akosombo Dam alone supplies Ghana with the bulk of its domestic electric power needs. In fact, the increasing demand for electricity in urban areas cannot even be met with power from the Akosombo Dam alone, which has traditionally provided 95 percent of hydroelectric power for Ghana. Consequently, between 1978 and 1981, another dam was constructed a short distance below the Akosombo Dam at Kpong to add another 160 megawatts to Akosombo's 912 megawatt generating capacity (Diemer 2008). To meet the ever-increasing urban demand for electricity, the Ghanaian government broke ground, once again, in 2007 to construct another dam—a 400 megawatt hydroelectric project at the Bui Gorge, on the Black Volta River, about 300 miles upstream of the Akosombo dam, scheduled to be completed by late 2011 or early 2012. A new urban area, Bui City, is to be constructed to accommodate over 500,000 people as part of the project. In Ghana, therefore, the water use is mainly urban-industrial rather than rural, especially since hydropower generation is the primary non-domestic water use.

Given the importance of the use and management of the Volta River's water among the two riparian countries of Burkina Faso and Ghana, located upstream and downstream of the river, respectively, and which together constitute 80 percent of the Volta basin, it is important to examine the basis and history of conflict and cooperation between the two countries. This is especially so since they share some common interests such as water demand for domestic, irrigation, and other agricultural usage as well as conflicting interests, such as disparities and priorities in rural vis-a-vis urban-industrial usage of the water. Andreini et al. (2000) note that the two countries with respect to the Volta River are intimately linked, a fact that perhaps was ignored when the damming of the river was first conceived.

THE BASIS AND HISTORY OF CONFLICT BETWEEN
GHANA AND BURKINA FASO

At the root of conflicts over water resources between Ghana and Burkina Faso, relative to water use based on the Volta River, is the shift from the traditional organic view of nature to a mechanistic view and associated actions, such as damming the river on a large scale—inter alia, for the purposes of irrigation and hydroelectric power generation—since such interventions influence the people's access to, and use of the shared water resource. Such interventions become necessary as traditional societies like Burkina Faso and Ghana change or develop. However, they may increase or decrease people's access to, or use of, water, as the case may be, thereby creating a basis for conflict. This is because water is an important development resource, and the riparian countries would want to exploit the basin's water resources as much as possible to develop their respective economies. The competing uses of water resources among different sectors within a country and between upstream and downstream countries both constitute factors for international conflict. The diverse use of water in one country, such as for irrigation, fishery, domestic water supply, and livestock watering purposes might negatively impact on another. Economic development geared at improving the livelihood of people in one country may even conflict with the need to preserve and protect the ecosystem in another for future generations (Andah and Gichuki 2005).

Also, as pointed out by Anthony Turton (2004), "Conflicts over water arise from the fact that under conditions of increasing scarcity, competition levels also increase" (Ofori-Amoah). Andreini et al. (2000) also note that rapid increases in the demand for water in the domestic, agricultural, mining, and industrial sectors, lead to conflicts over water use on the international level. This is particularly significant as the Volta basin population is expected to increase by as much as 80 percent over the next two decades, which would make access to water resources even scarcer (Andah and Gichuki 2005). In fact, population growth rates in the region are estimated at approximately three percent, which is expected to increase pressure on the water supply. The growth also means an intensification of land use in areas occupied by the rural population with spillovers to areas hitherto unoccupied. People who cannot survive in the rural areas will migrate into the cities, thereby further increasing the already growing demand for jobs, and consequently, create more demand for hydroelectric power to meet the needs of industry and the urban population. Even in the rural areas, there will be more aggressive fuel wood collection, increased cropping, and more extensive grazing, all of which will change the land surface with a profound effect on the sharing of the water (Andreini et al. 2002).

The prospect that water scarcity in the basin will increase is also compounded by diminishing precipitation, reduction in river flows, and falling water tables. In addition, there has been an increase in the amount of evapotranspiration—due to the construction of a myriad of large and small reservoirs in the basin and an inefficient use of the basin's water resources (Gao and Margolies 2009). In fact, Gyau-Boakye and Tumbulto (2000) also point out that the basin has seen a reduction in the amount of precipitation over the past 20 years. Andah and Gichuki (2005) note that groundwater is overexploited in the basin as a consequence of excessive pumping without regard to the recharge characteristics of the aquifers. They also note that lowering of the water tables has been observed in large parts of the basin with the prospect of saltwater intrusion in the southern part of the basin near the Gulf of Guinea coast. According to Ofori-Amoah (2004), such conflicts are tied to power politics as to who actually has the power to control the economy and population dependent on the water. She points out that in relation to industrial and agricultural uses, as in the case of Ghana and Burkina Faso, conflicts develop from the overuse and degradation of water resources, and the insufficient amount available for communities. Furthermore, Haftendorn (2004) notes that unevenly distributed water among people and countries also creates an imbalance among those who share water supplies. In general, as societies become more developed, they tend to use more resources, including fresh water (Klare 2001). Consequently, increased urbanization tends to increase the demand for water. Conflicts also arise in situations where upstream communities release or restrict flows without adequately informing downstream stakeholders about the actions taken upstream, especially among riparian developing countries as in the Volta basin, where formal mechanisms and institutions or water management structures are usually not in place to address such problems.

As noted by Andreini et al. (2002), the tension over the waters of the Volta River between Ghana and Burkina Faso can be characterized as a conflict between urban and rural communities, respectively, and the basic dichotomy could be defined as between those requiring water for the generation of hydroelectric power and those requiring water for irrigation. It must be noted here that even though Ghana's water demand is primarily tied to hydroelectric power generation for industry and the urban areas, its demand for irrigation is also very significant. It is therefore the rapid expansion of irrigation in Burkina Faso (Table 7.2) that is a major concern in Ghana, given that the former's demand is upstream and has consequences downstream in Ghana. As Gyau-Boakye and Tumbulto (2000) point out, anxiety exists in urban Ghana concerning irrigation and even drinking water development upstream of Lake Volta in general and in Burkina Faso in particular. This situation is

tied to the fact that the availability of surface water resources is not evenly
distributed throughout the Volta basin, especially since 67 percent of all the
water flowing into Lake Volta from outside Ghana comes through the Black
Volta, White Volta, and Oti Rivers (Fekete, Vörösmarty, and Grabs 2000).
This is evident by the fact that the Black Volta crosses the border near Bui
bringing 8.3 km^3 per year or 24 percent of the total inflow to Lake Volta.
The White Volta, entering from Burkina Faso near Pwalagu, has an average
yearly runoff of 3.9 km^3 (11 percent). Finally, 11.2 km^3 per year flows past
Sabari along the Oti River. Even though the Oti River contributes 32 percent,
the largest part, its basin is actually smaller than that of the White Volta
or Black Volta, showing that changes in some parts of the basin may have
more important downstream effects than changes in other parts (Andreini et
al. 2002). Consequently, the simple fact that most of Ghana's water comes
from outside the country is the major cause for its anxiety since it needs the
water for electricity, agriculture, and other uses. In fact, it was to reduce such
water-related tensions between the two countries, and perhaps to strengthen
Ghana's claim to use the Volta's water, that Ghana offered to sell hydroelectric power to Burkina Faso in 1998, arguing that it would be much cheaper
for Burkina Faso to buy hydroelectric power from Ghana than to build its
own hydropower plants.

The uneasiness between the two countries became apparent with the reaction of Burkina Faso to Ghana's offer. Ghana's effort is said to have been
"stopped at the border" (Ghana World Wide News 1998), as Burkina Faso
argued that it would be cheaper to generate power from thermal plants rather
than buy power from Ghana given that Ghana was charging US$0.09 per unit
whilst Burkina Faso was willing to pay US$0.06 (Africa News 1998). The
underlying rationale for the disagreement, as noted by Andreini et al. 2000,
was Burkina Faso's unwillingness to become dependent on Ghana's power
resources for political and security reasons rather than the reason of high cost
offered by Burkina Faso. This unwillingness runs at odds with the vested
interests of other riparian counties. Ghana's co-riparian and neighboring
countries of Côte d'Ivoire, Togo, and Benin, which consume seven percent of
Ghana's hydroelectric power, are certainly interested in uninterrupted power
supplies and consequently are necessarily interested in the maintenance of an
unreduced flow of the Volta River. They are also likely to be affected by the
installation of additional upstream generating capacity and withdrawals for
urban water supply in Burkina Faso, since such actions could have a negative impact on them. Such issues are also of immediate concern to Ghanaians
(Andreini et al. 2000).

Also, as noted by Andah and Gichuki (2005) and Gao and Margolies
(2009), the very weak capacity among the riparian countries including Ghana

and Burkina Faso to deal with environmental issues, such as loss of biodiversity, reduction of fisheries resources, groundwater resources depletion, flooding, and river pollution is also an important conflict issue. These problems are water related and transboundary in nature. In these two countries as in the other four, several different institutions are charged with responsibilities for managing water, food, and soil resources. This kind of arrangement results in overlapping of responsibilities and difficulties in coordination. Under such arrangements, coordination of activities among such institutions tends to be generally weak, and in some cases exists only on an ad hoc basis for crisis situations. With no cooperation, therefore, the potential for conflicts among the riparian countries tends to increase with rising water withdrawals (Andah and Gichuki 2005).

In general, despite the construction of major hydraulic works with considerable international implications beginning in the 1960s with the construction of the Akosombo Dam through the construction of others like the Bagré in 1992, it could be said that transboundary issues began to constitute a major concern only in the mid-1990s. Such issues included the following sources of tension:

a. In 1992, Burkina Faso built the Bagré Dam without any consultation with Ghana, which is downstream of Burkina Faso (Gao and Margolies 2009). The construction of this dam, and the flooding it causes in downstream Ghana, constitutes one of the most immediate issues in the basin that continually emerges as a cause of tension between the two countries.
b. In 1997, 1998, and since 2003 largely reduced water level behind the Akosombo Dam led to an energy crisis in Ghana and forced the Ghanaian Government to import energy from Côte d'Ivoire. Ghana accused Burkina Faso of causing the low water level in the Volta Lake with its upstream construction of dams and reservoirs for irrigation purposes and hydropower generation (van Edig et al. 2002).
c. In August 2007, there was a 50-year flood in Ghana, a flood that was aggravated by the opening of the floodgates of the Bagré Dam in Burkina Faso. Ghana was not notified at the time of the opening; therefore, it was not prepared for the sudden increase of water, and much damage was done. This opening of the gates was a unilateral decision by Burkina Faso. This action was not well planned, and the warning regarding dam activity was communicated at the last minute.
d. In August-September 2010, at least 17 people drowned and several farm areas in northern Ghana were destroyed after Burkina Faso released water from its overflowing dams by opening their spillway gates following heavy rains in the region. In this situation, it must be noted, Burkina Faso actually

alerted people in the most vulnerable areas to evacuate (Ghanaweb.com 2010). It was the communication process that was flawed.

Water conflicts arise largely at the local level (Carius et al. 2004), and as noted by Reenberg Oksen, and Svendsen (2003), transboundary issues with direct local impacts also occur. For example, the opening of spillways of the Bagré Dam in Burkina Faso in the rainy season not only results in floods, but also leads to health problems downstream in Burkina Faso and Ghana. In 1999, for example, 48 people died from an outbreak of cholera in northern Ghana following torrential rains and flooding, which also made some 9,000 people homeless (*Reuters*: September 14, 1999). Also, agricultural expansion following the construction of the Bagré Dam not only marginalized pastoralists who lost their grazing rights on fallow land, access to water, and other resources, but it also had a negative impact on the traditional herding contracts that regulated animal husbandry in the farming community (Reenberg, Oksen, and Svendsen 2003).

Even though this situation has not resulted in major conflict or destroyed relationships to date, it maintains a tension between the two countries. In the main, however, it could be said that it is lack of communication between the two countries that serves as the immediate source of conflict.

THE BASIS AND HISTORY OF COOPERATION BETWEEN GHANA AND BURKINA FASO

Historically, the fundamental basis for cooperation between the two countries is rooted in the fact that traditional practices and institutions prevalent in both countries are largely similar. As noted earlier, both Ghana and Burkina Faso traditionally deemed the environment as sacred and had a reverential "I-Thou" relationship with nature, and for that matter with water resources such as the common stake in the importance of the Volta River to their respective livelihoods—an environmental relationship that eschewed or minimized conflict, since the common traditional perception among the peoples of both countries ensured cooperation rather than conflict with each other, with respect to the use of the waters of the Volta River. According to Lautze and Youkhana (2006), sustainable water management practices were achieved through measures similar to those taken in the Volta's downstream portions. "Traditional [water] management is founded on practical logic," wrote a French observer to colonial Upper Volta (Institut des Sciences Humaines Appliquées, 1958; Ramatou 2002).

Given that the British colonial policies allowed for the persistence of certain levels of tradition (Lund 2006; Odame-Ababio 2002), and given that the French colonial impact on water use and management was somewhat minimal largely because of the inconsistency of French policies in Burkina Faso, then Upper Volta, it can be said that both countries shared a common and basic level of informal cooperation rooted in tradition. This perhaps explains why transboundary water issues began to constitute a major concern in the Volta basin only from the mid-1990s, even despite the construction of major hydraulic works on the Volta River with considerable international implications— beginning in the 1960s with the construction of Ghana's Akosombo Dam and others such as Burkina Faso's Bagré Dam by 1994.

In terms of cooperation among the six riparian countries, Gao and Margolies (2009) observe that development agencies and research institutes are the external driving forces, while increasing water demand and emergence of more environmental issues constitute the internal driving forces. The external driving forces are illustrated by the fact that there had not been any transboundary formal collaboration among the six riparian countries in the post-colonial period until 1975, when due to the initiative of the World Health Organization, the six countries signed an agreement governing the operations of its Onchocerciasis (river blindness) Control Program. Even in this case, the cooperative effort was limited to the control of water-borne diseases, and not water sharing or management (Gao and Margolies 2009). Some form of cooperation based on immediate national interest tied to access to electricity also existed. Ghana's electric power utility corporation, the Volta River Authority (VRA) has been supplying electrical power through the Communaute Electrique du Benin (CEB) to the neighboring co-riparian Republic of Togo and Benin since December 1972, under an international agreement signed in 1969. Also, the Ghana-la Côte d'Ivoire Electrical Networks were inter-connected in June 1983. In addition, the VRA has been exchanging electrical power with its Ivorian counterpart, Energie Electrique de la Côte d'Ivoire (EECI), since February 1984 under the Inter-Government Protocol for the interconnection. Since 1993, EECI's role as an electrical utility has been taken over by a private consortium, Compagnie Ivorienne d'Eliectricite (Yankah 1999).

Actual formal water sharing or management cooperation, however, really did not begin until the 1990s, and this was when outside involvement in national water strategies of the basin's riparian countries led to considerations of transboundary issues (Lautze and Youkhana 2006). The seeds were sown in 1992, when Burkina Faso built the Bagré Dam without any consultation with downstream Ghana. Repairing the lack of communication between the two countries was rightly identified as one major goal for an initiative by some international donors such as the World Bank. An initiative, the Volta Basin Water Resources Management Initiative, consequently concentrated on capacity building at national and international levels of the riparian countries. The World Bank took an active role in promoting communication with respect to water issues between the two countries in the mid-1990s as part of this initiative. It was within that framework that the Bank invoked its transboundary waters policy whereby a country "proposing to execute any project which will regulate, abstract or otherwise change river flows must notify co-riparian states of its intentions so that each state may consider whether it wishes to lodge an objection" (Ministry of Works and Housing 1998; World Bank 1995). As a result, in 1996, when Burkina Faso proposed to build another dam at Ziga, it complied with the policy by consulting with Ghana. A Ghanaian delegation then visited Burkina Faso and signed a "No-Objection" agreement on the construction of the Ziga Dam.

Water sector reform processes in Ghana and Burkina Faso were also instituted in the late 1990s under the World Bank-sponsored Structural Adjustment Programs to better meet their respective economic objectives, reduce poverty, and alleviate the effects of increasing water stress. As a result, all natural water resources within the two countries were nationalized (van Edig et al. 2003; Ministère de L'Environment et de L'Eau du Burkina Faso 2001). This led to the establishment of new water resource institutions at different societal levels and sectors within a broader framework of large-scale decentralization. As a de-facto form of cooperation under the auspices of the World Bank, the Ghanaian Water Resources Commission and the Burkina Faso Direction Général de l'Eau created new water sector policies and transformed the national water resources into economic goods, placing water resources allocation decisions within a demand-based framework (Fuest and Haffner 2005). These formal actions thus reinforce the simultaneous customary and "modern" natural resources management regulations in the basin.

It was, however, in 2004—a century after the "Exchange of Notes between France and Great Britain relative to the Boundary between the Gold Coast and Soudan" implemented in 1906 to establish the colonial boundary and to regulate the use of the waters from one side of the boundary to the other, and which had been the sole transboundary protocol in place—that a new and significant international institution was established. 2004 thus marks a major turning point in the history of cooperation between Burkina Faso and Ghana when the Volta Basin Technical Committee (VBTC) was launched to modernize the regulation of water management at the international level (Vlek). In April of 2004 the governments of Ghana and Burkina Faso signed the "Ghana-Burkina Joint Declaration" (Lautze and Youkhana 2006) which acknowledged common water and environmental issues—an expression of the internal driving forces—and stated their desire to collaborate on management of shared water resources through a Volta Basin Technical Committee involving all riparian countries (Direction Générale de l'Inventaire des Ressources Hydrauliques 2004). This declaration was followed by a conference in Ouagadougou on July 29 and 30, 2004, attended by representatives from Benin, Burkina Faso, Côte d'Ivoire, Ghana, Mali, and Togo. All six countries accepted a series of agreements acknowledging the need for a transboundary management institution and a timeline for its creation. In November 2004 the VBTC was formed and held its first meeting in December of the same year (Direction Générale de l'Inventaire des Ressources Hydrauliques 2004). The VBTC's mandate was to pave the way for the development of a new transboundary organization, the Volta Basin Authority (VBA), comprising National Water Directorate representatives of the six riparian countries. The VBA had its headquarters in Ouagadougou in Burkina Faso, and the ministers in charge of water resources of the six riparian countries signed a Memorandum of Understanding (MOU) for the creation of the VBA in Ouagadougou on December 6, 2005. This MOU provided the main legal framework and other formalities required for the establishment and empowerment of the VBA (African Development Bank 2006). The VBA was formed in 2006. According to the African Development Bank (2006), the immediate goal of the VBA was to improve the transboundary water resources, other natural resources, and ecosystems management in the Volta basin for the benefit of all affected stakeholders of the riparian states. The long term development goal of the creation of the VBA, however, is to contribute to economic growth, reduced poverty, and enhanced livelihood of all stakeholders in the Volta basin in keeping with the principles of integrated water resources management including environmentally sustainable water management and development.

In 2004, in response to the need for transboundary coordination and cooperation regarding the management of the Volta basin waters, and to demonstrate how to apply an ecosystem approach into river basin management, the Water and Nature Initiative (WANI) of the International Union for the Conservation of Nature (IUCN) initiated the "Volta Water Governance Project," commonly known by its French acronym PAGEV (Projet d'Amélioration de la Gouvernance de l'Eau dans le Bassin de la Volta). Although the project is ultimately to be implemented in the whole basin, Burkina Faso and Ghana were selected as experimental states because they are the two among the six riparian countries that share the largest proportion of the Volta basin's area (Odame-Ababio 2008).

The project's development and implementation is being carried out by the IUCN Regional Program for Central and West Africa (IUCNPACO) in partnership with the West African Water Partnership (GWP-WA), Ghana's Water Resources Commission (WRC), and Burkina Faso's Directorate General for Water Resources (DGRE). It also receives financial support from the Swedish International Development Cooperation Agency (SIDA) and The Netherlands Directorate General for International Development Cooperation (DGIS). The PAGEV approach is based on three key components: a water resources information base improvement component, a pilot IWRM component, and an institutional and legislative improvement component. Some of the innovative approaches adapted by PAGEV to mobilize multi-stakeholder support for the joint management of the White Volta sub-basin of the Volta basin, for example, resulted in significant results in the first three years of project implementation (mid-2004 to September 2007) (Odame-Ababio 2008). These included:

a. The establishment of river bank protection committees in communities on both sides of the Ghana-Burkina Faso border. These committees have undertaken re-vegetation of nearly 16 km of river banks to reduce soil erosion and protect water quality. Fruit trees and fuel-wood trees have also been introduced to combine environmental management and provision of new livelihood options.
b. The establishment of a set of multi-stakeholder forums for water resources management. The forums operate at local, national, and transboundary levels, and are also designed to mix the different levels, with the aim of increasing involvement by local communities in transboundary water management.
c. Supporting communities to dig wells and rehabilitate an irrigation dam in Ghana. These initiatives have created benefits (i.e., dry season vegetable farming, water supply for rice cultivation) for the communities while at the same time working with them to build awareness and capacity in sustainable water management and conservation of natural resources.
d. The formulation of a Code of Conduct on the shared management of the Volta River system between Burkina Faso and Ghana. The process involved stakeholder consultation, national workshops, and joint validation workshops.
e. The compilation of knowledge and decision-support information to support planning, decision making, and monitoring of interventions in the basin through a water audit of the basin; the production of maps and the collection of socioeconomic data on the riparian communities in the pilot zone.

Globaler Wandel des Wasserkreislaufs (GLOWA), which is part of a program financed by the German Federal Ministry of Education and Research, has played a crucial role as an external force for cooperation in the basin (Vlek). Since 2000, the GLOWA-Volta Project (GVP) has sought ways to lay the groundwork for an IRWM. Its aim has been to develop a scientifically sound decision support system for the assessment, sustainable use, and development of the Volta basin's water resources. Also, the GVP has aimed at creating a basis for the development of innovative technologies and cost-effective strategies relating to climate and environmental protection, in particular for management of water resources (Van Edig et al. 2003). The GVP could thus be seen as one of the first projects to contribute to transboundary water co-operation (van Edig et al. 2003; van Edig et al. 2001; Andreini et al. 2002). The logical partner in this endeavor is the newly established VBA, which serves the six governments in the region. This scientific project also attempts to strengthen international efforts that are ongoing in the Volta basin such as by Green Cross International, the Global Environmental Facility (GEF), the United Nations Environment Program (UNEP), the European Union (EU), and the World Conservation Union (IUCN) (Lautze and Youkhana 2006). Overall, the project has sought the avoidance of conflict and the equitable access to water and water-related resources throughout the Volta basin.

More evidence of recent cooperation between Burkina Faso and Ghana is related to the Bagré Dam. In order to prevent the frequent spillage from the dam, which has for the past few years compounded the effects of floods in the upper east region of Ghana, the Burkinabe government has renovated and expanded the dam to enable it to hold more water to alleviate the downstream problems. In this regard, in 2008, the height of the dam was increased by 1.5 meters and renovations were done to strengthen its banks, at a cost of US$18 million, provided by the French Aid for International Development. This was in addition to earlier improvements made at the cost of US$33 million. The Burkinabe government acknowledges that further works need to be done to increase the capacity of the reservoir to limit the flooding from spillage, which has adverse effects in northern Ghana (Ghanaweb.com 2008).

Prior to 2004, each country had largely acted independently in harnessing the Volta River despite the protocol, which guaranteed the continuity of customary practices related to water withdrawal and use. At a local level, stakeholders were largely unaware of the colonial agreements, and certainly were not waiting for new international agreements. They have been coping as best they can, but as per the "Agreement between France and Great Britain relative to the frontier between French and British possessions from the Gulf of Guinea to the Niger (Southern Nigeria and Dahomey)," which permitted cross-border "native access," people from both countries cross the border in order to undertake different economic activities. For example, Ghanaian fishermen go to the

Bagré Dam in Burkina Faso to find new fish stocks; cattle herders who were displaced because of the introduction of larger irrigation projects around the Bagré Dam migrate seasonally to Ghana in order to find fallow land for grazing. Traditional courts successfully resolve problems related to the intrusion of Fulani cattle herders. Thus, communication structures exist and function across national boundaries. Likewise, social networks (marriage system) facilitate the access to land for people beyond the border (Vlek).

Despite these various forms of cooperation—formal and informal—so much more needs to be done. The establishment of the VBA stands out as the most significant institution to date regarding cooperation pertaining to water resource management in the Volta basin. Even in that case, Gao and Margolies (2009) point out that the institution has not been functional since stakeholders have not utilized it to plan projects or to resolve water conflicts. Three reasons for the VBA's lack of success have been pointed out: lack of institutional integration; unclear decision-making processes; and lack of transformation of the conventions and statutes into actions.

LACK OF INSTITUTIONAL INTEGRATION

Although the institutional structure for formal cooperation is largely established, the necessary lateral and vertical integration have still not been achieved. Laterally, the national institutions of water management possess differing levels of capacity. The most developed national water institution in the basin is the Ghanaian Water Resources Commission (WRC), a governmental body responsible for water allocation and management in Ghana. The WRC recognizes that national and international institutional capacity building and initiatives are intertwined (for example in the field of data exchange), hence it is designed to deal with national as well as with international management issues (van Edig et al. 2003). This institution takes a formal, top-down approach to water resources management. In contrast, its equivalent in Burkina Faso is highly uncoordinated; while its Malian counterpart relies on water law created in 1928 (van Edig et al. 2001). This discrepancy in capacity and resources among the member states is thus problematic for the work of the VBA. Also, the unequal relationships between participants tend to affect power dynamics in negotiations thereby negatively impacting on agreements. In some countries, many institutions are charged with responsibilities for managing water, food, and soil resources, which result in overlapping of responsibilities and difficulties in coordination for the VBA (Gao and Margolies 2009).

Vertically, there is a lack of integration between the VBA nations and the stakeholders at the lower levels, in the sense that there is a lack of involvement of the grassroots stakeholders. An active role of traditional leadership in water management, and traditional practices, which have evolved with the biophysical and cultural settings in the society, are generally sustainable; however, village water resources are expropriated and controlled in a top-down approach by agencies such as the WRC, a process that has occurred without consultation with local leaders or the provision of compensatory packages for the value of the resources lost. "Instead of providing incentives for traditional institutions to cooperate, the WRC's policy of neglecting traditional practices of water rights allocation, which is backed by the current rule of law, provides disincentives for cooperation by diminishing the chiefs' responsibilities and ability to collect funds" (Van Edig et al. 2002). This style of aggressive institutional behavior is not conducive to collaboration (Gao and Margolies 2009).

UNCLEAR DECISION-MAKING PROCESSES

The degree of success regarding VBA's water management is invariably tied to the characteristics of decision-making processes. Consequently, Gao and Margolies (2009) point out that the processes needed to spur action in the VBA are not explicitly defined, especially since the VBA is composed of National Water Directorate representatives of all the six riparian countries. It also ignores the needs of all stakeholders involved. By excluding civil society representatives, the VBA may create problems for the process, as spoilers may emerge and prevent sustainable agreements (Gao and Margolies 2009).

Another unclear aspect of the decision-making process relates to the fact that one of VBA's mandates is to authorize the development of infrastructure and projects planned by the various riparian countries—projects that could have substantial impact on the water resources of the basin. It is however not clear as to how this should be done in terms of coordination and the implications or externalities of such projects. This, Gao and Margolies (2009) point out, is a very important role that VBA can play in solving water-related conflicts in the basin, but there has not been a standard procedure created to allow VBA to carry out this role.

CONVENTIONS AND STATUTES HAVE NOT BEEN TRANSFORMED TO ACTIONS

The signed VBA convention and statues have largely not been enforced due to the absence of an effective mechanism to transform the already accepted rules into action. This is why flooding caused by the Bagré Dam in Burkina

Faso, for example, continues to be a cause of tension between Ghana and Burkina Faso.

As noted earlier, the opening of the floodgates of the Bagré Dam in 2007 was unilaterally decided by Burkina Faso, and Ghana was informed of the action much later. Gao and Margolies (2009) also point out that there is no mechanism for the member states to define problems and prioritize projects. The definition of the problems and the prioritization of the development projects necessarily require inputs from various stakeholders as well as data from the member states based on studies and assessments of the basin. However, such a data sharing system does not exist due to the fact that most of the riparian countries lack the funding and capacity to collect sufficient hydrologic and meteorological data, and the constraining roles of bureaucracy and red tape in the sharing of resources among different government agencies in these countries. It is quite evident that the many direct and indirect challenges facing the forthcoming VBA are rather complex, and in fact include land degradation concerns, wise use and sharing of scarce water resources, preservation of biodiversity, flood attenuation, mitigation of water borne diseases, reduction of aquatic weeds, coastal erosion mitigation, water quality aspects, and fisheries (Odame-Ababio 2008). Strengthening of transboundary water resources management may have benefits beyond the boundaries of the Volta basin through increased production of hydroelectricity, increased agriculture outputs, and enhanced fisheries. As the most significant institution on water resource management in the Volta asin, the VBA needs more effective governance of the already accepted rules of cooperation.

HOW TO FURTHER COOPERATION AMONG THE RIPARIAN COUNTRIES IN THE VOLTA RIVER BASIN

Despite tensions and concerns in urban Ghana regarding irrigation and drinking water development upstream of Lake Volta in general and in Burkina Faso in particular, there has not been any major conflict between the two countries. This suggests that there exists some limited degree of informal and formal cooperation like the recent establishment of the VBA. This provides the basis for further cooperation between these two and the other riparian countries, which could benefit from conscious efforts among those countries to avoid boiling conflicts, and the assistance of the international community and organizations like the IUCN, GCI, and GWP. Informally, there already exists a centripetal force which could be utilized as a basis for further cooperation in the basin based on:

a) The traditional foundations relating to culture, and rooted in religion, namely the shared similar traditional water management structures prior to the arrival of the British and the French in Ghana (Ramatou 2002). As discussed above, the VBA constitutes the primary basis for formal cooperation, albeit with some teething constraints and challenges such as the lack of institutional integration, unclear decision-making processes, and the lack of transformation of the conventions and statutes into actions. Regarding the lack of institutional integration among the membership of the VBA, it is suggested by Gao and Margolies (2009) that capacity-building efforts in the form of lateral integration are needed at the national level. In this regard, member countries which are best situated could provide support to their weaker counterparts. Ghana is the most appropriate actor in this sense, as the Ghana WRC has the most advanced water allocation methodology in the basin. The VBA should organize capacity training workshops for the member states and assist the member states to improve their water laws and policy. Funding and technical assistance from international development agencies or foreign aid will be necessary to support capacity-building efforts. Vertically, they suggest that integration should begin on the village level, eventually scaling to the national level and finally, to the international.

Gao and Margolies (2009) also note that water governance in the Volta River basin must take traditional values into account, especially since the traditional or religious leaders, for example, have control over various aspects of allocation and use of natural resources in rural Africa, and thus affect the right of the villagers to fish and farm. In relation to this, and mindful of the variations in custom and culture across the six riparian signatory countries, they suggest that the traditional leaders, namely the chief and highly respected senior members of the village, will need to be consulted regarding water disputes that occur among villagers. The resolution reached by those traditional leaders should then be final. Since the chief is entrusted with the land, site selection of any irrigation scheme at the village level must be agreed on by the chief. In incorporating such traditional systems, they suggest that it is must be done in a manner that is comprehensive but also feasible. Also, integration on the international scale will only be possible if cooperation is achieved among the grassroots village level and the national level, and NGOs become involved. Therefore, it is evident that for such an international basin management to be effective, the mechanism must also embrace a bottom-up approach to include the participation of grassroots actors.

As regards the unclear decision-making processes, many considerations, including the variations in custom and culture across the six riparian signatory countries, need to be taken into account in order to spur action in the VBA. First, the decision-making processes themselves must be defined, since it is unclear what kind of principles, procedures, and processes the VBA utilizes to negotiate policies and action plans. This is of particular significance given that the VBA's small coalition of actors comprising National Water Directorate representatives of the six countries may engender an exclusive, constraining process that, inter alia, may not meet the needs of all stakeholders involved. For example, by excluding other actors such as civil society representatives, the VBA may create problems for the process, as spoilers may emerge and prevent sustainable agreements. Although it may be unreasonable or impractical to include a multitude of actors with a stake in the process, the inclusion of other key decision-makers in the region would expand the possibilities for lasting agreements (Gao and Margolies 2009).

b) The subsequent colonial "Agreement between France and Great Britain relative to the frontier between French and British possessions from the Gulf of Guinea to the Niger (Southern Nigeria and Dahomey)," which permitted cross-border "native access" to water resources (The African Transboundary Water Law 2008; Gao and Margolies 2009).

Also, in order to enforce the conventions and the statutes, a long-term development strategy, which is currently nonexistent, should be created as a guiding document for the VBA and its member states to develop their respective water projects. This should be developed concurrently with a development plan based on this strategy that is reviewed on a regular basis (e.g., every five years) and that should be made available to the public. This necessarily requires that the member states provide the inputs for the development plan. Inputs from studies and assessments of the basin are also needed to make such a plan. Data sharing—hydrologic, meteorological, etc.—between the VBA and each of its member states and among the member states is thus essential for good planning and building cooperation and trust instead of bureaucracy and red tape. It is with respect to the inputs and assessments that Lautze and Youkhana (2006) point out that in order to share scientific knowledge and identify management options among the riparian countries, there is the need to acknowledge and to incorporate indigenous knowledge, communication structures, and networks as well. They therefore suggest that local under-standing of environmental processes and indigenous strategies to cope with the capricious nature of water and other environmental resources, have to be incorporated into international initiatives as well. This is because from their perspective, transboundary or trans-district water re-sources allocation decisions can be contested at the local level, where traditional structures of authority and power often determine the distribution of water (Opoku-Agyemang 2005) and where most decisions are made on the basis of customary practices as well as indigenous knowledge and belief systems. In other words, where local or indigenous allocation and decision-making protocols exist, international policies and regulation will have a limited impact unless these arrangements are recognized and properly accommodated. Participatory approaches to cooperation developed locally have often turned out to be sound strategies for conflict prevention, as demonstrated at the Bagré Dam and in the Nakambé River Basin (Kibi 2004). Consequently, attempts to establish transboundary water management structures therefore need to encompass local knowledge systems in order to develop an Integrated Water Resources Management system (IWRM) and to avoid water-related conflicts. This is also tied to the view that conflicts arise largely at the local level (Carius et al. 2004), hence the need to understand how local knowledge is used to address future water management needs, particularly in the case of transboundary waters as in the case of the Volta basin.

As to the lack of a mechanism for the member states to define problems and prioritize projects, it is suggested that the problems in the basin should be defined and the corresponding mitigation measures must be prioritized in a joint fact-finding mission carried out by all six riparian countries and other major stakeholders in the basin, such as representatives of traditional authority and environmental groups.

CONCLUSION

From a geographic perspective, this chapter has discussed the areas of current and potential conflict and cooperation among the six riparian countries of the Volta River basin in West Africa. It has focused primarily but not exclusively on transboundary cooperation and conflict between the downstream country of Ghana and the upstream country of Burkina Faso, which together constitute the main countries, the bulk of whose territories are drained by the Volta River system. Even though both countries are largely agrarian, Ghana's main use of the Volta River is tied to the generation of hydroelectric power primarily for urban and industrial use, while Burkina Faso's is tied to agriculture, particularly for irrigation. And despite the tensions and concerns felt in urban Ghana regarding irrigation and drinking water development upstream of Lake Volta in general and in Burkina Faso in particular, there has not been any major conflict between the two countries, which suggests that there exists some limited degree of informal and formal cooperation among the nations that could be harnessed for the good of all the countries sharing the basin. Informally, the traditional foundations relating to culture, and rooted in religion, namely the shared similar traditional water management structures prior to colonialism, and the subsequent colonial policies, which permitted cross-border "native access" to water resources, could be utilized as a basis for further cooperation. Formally, transboundary institutions like the VBA and other national and international institutions need to be developed. An important aspect of such institutions or mechanisms should be to facilitate communication and to monitor the agreements among the riparian countries. With these measures developed and nurtured, conflicts could be minimized in the Volta basin. Kofi Annan, the former Secretary General of the United Nations, was quoted in Carius et al. (2004) on transboundary water issues, in terms of conflict and cooperation: "Water problems of our world need not be only a cause of tension; they can also be a catalyst for cooperation . . . If we work together, a secure and sustainable water future can be ours."

REFERENCES

Acheampong, Steve, Y. 2010. "Opening of Bagré Dam spillway—For How Long Should This Annual Killing Ritual and Property Destruction Continue?"http://www.ghanaweb.com/GhanaHomePage/features/artikel.php?ID=190248. Accessed 5/19/2011.

African Development Bank. 2006. "Volta Basin Technical Committee: Support for the Creation of Volta Basin Authority—Appraisal Report." http://www.africanwaterfacility.org/fileadmin/uploads/awf/projects-activities/AWF_APPRAISAL_REPORT_ESTABLISHMENT_VOLTA_BASIN_AUTHORITY_13_MARCH.PDF. Accessed 5/5/11.

Africa News Online 1998. "Ghana and Burkina Faso Discuss Energy Crisis." At:http://www.africanews.org/west/stories/19980326_feat2.html.

Andah, W., and F. Gichuki. 2003. *Volta Basin Profile: Strategic Research for Enhancing Agricultural Water Productivity (Draft).* Accra: International Water Management Institute, Challenge Program on Water and Food.

Andah, W. and F. Gichuki, eds. 2005. *Volta River Basin Profile: Enhancing Agricultural Water Productivity through Strategic Research.* Sri Lanka: International Water Management Institute.

Andreini, M., N. van de Giesen, A. van Edig, M. Fosu, and W. Andah. 2000. "Volta Basin Water Balance." Zentrum für Entwicklungsforschung (ZEF)—Discussion Papers on Development Policy No. 21, Center for Development Research, Bonn, March 2000. http://www.zef.de/fileadmin/webfiles/downloads/zef_dp/zef-dp21–00.pdf. Accessed 4/22/2011.

Andreini, Marc, et al. 2002. "Water Sharing in the Volta Basin." Regional Hydrology: Bridging the Gap between Research and Practice (Proceedings of the Fourth

International FRIEND Conference, Cape Town, South Africa. March 2002), IAHS Pub. No. 274.

Buber, Martin. 1958. *I and Thou.* Translated by Ronald Gregor Smith. New York: Charles Scribner's Sons.

Carius, Alexander, et. al. 2004. "Water, Conflict and Cooperation." http://www.wilsoncenter.org/news/docs/Carius_Dabelko_Wolf.pdf. Accessed 5/18/11.

Diemer, Andie. 2008. "Bui Dam." Visions Magazine Spring 2008. http://bradhartland.com/Print%20Docs/Visions_BD.pdf. Accessed 4/16/11.

Direction Générale de l'Inventaire des Ressources Hydrauliques. 2004. "The Volta Basin Countries: (Benin-Burkina-Cote d'Ivoire-Ghana-Mali-Togo) Heading for a Basin Organization." Government of Burkina Faso.

Falk, D. and Ü. J. Attfield. (Undated). "Sourou (Burkina Faso, Sahel)—Regional Self-Sufficiency in Farming." Diercke International Atlas. http://www.diercke.com/kartenansicht.xtp?artId=978–3-14–1007909&seite=159&id=17661&kartennr=4. Accessed 4/11/11

Fekete, B. M., C. J. Vörösmarty, and W. Grabs. 2000. "Global, Composite Runoff Fields Based on Observed River-Discharge and Simulated Balances." CD-rom, Univ. of New Hampshire. Durham, New Hampshire, USA and Global Runoff Data Centre, Koblenz, Germany.

Food and Agriculture Organization of the United Nations (FAO). 1997- Irrigation Potential in Africa: A basin Approach. Chapter 6: Review of Existing Information on Irrigation Potential- the Volta Basin, FAO Land and Water Bulletin 4. http://www.fao.org/docrep/w4347e/w4347e00.htm, accessed 1/20/11.

Fuest, Veronika, and Stefan A. Haffner. 2005. Mapping the Water Sector of Ghana. An Inventory of Institutions and Actors. Unpublished paper. Bonn: Center for Development Research. In Vlek, Paul L.G. Undated. "Transboundary Management of Natural Resources—The Example of Volta Basin." http://www.ghana.diplo.de/Vertretung/ghana/en/03/Vlek/Volta.html. Accessed 5/5/11.

Gao, Yongxuan and Amy Margolies. 2009. Transboundary Water Governance in the Volta River Basin. https://wikis.uit.tufts.edu/confluence/display/aquapedia/Transboundary+Water+Governance+in+the+Volta+River+Basin. Aquapedia, Tufts University. Accessed 5/18/2011.

Ghanaweb.com. 2008. "Bagre Dam in Burkina Faso Expanded to Prevent Frequent Spill Over," General News of Monday, July 14. http://www.ghanaweb.com/GhanaHomePage/NewsArchive/artikel.php?ID=146821

Ghanaweb.com. 2010. "Dam Spill Kills 17 in Ghana." General News of Friday, September 10. http://www.ghanaweb.com/GhanaHomePage/NewsArchive/artikel.php?ID=190164. Accessed 5/6/11.

Ghana World Wide. 1998. Rawlings Receives Ministers of Benin and Togo. At:http://www.ghana.com/politics/p67.htm.

GLOWA. 2008. "Global Change and the Hydrological Cycle: Towards Sustainable Development." http://www.glowa-elbe.de/pdf/glowaiii/GLOWA_Broschuere_2008.pdf.Globaler Wandel des Wasserkreislaufes. Koblenz, Germany. Accessed 5/19/2011.

Government of Ghana. 1961. "The Volta River Project," Statement by the Government of Ghana, 20th February 1961, WP No. 1/61, The Ministry of Information. The State Publishing Corporation, Accra-Tema, Ghana.

Gyau-Boakye, P. and Tumbulto, J. W. 2000. "The Volta Lake and Declining Rainfall and Streamflows in the Volta River Basin" *Environment, Development and Sustainability* 2: 1–10.

Haftnedorn, Helga. 2004. *Water and International Conflict.* [Internet] http://www .ciaonet.org. April 27.

Hart, D. 1980. *The Volta River Project: A Case Study in Politics and Technology.* Edinburgh: University Press.

Kibi, N. 2004. "Resolving Water Conflicts through Participatory Decision Making: A Case Study from the Nakanbé River Basin." http://www.iascp2004.org.mx/ downloads/paper_110f.pdf.

Klare, Michale T. *2001. Resource Wars: The New Landscape of Global Conflict.* New York: Owl Books.

Lautze, J., B. Barry, and E. Youkhana. 2006: "Changing Interfaces in Volta Basin Water Management: Customary, National and Transboundary." Zentrum für Entwicklungsforschung (ZEF) Center for Development Research Working Paper Series 16. University of Bonn. Germany. http://www.zef.de/fileadmin/webfiles/ downloads/zef_wp/wp16.pdf. Accessed 4/9/11.

Leemhuis, C., G. Jung, R. Kasei, and J. Liebe. 2009. "The Volta Basin Water Allocation System:Assessing the Impact of Small-Scale Reservoir Development on the Water Resources of the Volta Basin, West Africa." *Advances in Geosciences* 21: 57–62. http://www.advgeosci.net/21/57/2009/adgeo-21–57–2009.pdf. Accessed 2/15/11.

Ministère de L'Environnement et de L'Eau. 2001. Etat des lieux des ressources en eau du Burkina Faso et de leur cadre de gestion. Government of Burkina Faso. In Vlek, Paul L.G. Undated. "Transboundary Management of Natural Resources— The Example of Volta Basin." http://www.ghana.diplo.de/Vertretung/ghana/en/03/ Vlek/Volta.html. Accessed 5/5/11.

Ministry of Works and Housing (MoWH). 1998a. *Ghana's Water Resources: Management Challenges and Opportunities.* Accra: Ministry of Works and Housing.

Ministry of Works and Housing. 1998b. *Institutions and Participation.* Accra: Environmental Management Associates Ltd..

Obeng-Asiedu, P. 2004. "Allocating Water Resources for Agricultural and Economic Development in the Volta Basin." European University Studies, Series 5, Economics and Management, Vol. 3096.

Odame-Ababio, K. 2002. *The Changing Focus in the Development and Management of Ghana's Water Resources.* Accra: Ghana Water Resources Commission.

Odame-Ababio, Kwame. 2008. "Stimulating Stakeholders' Support for Managing Shared Waters—Experiences from the Volta Basin." Paper presented at the IV International Symposium on Transboundary Waters Management, Thessalonica, Greece. October 2008.

Ofori Amoah, Abigail. "Water Wars and International Conflict." http://academic
.evergreen.edu/g/grossmaz/OFORIAA/. Accessed 3/26/2011.

Opoku-Agyemang, M. 2001a. "Shifting Paradigms: Towards the Integration of Customary Practices into the Environmental Law and Policy in Ghana." Proceedings from Securing the Future International Conference on Mining and the Environment. Skelleftea, Sweden.

Opoku-Agyemang, M. 2001b. "Water Resources Commission Act and the Nationalisation of Water Rights in Ghana." Proceedings from Securing the Future International: Conference on Mining and the Environment: Skelleftea, Sweden.

Opoku-Agyemang, M. 2005. "The Role of the District Assemblies in the Management of Transdistrict Water Basins in Ghana." Working Paper at the International Workshop on African Water Laws: Plural Legislative Framework.

Owusu, J. Henry. 1998. "Current Convenience; Desperate Deforestation: Ghana's Adjustment Program and the Forestry Sector." *The Professional Geographer* 50 (4): 418–436.

Oxfam. 2000. Burkina Faso—Country Report by On the Line. http://www.ontheline .org.uk/mawards/downloads/burkina.doc.

Ramatou, T. 2002. "La Place du savoir traditionnel dans la géstion des ressources en eau dans le bassin du Nakambé." From Forum technique et de communication sur les comités de gestion des points d'eau en milieux et semi-urbain dans le bassin du Nakambe au Burkina Faso. International Development and Research Center: Ottawa.

Reenberg, A., P. Oksen, and J. Svendsen. 2003. "Land Use Change Vis-a-Vis Agricultural dDevelopment in Southeastern Burkina Faso: The Field Expansion Dilemma." *Geografisk Tidsskrift, Danish Journal of Geography* 103 (2).

TFDD. 2004. Transboundary Freshwater Dispute Database. Available on-line at:http://www.transboundarywaters.orst.edu/.

The African Transboundary Water Law. http://www.africanwaterlaw.org/html/ basinsearchresult.asp. Accessed 5/5/11.

Turton, Anthony. 2004 *Water and Conflict in an African Context.* http://www.accord. org 27.

Van Edig, A., S. Engel, and W. Laube. 2002. Ghana's Water Institutions in the Process of Reform: From the International to the Local Level. GLOWA Volta Project; 31–51.

Van Edig, Annette, Nick van de Giesen, Marc Andreini, and Wolfram Laube. 2003. "Transboundary, Institutional, and Legal Aspects of the Water Resources Commission in Ghana." *Center for Development Research* (2003): 1–10.

Vlek, Paul L. G. Undated. "Transboundary Management of Natural Resources—The Example of Volta Basin." http://www.ghana.diplo.de/Vertretung/ghana/en/03/ Vlek/Volta.html. Accessed 5/5/11.

Yankah, E. 1999. "What is the Volta River Authority?" The Unofficial Volta River Authority Home Page. http://ericyankah.tripod.com/vrabinfo.html. Accessed 5/6/11.

Youkhana, Eva, Charles Rodgers, and Oliver Korth. 2006. "Transboundary Water Management in the Volta Basin." Extended Abstract for the III International Symposium on Transboundary Water Management., University of Castilla-La Mancha Ciudad Real, and co-organised by UNESCO and SAHRA.30th May—2nd June 2006, Ciudad Real, Spain. http://www.zef.de/fileadmin/webfiles/downloads/press/transboundary_water_managemet_volta.pdf. Accessed 3/15/11.

Chapter Eight

Conclusion

Dhirendra K. Vajpeyi

A review of the preceding chapters in this anthology and the pertinent literature related to global water scarcity illustrates that the emerging role of water for human development, and judicious usage of transboundary rivers by riparian countries, are issues that will define economic and political relationships in many regions, especially in the most water-stressed regions of the world. Several states have already adopted harnessing of water—using new technologies not only to construct mega-hydroelectric projects but even diverting the direction of rivers—as part of their national security agenda, therefore injecting a defense component to their water policies, raising concerns and anxieties among neighboring countries that share transboundary rivers with them. These case studies point out that while low intensity diplomatic tensions have emerged on water sharing between China and India; Pakistan, Bangladesh, and India; Turkey, Iraq, and Syria; and Egypt and Ethiopia, no major armed conflicts or confrontations have taken place so far. Most of these disputes and disagreements have been resolved either by bilateral or multilateral efforts, even in the most volatile areas such as South Asia. However, unplanned minor incidents unrelated to water could ignite more serious confrontations. Nationalism, defined in narrow terms, is "the last infirmity of the noble mind." Water may not be the sole trigger factor in starting an armed conflict between states with a history of distrust and severe tensions. Water disputes as a shadow issue could be used as a pretext for conflict. Other factors, such as territorial disputes (India-Pakistan; China-India), ethnic tensions (Central Asia), and other power equations (the Middle East) might be the real reasons to justify conflicts.

"Water scarcity may amplify conventional international security problems related to militarization, weak institutions, and ethnic and other sources of hostility and tension" (Chou et. al 1997, 98). Two major case studies in this collection (Chapters 4 and 5) are excellent examples of the above concerns. In South Asia, mainly India-Pakistan, and the Middle East, mainly Israel-Jordan and Syria, water-sharing issues have brought these countries almost to the brink of war. In both cases, water has been an excuse, a pretext, and a shadow issue to settle other scores. Territorial issues have created a hostile environment in both regions. In the Indian subcontinent, potential for an armed conflict, however limited, could engulf India and Pakistan in an armed confrontation. Both have several non-water issues such as Kashmir. They have fought four wars. Several major rivers that flow into Pakistan originate from Kashmir. In recent years India has repeatedly announced its intentions to build hydroelectric projects by reducing the flow of water to Pakistan's breadbasket state of Punjab. In both countries, ultra-nationalist groups have raised threatening voices on water issues, demanding that their respective governments should take a harder stand, including armed actions. Pakistan is almost a failed state, a hub of international jihad extremists and terrorists, and lawlessness with an obsessive fear of India, and could launch a mis-guided adventure such as in Kargil to distract its population's attention from domestic problems. India-China disputes over their border and water sharing are less likely to produce a serious armed confrontation. Despite mistrust of each other, and recent acrimony on water sharing, they have diplomatically diffused these tensions. Both countries are stable and are emerging as global economic and political powers. Both stand to lose too much in an event of serious armed confrontation. Hence, both will hurl verbal threats and a bar-rage of propaganda at each other but will prefer to settle into an unsettled cold war on sharing of water. This is the case at least for the near future.

The Middle East, however, presents a quite different scenario. It is one of the most unstable, violent, and volatile regions in the world. Arab-Israeli, Shi'a (Iran and Bahrain), Sunni (mainly Arabs), and other ethnic tribal ten-sions (Kurds, Baluch) are real issues that have plagued the region for a long time. It is one of the regions where armed actions (Israel-Jordan) have taken place on the issue of transboundary water sharing (Chapter 3). In other parts of the Middle East several factors will determine water-sharing relation-ships between Turkey, Syria, Iraq, Egypt, and other countries. The most important of these factors is the power equation between these countries. Turkey—militarily, economically, and politically—is the predominant, stable country. Iraq and Syria, individually and collectively, are not in a position to challenge Turkey on any issue including Turkey's unilateral water resource utilization policies. Syria and Iraq are too unstable and weak to challenge Turkey (Chapter 2). At least for the present, a similar situation exists between Egypt and other upstream countries sharing the waters of the Nile

(Chapter 3). The current power equation favors Egypt; however, political and economic changes and massive assertiveness of the countries in the region might change the equation. In Central Asia, despite its economic stagnation, political corruption, authoritarian regimes, instability, and ethnic tensions, the possibility of an armed confrontation between these "Stans" is very remote, mainly due to the involvement and commitment of international regimes and organizations such as the World Bank in helping these countries to negotiate. However, ethnic and economic tensions do exist and have the potential to create low intensity conflicts and political instability in this very strategic region (Chapter 6). In West Africa, international involvement, traditional value systems, and domestic efforts have kept differences on water sharing issues to a very manageable non-confrontational stage. Factors such as territorial disputes, ethnic tensions, and egocentric political leaders and bureaucrats have, by and large, diffused misunderstandings and differences (Chapter 7). The above review presents us with the following:

Table 8.1. Water Resource Conflicts and International Regional Security

Region/Countries	Degree of Conflict Potential
Middle East:	
a. Israel-Arabs	High
b. Turkey-Iraq-Syria	Low
c. Egypt and others	Medium-Low
South Asia	
a. India-Pakistan	High
b. India-Bangladesh	Low
c. India-Nepal	Low
d. India-China	Medium-Low
Central Asia	Medium-Low
West Africa (Ghana-Burkina Faso)	Low

Our study also pinpoints several economic, political, environmental, and demographic factors, which have potential to create a confrontational situation between neighbors sharing transboundary rivers and lakes. They include:

a. Increased demand and reduced water supply due to severe droughts, climate change, and population explosion in other parts of the world besides China and India.

b. Miscalculation on the part of water policy planners, and more importantly by politicians, in taking unilateral actions without considering
   the needs of other riparians—the hubris factor. Conflicts may also arise
   when upstream communities release or restrict water flows without adequately warning downstream stakeholders.
c. Territorial disputes and ethnic tensions.
d. Any combination of the above.
e. Absence of coordination and mutual trust.
f. Absence of an institutional framework and arrangements to resolve
   disputes, policymaking, and implementation. Unclear decision-making
   process.

In view of the above discussion, certain policy observations could be made
to create a more conducive and less conflict-prone regional-international
environment to settle water resource conflicts. First, regional and bilateral
arrangements are more effective than externally brokered arrangements. They
tend to thwart political conflicts in a more effective manner. In most of the
cases, water-sharing disputes are between neighbors, and whether they like it
or not they have to accommodate their differences or live in constant fear and
anxiety. Secondly, however, the crucial role of international arrangements,
organizations, and treaties should not be minimized. International organizations not only bring new ideas and approaches but also act as honest brokers
in solving disputes. Efforts should be made to chart more comprehensive,
internationally acceptable water laws, and strongly support the existing ones
such as the U.N. Convention on the Law of the Non-Navigational Uses of
International Waterourses. Internationally arranged mediations can serve a
very useful function, especially at the earlier phases of misunderstanding.
Multilateral aid organizations and nongovernmental agencies, such as the
World Bank, World Water Forum, and regional development banks have
much to offer from their experiences in other parts of the world. In the
1950s, the World Bank facilitated the Indus Water Treaty between India and
Pakistan. Several donors have played a crucial and constructive role in the
Central Asian Republics. These agencies need support from the international
community. At present, several major international resolutions and laws
stipulate codes of conduct on the usage of transboundary rivers and lakes.
They mandate that states that share an international watercourse cooperate,
communicate, and coordinate with each other to avoid conflicts. According to
Wolf (1999, 3–30), equitable distribution of the water is the heart of sharing
arrangements.

Thirdly, the international community under an umbrella must not only
formulate water-sharing policies but also have efficient and effective water

regimes. Water is too precious and important of a resource to be wasted. Billions of people depend on it for their everyday sustenance. It affects every aspect of human life and must be considered as one of the most important human rights. Humanity cannot survive without clean, unpolluted water. Conflicts and confrontations on sharing water will not solve the problem. Cooperation will. Lastly, modern organizational techniques to diffuse water tensions must not discard or ignore communitybased, old, informal ways. These old ways have worked very well in many societies where traditional rules are still highly respected and valued. To quote Kofi Annan, "Water problems of our world need not to have only a cause of tension; they can also be a catalyst for cooperation. If we work together, a secure and sustainable water future can be ours."

REFERENCES

Wolf, Aron T. 1999. "Criteria for Equitable Allocation: The Heart of International Water Conflicts." *National Resource Forum* 23:
Chou, Sophie. et al. 1997. "Water Scarcity in River Basins as a Security Problem."In *Environmental Change and Security Project*, 96–105. Washington: Woodrow Wilson Center.

Selected Bibliography

Ahmad Tufail, 2009. *Pakistan's Water Concerns: Water Disputes between India and Pakistan- A Potential Casus Belli*, Noor Ul Haq and Muhammad Nawaz Khan (eds.), http://www.henryjacksonsociety.org/stories.asp?id=1230, 4–5. July 31.

Ahmed, Q. K., Biswas, A. K., and Rangachari, R., 2001. *Ganges, Brahmaputra, Meghna Region: A Framework for Sustainable Development*, Dhaka: The University Press Limited.

Andah, W., and Gichuki, F. (ed.), 2005. *Volta River Basin Profile: Enhancing Agricultural Water Productivity through Strategic Research*. Sri Lanka International Water Management Institute.

Bagis, A. I., 1997. "Turkey's Hydropolitics of the Euphrates-Tigris Basin," *Water Resources Development*. Vol. 13, 567–581.

Bandyopadhyay, Jayanto, 1988. "The Ecology of Drought and Water Scarcity," *Ecologist*, Vol. 18, Issues 2/3.

Barnett, J., and Ager, N., 2007. "Climate Change, Human Security, and Violent Conflict," *Journal of Political Geography*, 26 (6) 639–655.

Briscoe, John, et al., 2005. *India's Water Economy: Bracing for a Turbulent Future*. Washington: World Bank, 4.

Brown, Lester R. 1995. *"Who Will Feed China?"* New York: W. W. Norton and Company, Inc.

Brunée, J., and Toope, S. J., 1997. "Environmental security and freshwater resources: Ecosystem regime building," *The American Journal of International Law*. Vol. 91, 26–59.

Chou, Sophie, BeZark, Ross, and Wilson, Anne, 1997. "Water Scarcity in River Basins as a Security Problem," in *Environmental Change and Security Project*, Washington, D.C. Woodrow Wilson Center. 96–105. http://wilsoncenter.org/topics/pubsacf26e.pdfaccess20070726.

Conca, K., and Dabelko, G. D., 1997. *Environmental Peacemaking*. Washington: Woodrow Wilson Center.

Davutoglu, A., 2010. "Turkey's zero-problems foreign policy," *Foreign Policy*, 20 May, available at http://www.foreignpolicy.com/articles/201 ys_zero_problems_foreign_policy.

de Chazournes, L. B., 2006. "The Aral Sea basin: legal and institutional aspects of governance." *The Multi-Governance of Water: Four Case Studies*. Tamiotti, L., Allouche, J., and Finger, M. (eds.). New York: State University of New York Press. 147–171.

Detraz, Nicole, and Betsill, Michele M., 2009 "Climate Change and Environmental Security for Whom the Discourse Shifts," *International Studies Perspectives*, 10.

Dinar, Shlomi, 2010. "Scarcity and Cooperation along International Rivers," *Global Environmental Politics*, February. 109–135.

Falkenmark, M., Lundquist, J., and Widstrand, C., 1989. Macro-scale water scarcity requires micro-scale approaches: Aspects of vulnerability in semi-arid development. *Natural Resources Forum*, Vol. 13, no. 4: 258–267.

Elhance, Arun P., 1997. "Conflict and cooperation over water in the Aral Sea basin." *Studies in Conflict & Terrorism*. Vol. 20. No. 2. 207–218.

Foster, Gregory D., 1989. "Global Demographic Trends to the Year 2010: Implications for National Security," *The Washington Quarterly*, Spring.

Garg, S. K., 1999. *International and Interstate River Water Dispute*, New Delhi: Manoher.

Gargan, Edward A., 2002. *The River's Tale: A Year on the Mighty Mekong*. New York: Alfred A. Knoff.

Glantz, Michael H., 1998. "Creeping environmental problems in the Aral Sea basin." In *Central Eurasian Water Crisis: Caspian, Aral, and Dead Seas*, Kobori, Iwao, and Glantz, Michael H. (eds.). New York: United Nations University Press. 25–52.

Gleditsh, Nils Peter, 1998. "Armed Conflict and Environment: A Critique of the Literature," *Journal of Peace Research*, Vol. 35 (3). 381–400.

Gleditsch, Nils et al., 2006. "Conflicts Over Shared Waters: Resource Scarcity or Fuzzy Boundaries," *Political Geography*, Vol. 25. 361–382.

Gleick, Peter H. (ed.), 1993. "*Water in Crisis: A Guide to the World's Fresh Water Resources*," New York: Oxford University Press.

Gleick, Peter H., 2008. *Water Conflict Chronology*, Oakland, Pacific Institute www.worldwater.org/conflictintro.htm.

Goldman, Michael, 2007. "How "Water for All!" Policy became hegemonic: The Power of the World Bank and its transnational policy networks." *Geoforum*.

Gulati, Chandrika J., 1988. *Bangladesh: Liberalism to Fundamentalism*, New Delhi: Manoher

Gulhati, N. D., 1973. "Indus Waters Treaty: An Exercise in International Mediation," Bombay: Allied.

Gupta, Sisir, 1960. "The Indus Water Treaty," *Foreign Affairs Reports*, Vol. 9, no. 12

Gyawali, Dipak, and Ajaya, Dixit, 1999. "Mahakali Impasse and Indo-Nepal Water Conflict," *Economic and Political Weekly*, Vol. 34, No. 9, Feb. 27—Mar. 5, 553–564.

Hart, D., 1980. *The Volta River project: A case study in Politics and Technology.* Edinburgh: University Press.

Harris, L. M., and Alatout, S., 2010. Negotiating hydro-scales, forging states: Comparison of the upper Tigris/Euphrates and Jordan River Basins. *Political Geography.* Vol. 29:148–156.

Hirji, Rafik, and Davis, Richard, 2009. "Environmental Flows in Water Resources Policies," *Plans and Projects.* World Bank Publications. 49–51.

Homer-Dixon, Thomas, 1999. *Environment Security and Violence*, Princeton: Princeton University Press.

Iyer, R. Ramaswamy. "Dispute and Resolution: The Ganges Water Treaty," *Indian Foreign Policy Agenda for the 21st Century*, (Vol. 2), New Delhi: Foreign Service Institute.

Jongerden, J., 2010. Dams and politics in Turkey: Utilizing water, developing conflict. *Middle East Policy.* Vol. 17, no. 10, 137–143.

Joshi, Bhuvan Lal, 1951. *Indo-Nepal Economic Cooperation*, Kathmandu; Indian Cooperation Mission.

Kaplan, Robert, 2010. *Monsoon- The Indian Ocean and the Future of American Power*, New York: Random House.

Karaev, Zainiddin, 2005. "Water Diplomacy in Central Asia." *Middle East Review of International Affairs.* 63–69.

Kay, R. Gresswell, and Huxley, Anthony (eds.), 1965. *Standard Encyclopedia of the World's Rivers and Lakes*, London: Weidenfield & Nickelson Ltd.

Khadka, Narayan, 1991. *Foreign Aid, Poverty and Stagnation in Nepal*, New Delhi: Vikas.

Khurshid, Begum, 1987. *Tension Over the Farakka Barrage, A Techno-Political Tangle in South Asia*, Dhaka: Calcutta Port Trust.

Khor, Martin, 2008. 'The Food Crisis, Climate Change, and the Independence of Sustainable Agriculture' *Third World Network.* Penang, Malaysia. www.townside .org.sq/title/end/pdf/end08.polf.

Kibaroglu, A., 2008. The role of epistemic communities in offering new cooperation frameworks in the Euphrates-Tigris rivers system. *Journal of International Affairs.* Vol. 61, no. 2, 183–198.

Kibaroglu, A., Klaphake, A., Kramer, A., Scheumann, W., and Carius, A., 2005. *Cooperation on Turkey's transboundary waters: Final report—October 2005.* Berlin: Adelphi Research.

Kibi, N., 2004. "Resolving Water Conflicts through participatory Decision making: A Case Study from the Nakanbé River Basin" http://www.iascp2004.org.mx/ downloads/paper_110f.pdf. Quoted in Youkhana et. al.2006.

Klare, Michael, 2006. "Resource Wars," *Foreign Affairs*, Vol. 80 (3). 49–61.

Klare, Michael T., 2001. *Resource Wars: The New Landscape of Global Conflict.* New York: Owl Books. 2001

Kolars, J., 1994. "Problems of international river management: The case of the Euphrates," *International Waters of the Middle East from Euphrates-Tigris to Nile*, (ed.) Asit Biswas. Oxford: Oxford University Press. 44–94.

Kolars, J. F., and Mitchell, W. A., 1991. *The Euphrates River and the Southeast Anatolia Development Project.* Carbondale and Edwardsville: Southern Illinois University Press.

Kut, G., 1993. "Burning waters: The hydropolitics of the Euphrates and Tigris," *New Perspectives on Turkey.* Vol. 9, 1–17.

Lamners, Richard B., et al., 2000. 'Global Water Resources: Vulnerability from Climate Change and Population Growth.' *Science.* 289. 54–77.

Lauener, Paul, 2010. "A Sea returns to life, a Sea slowly dies." *New Internationalist,* November 1. 16–19.

Li Ling, 1990. *How Tibet's Water Will Save China.* Beijing, Ministry of Water Development

Mattoo, Amitabh, 2010. "Pakistan's Water Concerns," *News International* (Rawalpindi), May 11.

McCully, P., 2001. *Silenced Rivers: The Ecology and Politics of Large Dams.* London: Zed Books.

Murakami, Masahiro, 1995. *Managing Water for Peace in the Middle East: Alternative Strategies,* Tokyo: United Nations University Press.

Murthi, Y. K., 1975. *Souvenir: Farakka Barrage Project,* Calcutta.

Nepal, B. H., and Alam, Imtiaz (eds.), 2001. *Water Resources Strategy—Nepal.* Kathmandu: Ministry of Water Resources.

NICOH Nepal India Cooperation on Hydropower, Independent Power Producers' 2006. New Delhi: Association Nepal Confederation of Indian Industry, January 2006.

O'Hara, S., 2000. "Central Asia's water resources: contemporary and future management issues." *Water Resources Development.* 423–441.

Odame-Ababio, K., 2002. *The Changing Focus in the Development and Management of Ghana's Water Resources.* Accra: Ghana Water Resources Commission.

Peachey, Everett J. 2004. "The Aral Sea Basin Crisis and Sustainable Water Management in Central Asia." *Journal of Public and International Affairs.* 15: 1–20.

Pomeranz, Kenneth, 2009. "The Great Himalayan Watershed: Water Shortages, Mega Projects and Environmental Politics in China, India, and Southeast Asia," *Asia Pacific Journal,* Vol. 30. July 27. 2–9.

Postel, Sandra, 1996. "*Dividing the Waters: Food Security, Ecosystem Health, and the New Politics of Scarcity,*" Washington D.C., Worldwatch Institute Paper no. 132.

Qureshi, M. L., 1981. *Survey of Economy: Resources and Prospects of South Asia,* Colombo: Marga Institute.

Ragnhild, Nordas, et al., 2007. 'Climate Change and Conflict,' *Political Geography.* Vol. 27.

Raleigh, Clionadh, and Urdal, Henrik, 2007. "Climate Change, Environmental Degradation, and Armed Conflict," *Political Geography* (26) 674–694.

Rao, K. L., 1975. *India's Water Wealth, Its Assessment, Uses and Projections,* New Delhi: Orient Longman.

Reuveny, Rafel, 2007. "Climate Change- Induced Migration and Violent Conflict" *Political Geography,* Vol. 26, 656–673.

Sinha, Rajesh, 2006. "Two Neighbors and a Treaty: Baglihar Project in Hot Waters," *Economic and Political Weekly*, February 18. 81–87.

Spoor, Max, 1998. "The Aral Sea Basin Crisis: Transition and Environment in Former Soviet Central Asia." *Development and Change*. 29. 409–435.

Spoor, Max, and Krutov, Anatoly, 2003. "The 'Power of Water' in a Divided Central Asia." *Perspectives on Global Development & Technology*. 593–614.

Sridhar, 2005. "Indus Water Treaty," *Security Research Review*

Starr, Joyce R., 1991. "Water Wars," *Foreign Policy*, Spring.

Tenkin, A., and Williams, P. A., 2011. *Geo-Politics of the Euro-Asia Energy Nexus: The European Union, Russia and Turkey*. Houndsmills, New York: Palgrave MacMillan.

Upreti, B. C., 1993. *Politics of Himalayan River Waters*, New Delhi: Nirmala Publications

U.S. Congress. Senate. Committee on Foreign Relations. "Avoiding Water Wars: Water Scarcity and Central Asia's Growing Importance for Stability in Afghanistan and Pakistan." 112th Congress. 1st sess., 2011. Committee Print, 1–22.

Vajpeyi, Dhirendra, and Zhang, Tingting, 1998. "Dam or Not to Dam: India's Narmada River," *Water Resource Management-A Comparative Perspective*, Vajpeyi, Dhirendra (ed.), London: Praeger. 93–106.

Verghese, B. G., 1990. *Waters of Hope, Himalaya-Ganga Cooperation for a Billion People*. Oxford: Oxford-IBH.

Vinogradov, Sergei, 1996. "Transboundry water resources in the former Soviet Union: Between Conflict and Cooperation." *Natural Resources Journal*. 393–415.

Warikoo, I. K., 2001. "Peace as Process: Reconciliation and Conflict Resolution in South Asia," Ranabir, Samaddar, and Helmut, Reifeld (eds.), *'Perspectives of the Indus Water Treat,'* New Delhi: Manohar Publications.

Williams, Rushbrook, 1955. *'The Indus Canals Water Dispute,'* *Leader*, Allahabad, 5 June.

Wegerich, Kai, 2008. "Hydro-hegemony in the Amu Darya Basin." *Water Policy*. 71–88.

Weinthal, Erika, and Watters, Kate, 2010. "Transnational environmental activism in Central Asia: the coupling of domestic law and international conventions." *Environmental Politics*. 782–807.

Weinthal, Erika, 2000. 'Making waves: third parties and international mediation in the Aral Sea Basin.' Greenberg, M., et al. (eds.), *Words over War: Mediation and Arbitration to Prevent Deadly Conflict*. Lanham: Roman and Littlefield.

Yuksel, I., 2010. "Energy production and sustainable energy policies in Turkey," *Renewable Energy*. Vol. 35, 1469–1475.

Zawahari, Neda, 2008. "International Rivers and National Security: The Euprhrates, Ganges Brahmaputra, Indus, Tigris, and Yarmuk Rivers," *Natural Resources Forum*, Vol. 32, no. 1, 280–289.

Index

About the Editor and Contributors

Pia Malhotra-Arora holds a M.A. in International Relations from New York University. Presently she is a senior sub-editor on International Relations with DNA Newspaper, Mumbai (India). She has extensively published on Watershed Management and other issues related to water disputes between Nepal, India, Bangladesh and China.

Brittany Brannon is presently a Graduate Student at Portland State University, Oregon. Her research interests include Environmental Policy, Disaster Management and Sustainable Development.

J. Henry Owusu has a Ph.D from the University of Iowa specializing in Regional Development. Presently he is an Associate Professor of Economic and Cultural Geography and African Development at the University of Northern Iowa, Cedar Falls, Iowa. He also is a research associate of the International Institute. His research focuses on Industrialization, International Development Policies and Development in Sub-Saharan Africa, particularly Ghana, Tropical Timber Trade, the Environment and development in Sub-Saharan Africa, regional economic restructuring, decentralization, Local Livelihoods and Sustainable Forest Management in Sub-Saharan Africa. He has published in several scholarly journals such as *the Professional Geographer, Journal of African Economies, The Journal of Modern African Studies, African Geographical Review, and Review of Human Factor Studies.*

Sanghamitra Patnaik obtained her Ph.D from the School of International Studies, Jawaharlal Nehru University in New Delhi (India). Presently she is an Associate Professor at the Advanced Centre for American Studies, Osmania

239

University, Hyderabad, India. Her research interests and publications are Indo-U.S. Relations, International Relations, and International Environmental Issues. She has published books and several articles on the above subjects.

Sheila Rai has a Ph.D. in Political Science from the University of Rahasthan, India and is presently an Assistant Professor there. Her teaching and research interests focus on Environmental Policymaking, Comparative Bureaucracies, and Indian Politics. She has presented scholarly papers at national, regional and international conferences, and has published extensively in scholarly journals both in India and abroad. Presently she is an active member of the Advisory Board IPSA Research Committee 35 and the Secretary of the Research Committee in 2004.

Hillery L. Roach is finishing her graduate degree at The American University in Cairo (Egypt). Her scholarly focus areas are Grassroots Politics in Egypt, Water Resource Management in the Middle East and U.S. Egyptian relations. She has presented several papers on the above topics at regional and international conferences.

Teagan E. Ward has a M.A. on Environmental Management from Duke University, Durham, North Carolina, U.S.A. Her areas of research interests include Water Resource Management and Policy, Environmental Law, Water and Sanitation in less developed countries with an emphasis on the Jordan River Basin, and Community Based Environmental Management. Presently Ward is an Environmental Policy and Outreach Intern with Americorps, city of Bellingham, Washington. As a water efficiency analyst she has conducted research on water scarcity issues. She has published several articles and research papers on water efficiency and social justice at national and international fora.

Paul A. Williams holds a Ph.D in Political Science from the University of California, Los Angeles and is currently Assistant Professor in the Department of International Relations at Bilkent University in Ankara, Turkey. He and Ali Tekin are the co-authors of *Geo-Politics of the Euro-Asia Energy Nexus: The European Union. Russia, and Turkey* (Houndmills, UK and New York, NY: Palgrave MacMillan, 2011).

Dhirendra Vajpeyi is Professor of Political Science at the University of Northern Iowa. He has authored, co-authored, and edited fifteen books and numerous articles. They include: *Environmental Policies in the Third World; Technology and Development; Local Government and Politics in the Third*

World; Indira Gandhi's India; Deforestation; A Comparative Analysis; Civil Military Relations, Nation Building, and National Identity; Local Democracy and Politics in South Asia; Religious and Minority Politics in South Asia; Modernizing China; Water Resource Management: A Comparative Perspective; Law, Politics and Society in India; Politics, Technology and Bureaucracy in South Asia; and Globalization, Governance, and Technology: Challenges and Alternatives. Vajpeyi has lectured at universities in Moscow, St. Petersburg (Russia), People's Republic of China, Nigeria, Chile, and Klagenfurt (Austria). He was a Senior Research Fellow at Hoover Institute at Stanford University (California). Currently he is the Chair of the IPSA Research Committee 35, on Technology and Development. He is also a member of the Advisory Committee of IPSA (RC04 and RC48). He holds a Ph.D in Political Science from Michigan State University.